Third Edition

Softball

STEPS TO SUCCESS

Diane Potter
Professor Emerita, Springfield College
Springfield, Massachusetts

Lynn V. Johnson
Associate Professor, Plymouth State University
Plymouth, New Hampshire

Human Kinetics

Library of Congress Cataloging-in-Publication Data

Potter, Diane L., 1935-
  Softball : steps to success / Diane Potter, Lynn V. Johnson. -- 3rd ed.
      p. cm.
  ISBN-13: 978-0-7360-5953-4 (soft cover)
  ISBN-10: 0-7360-5953-9 (soft cover)
  1. Softball--Training. 2. Slow pitch softball--Training. I. Johnson,
Lynn V., 1955- II. Title.
  GV881.4.T72P68 2007
  796.357'8--dc22   2006100910

ISBN-10: 0-7360-5953-9
ISBN-13: 978-0-7360-5953-4

The Web addresses cited in this text were current as of January 28th, 2007, unless otherwise noted.

Acquisitions Editor: Jana Hunter
Developmental Editor: Cynthia McEntire
Assistant Editor: Scott Hawkins
Copyeditor: Patrick Connolly
Proofreader: Julie Marx Goodreau
Graphic Designer: Nancy Rasmus
Graphic Artist: Kim McFarland
Cover Designer: Keith Blomberg
Photographer (cover): Ezra Shaw/Getty Images
Art Manager: Kelly Hendren
Field diagrams: Al Wilborn
Line art: Tim Offenstein
Printer: United Graphics

Human Kinetics books are available at special discounts for bulk purchase. Special editions or book excerpts can also be created to specification. For details, contact the Special Sales Manager at Human Kinetics.

Printed in the United States of America   10 9 8 7 6 5 4 3 2 1

Human Kinetics
Web site: www.HumanKinetics.com

United States: Human Kinetics
P.O. Box 5076
Champaign, IL 61825-5076
800-747-4457
e-mail: humank@hkusa.com

Canada: Human Kinetics
475 Devonshire Road Unit 100
Windsor, ON N8Y 2L5
800-465-7301 (in Canada only)
e-mail: orders@hkcanada.com

Europe: Human Kinetics
107 Bradford Road
Stanningley
Leeds LS28 6AT, United Kingdom
+44 (0) 113 255 5665
e-mail: hk@hkeurope.com

Australia: Human Kinetics
57A Price Avenue
Lower Mitcham, South Australia 5062
08 8372 0999
e-mail: liaw@hkaustralia.com

New Zealand: Human Kinetics
Division of Sports Distributors NZ Ltd.
P.O. Box 300 226 Albany
North Shore City
Auckland
0064 9 448 1207
e-mail: info@humankinetics.co.nz

■ Contents

Climbing the Steps to Softball Success

Softball is a game for participants of all ages. This book takes players through a progression of practice to enhance development of skills and game concepts. You will move from practicing individual skills to combining two, three, and four skills in gamelike drills, and then apply them in modified games. Finally, you will be given the opportunity to display your skills and knowledge in regulation game play.

This new edition focuses on skill development applicable to both slow-pitch and fastpitch softball. However, since fastpitch is becoming increasingly popular, new material has been added to increase the coverage of fastpitch. A new step provides more extensive coverage of the short hitting game widely used in fastpitch. Because of the emphasis on pitching in fastpitch, additional material was added to the pitching step. New steps increase the coverage of offensive and defensive tactics, especially those used in fastpitch.

Players who are new to the game are typically at a beginning skill level and have not had much experience in real-game situations. A player with more experience has likely had many opportunities to develop the skills needed to play at a more advanced skill level. This book is designed to give both less experienced and more experienced players a variety of challenging opportunities to further develop skills as they progress through the steps.

Each step is an easy transition from the one before. The first few steps provide a solid foundation of basic skills and concepts. As you progress, you will combine the single skills in ways that they are typically used in games. As you refine your skills, you will apply combinations in gamelike drills and modified games. Being able to anticipate, being ready, and becoming proficient at reading and reacting to game situations enable you to more fully and actively participate. You will learn to anticipate while batting, running, fielding, and throwing so that you can select the proper plays and fulfill the various responsibilities of your offensive and defensive positions. As you near the top of the staircase, you'll find that you have developed confidence in your playing ability that makes further progress a real joy.

Follow this sequence each step of the way:

1. Read what is covered in the step, why the step is important, and how to execute or perform the step's focus.

2. Follow the illustrations to execute each skill successfully.

3. Read the directions and review the success checks for each drill; these are the key points to remember when performing the skill. Drills help you improve your skills through repetition and purposeful practice, so practice accordingly and record your score.

4. Based on your score, follow the "To Increase Difficulty" or "To Decrease Difficulty" variations. The drills are arranged in an easy-to-difficult progression to help you achieve continued success. Pace yourself by adjusting the drills to increase or decrease difficulty.

5. Have a qualified observer—such as your teacher, coach, or trained partner—evaluate your basic skill technique when you have completed each set of drills. The observer can use the success checks to evaluate your execution of the skill.

6. Use the chart at the end of each step to total your drill scores. Once you have achieved the recommended level of success for the step, move on to the next step.

Enjoy your step-by-step journey to enhancing your softball skills, building confidence, experiencing success, and having fun!

◧ Acknowledgments

The preparation of this book was made possible through the assistance of many people, not all of whom can be mentioned by name. Over the years, many Springfield College and University of Vermont students and players we have taught and coached have challenged our views of softball and how it should be taught. For Diane Potter, coaching 7- to 10-year-old youngsters in the Brimfield Youth Sports softball program several years ago did much to confirm for her the importance of developing fundamental skills and game concepts, especially for young players who wish to continue to play as members of school varsity and recreational teams. We have learned from all of our students and players and thus have developed the instructional approach presented in this book. To all of you, we are forever indebted.

Once again, our sincere thanks go to five Springfield College students who were responsible for the pictures provided to the illustrator for the first edition of this book: to David Blizard for his excellent photography; to Jody Dobkowski, Shelly Quirk, and Christopher Mayhew, who were the models for the pictures; and to Tammy Oswell, who developed film and printed photographs. Many of these illustrations continue to be used in this third edition. Our thanks to Erin Barney, Whitney Borisenok, Sara Burke, Angie Hill, and Amy Kern from the University of Vermont for serving as the model for several fastpitch technique photographs. A special thanks to two young players, Kyle and Anna Dunphey, who volunteered as subjects for some new photographs provided to the illustrator for this third edition. We especially thank colleague Diane Schumacher, Softball Hall of Famer and former Springfield College player, for her consultation and suggestions regarding pitching (which were used in the development of step 3).

One learns much as a player of the sport. Diane Potter wishes to especially acknowledge the influence of Ralph Raymond, coach of the 1996 and 2000 gold-medal-winning U.S. Olympic softball teams, as her inspiration for and essence of this book. Diane's passion for the game, emphasis on fundamentals, and pride in the execution of quality play are a direct result of his coaching years ago when she was a player on his Cochituate Corvettes team. Lynn Johnson would like to thank Diane Potter for instilling her with an undying passion for the game of softball. She would also like to thank all of her former teammates and players for making the game so special. We hope that players, teachers, and coaches of all ages who use this book will be fortunate enough to have experiences with the sport of softball that are comparable to ours.

Diane Potter thanks Sydney Stewart—and Lynn Johnson thanks Pam Childs—for their diligent work in editing our drafts before the submission of the manuscript to Human Kinetics. Lynn Johnson would also like to thank Pam Childs for sharing her softball expertise and for the many technical discussions that occurred during the writing of the manuscript.

We acknowledge with deep appreciation the contributions of Dr. Gretchen Brockmeyer, coauthor of the first two editions of this book. Dr. Brockmeyer, a master teacher, was instrumental in the development of the instructional focus that is continued in this third edition.

We would like to express our appreciation to the staff at Human Kinetics—especially to Jana Hunter, acquisitions editor, and Cynthia McEntire, developmental editor of this third edition—for their encouragement, for serving as sounding boards for our ideas, and for their support throughout the preparation of the manuscript.

The Sport of Softball

The game we know today as softball was invented by George Hancock in 1887 at the Farragut Boat Club in Chicago. Hancock intended softball, then called *kittenball,* to be a game that the rich members of the boat club could play indoors. Later, however, an outdoor version of the game was developed by Lewis Rober, who introduced it to his fellow Minneapolis firemen. Currently, *softball* (as it was finally named at a 1926 YMCA convention) is played all over the world by millions of people from all walks of life.

The sport of softball has several variations, each with a unique set of rules that differentiate the games. There are official rules for men's and women's fastpitch, slow pitch, and modified pitch; coed slow pitch; and boys' and girls' (youth) fastpitch and slow pitch. The rules of men's and women's games vary only slightly; however, the rules for fastpitch and slow pitch make the games distinct from each other. The United States Specialty Sports Association (USSSA) has additional sets of rules for 16-inch and super slow pitch.

Today, participation opportunities abound for softball enthusiasts of all ages and abilities. The Amateur Softball Association (ASA) is the governing body for softball in the United States. Under the sponsorship of the ASA, over 250,000 teams with a membership of more than 4 million participate each year in a wide variety of classifications of fastpitch and slow-pitch programs. In addition, a full ASA program for youth teams, known as the *Junior Olympic program,* includes over 80,000 teams and 1.3 million players. Softball is played by millions of people around the world, and international competition opportunities are growing every year. The International Softball Federation regulates rules of play in more than 113 countries, including the United States and Canada.

However, it was not always so. The women's fastpitch game is the game currently gaining the most attention. The Women's NCAA National Collegiate Softball Championships can be seen on television, and women's fastpitch softball finally became an Olympic sport at the 1996 Atlanta Games. The road to that historic event was a long and arduous one, starting in 1965 with the first International Softball Federation (ISF) World Championships held in Melbourne, Australia. Australia defeated the highly favored U.S. team to become the first world champions. The second world championship was held in Japan in 1970, and the host Japanese team defeated the United States to become the new world champions. Finally, in 1974, at the world championship held in Stratford, Connecticut, the United States, represented by the Raybestos Brakettes, won the third world championship. Softball was first played at the Pan American Games in 1979, and that event continues to provide strong international competition for the U.S. national team as it prepares for the world championships and now the Olympics. The U.S. national team won the Olympic gold medal in Atlanta in 1996, in Australia in 2000, and again in Greece in 2004. Young girls and women in the late 1990s and early 2000s had their own female role models in Olympic star pitcher and hitter Lisa Fernandez, shortstop Dot Richardson, and outfielder Laura Berg. In the 2004 Olympics, Lisa Fernandez continued her dominance of Olympic Games with a 4-0 pitching record and an Olympic record .545 batting average, as the U.S. team went undefeated (9-0)—including 8 consecutive shutouts—to win the gold medal. Three new young pitchers—Jennie Finch, Cat Osterman, and Lori Harrigan—combined for the other five victories in the 2004 Olympics. Natasha Watley, the team's shortstop, stole five bases, setting a new Olympic record. Young players today have many outstanding women softball players as role models.

The success of the U.S. national team, the increased exposure from the Olympics, and the restructuring of the Women's Pro Softball League to National Pro Fastpitch (providing more professional playing opportunities for elite softball players) have caused a trickle-down effect to reach school and local recreation programs. The result is that more girls and women have an interest in participating in fastpitch softball. With the inclusion of softball in the National Sports Festival (now the U.S. Olympic Festival), the development of Olympic-level competitors is an ongoing process.

For those who do not aspire to Olympic-level competition, hundreds of thousands of recreational teams provide opportunities for partici-pation at every level of ability. Softball truly is a sport for everyone:

- It can be played and enjoyed by all ages and abilities, from 10-and-under to 50-and-over leagues.
- It is an excellent coed activity with special coed rules.
- It can be played on the local sandlot as well as in an Olympic stadium.
- It requires you to participate mentally as well as physically.
- It provides a social occasion for you to enjoy old friends and make new ones.

The skills needed to play the game are few; basically, a person must be able to catch, throw, hit, and run bases with a moderate degree of skill.

Now grab a ball and take the field!

RULES OF PLAY

Official softball games are played on a field like that depicted in figure 1. The *playing field* is the area within which the ball may be legally played and fielded. The boundaries of the playing field are usually an outfield fence as well as two side fences extending from the ends of the backstop to the outfield fence and running parallel to and 25 to 30 feet (7.6 to 9.1 meters) from the foul lines. The area outside the playing field is the *out-of-play,* or *dead-ball, territory.* The playing field is made up of fair territory and foul territory. *Fair territory* is the part of the playing field between and including the first- and third-base foul lines and the outfield fence, including the airspace above. *Foul territory* is the part of the playing field between the first- and third-base foul lines and the out-of-play territory.

The playing field is further divided into *infield* (that portion of fair territory that includes areas normally covered by infielders) and *outfield* (that portion of fair territory that is outside the diamond formed by the baselines, or the area not normally covered by an infielder between first and third bases and the outfield fence). Most softball playing fields have a dirt infield (see the shaded area in figure 1) and a grass outfield.

Distances between bases, pitching distances, and distances from home plate to the outfield fence vary, depending on the game being played. Unofficial games are played on all kinds of fields that have at least a home plate and three bases set out in a diamond or square configuration.

Any variety of softball involves two teams alternately playing offense and defense. A team is on offense when it is at bat, attempting to score runs. The defensive team is the team in the field, attempting to prevent the team at bat

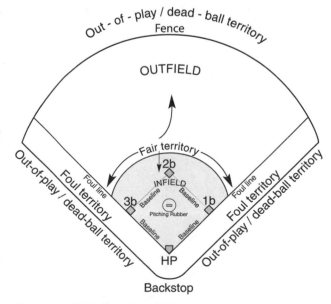

Figure 1 Softball playing field.

from scoring runs. Fastpitch and modified-pitch teams have 9 players in the field on defense, whereas all slow-pitch teams have 10 defensive players, although some allow extra players to bat. Defensive positions for fastpitch are identified by the numbers 1 through 9 as follows: pitcher (1), catcher (2), first baseman (3), second baseman (4), third baseman (5), shortstop (6), left fielder (7), center fielder (8), right fielder (9). In the slow-pitch game, 10 defensive players are used. The additional player is usually an outfielder, and for most teams, the center fielder is replaced by a left center fielder and a right center fielder. The starting positions are depicted in figure 2. The outfield, first baseman, and third baseman positions are labeled in lowercase letters for fastpitch. For slow pitch, these positions are labeled in capital letters. The starting positions for the pitcher, catcher, second baseman, and shortstop are the same for both fastpitch and slow pitch (those positions are labeled only once). The left fielder, center fielder, and right fielder—as well as the left center fielder and right center fielder for slow pitch—are called *outfielders*. *Infielders* are the first baseman, second baseman, third baseman, and shortstop. The pitcher and catcher, though playing in the infield and having some of the same kinds of responsibilities as infielders, are usually called the *battery,* rather than infielders.

A regulation softball game consists of at least seven innings. In each inning, each team bats until three batters or runners have been put out. An *out* occurs when an offensive player does not reach a base safely. In competitive play, the choice of first or last at-bat in an inning is decided by a coin toss, unless stated differently in the rules of the organization governing the game. The *visiting team* is up to bat first in an inning; the *home team* bats last. Typically, in any kind of league play, the team whose field the game is being played on is the home team.

A *run* is scored each time a baserunner legally touches first base, second base, third base, and home plate before the defensive team makes the third out of the inning. The winner of a game is the team that scores the greater number of runs.

In addition to these basic rules of play, other rules are introduced and explained as they apply to specific skills and concepts in this book. Reference is made throughout the book to official and modified rules of play. *Official* rules are those used in an official game between two high school, college, summer league, or Olympic teams.

High schools play under the fastpitch rules of either the National Federation of State High Schools Association (NFHS) or the Amateur Softball Association (ASA). College women play under the fastpitch rules of either the National Collegiate Athletic Association (NCAA) or the ASA. Fastpitch and slow-pitch recreational teams play under the rules of the ASA or the National Softball Association (NSA). The United States Specialty Sports Association (USSSA) governs play in some slow-pitch leagues. International play is governed by the rules of the International Softball Federation (ISF). The majority of the official fastpitch softball rules for high schools, colleges, and for the ASA are the same because they follow the rules made by the ISF. However, these organizations do have a few rules that apply only to their own competitions. For the purposes of this book, discussion of rules as they occur in the learning progressions is based on the ASA's *Official Rules of Softball*.

Modified rules, on the other hand, are rules that the teacher or coach makes up, usually to encourage students to focus on a particular skill or combination of skills. The player rotation rules used in the modified game called Scrub (step 10, page 204), for example, are designed to ensure that every player experiences playing all the defensive field positions. Those rules are not official and would not be used during any official game.

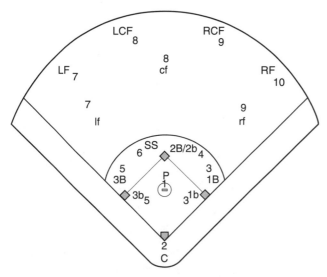

Figure 2 Starting positions shown by the numbers.

EQUIPMENT SELECTION AND SAFETY CONCERNS

To play softball safely, you need to have reliable equipment and practice facilities free from danger. Here are some suggestions for selecting personal equipment and for safety checks before practicing softball skills.

Gloves

A fielder's glove should be all leather, including the laces and bound edges of the hand opening. Be especially wary of plastic or synthetic materials in laces and edges. The glove should have an easily adjustable strap over the back of the hand (Velcro is nice). Size is somewhat dependent on the position you play, but the following guidelines will help you select the proper glove:

- The glove needs to be manageable. Many manufacturers provide age guidelines for youth gloves.
- A glove for a second baseman, third baseman, or shortstop should have a shorter finger length.
- Gloves should have a longer finger length for outfielders, first basemen, and catchers for slow-pitch play (if a fielder's glove rather than a mitt is used at first base or catcher).
- Faspitch catchers should purchase a catcher's mitt designed specifically for softball.

Bats

Bat technology has advanced enormously over the past several years, and this has made selecting a bat more complicated and purchasing a bat much more expensive. Depending on your level of play and your commitment to softball, your choices can range in price from $25 to over $400.

The length and weight of the bat should enable you to easily swing the barrel of the bat into the contact zone. Bat selection, therefore, may depend on your bat speed, strength, and the speed of the pitch. Bat weights are identified by ounces and might be indicated with plus or minus numbers—for example, if a bat is 34 inches long and is minus 8 weight, it weighs 22 ounces. Slow-pitch bats are typically heavier than fastpitch bats. All bats used in ASA (fastpitch or slow pitch) and NCAA competition must bear the ASA-approved certification mark.

The bat's grip should feel comfortable in your hands. Grip composition needs to ensure a secure grip for your hands on the handle. A safety grip is required on all bats and may be made of rubber, leather, or a synthetic material.

Bat composition has changed significantly in recent years. Hardwood bats are rarely seen in softball today. Bats are made of aluminum, steel, composites, metal alloys, and titanium. Manufacturers have used technology to make bats much more responsive, hoping to increase the offensive aspect of the game. The most inexpensive bats used in softball today are made from an aluminum alloy. Your bat selection may be governed more by price than by material, although those two factors are closely related. For recreational use, aluminum bats are durable and will last longer than some other bats; however, they are much less responsive and often do not give you a choice of weight. A major disadvantage of the new materials used to make today's bats is that they are not durable. Many bats costing $200 or more will not last a season and are often not returnable. Therefore, when selecting the composition of your bat, you should take into consideration your budget, your level of play, and your commitment to the game.

Batting Gloves

The batting glove, initially worn only on the hand holding the bottom end of the bat, was first used in baseball to ensure a more secure grip on a wooden bat. Unlike wooden softball bats that by rule must have a composition grip attached to the handle area, by rule the wooden baseball bat had to be made from one solid piece of wood with the grip area free from any foreign substance. Often, sweaty bare hands on bare wood resulted in the bat flying out of the batter's hands.

The softball bat used today typically has a replaceable grip that offers a secure handhold. Although the safety need for the batting glove in softball is not the same as for baseball, the trend is for players to mimic the major league player and wear not one but two batting gloves. For defensive players, especially the catcher and the first baseman, wearing a batting glove under the fielding glove offers additional protection for the hand catching the ball. Batting-style gloves that have extra padding are made specifically to wear under a glove or mitt to protect the hand.

Footwear

Shoes with soft or hard rubber cleats are the footwear of choice for most youth and recreational softball programs. Metal sole or heel plates are allowed in some levels of play, including college, if the cleat on the plate is not longer than three-quarters of an inch (1.9 centimeters). Round or track-type spikes are not allowed. Before selecting your footwear for softball, be sure to check the rules governing your specific level of play.

All equipment must be in compliance with the rules governing play. For example, if play is governed by ASA rules, the bat must be approved by the ASA. A bat marked "Little League"—even if it complies with ASA requirements of length, weight, maximum barrel size, and so on—could not be used by a player in a game being played under ASA rules.

For safety's sake, before practicing or playing softball, you should check your personal equipment and the playing field.

- Check your glove for broken laces, especially in the web area.
- Check all bats for dents, loose or torn grips, or displaced end caps.
- Make sure your footwear is well fitting, has strong arch support, and has soles that provide good traction, especially on wet or damp ground. Shoes should not have holes.
- Make sure your shirt is loose fitting so that it does not restrict your movements, especially for throwing. Pants or shorts should also be loose fitting for free movement.
- If you use sunglasses, be sure that they have nonbreakable safety lenses.

Check the playing field for glass and other sharp objects, holes in the field, and dangerous obstructions, such as football blocking sleds, lacrosse or field hockey goals, and so on. Remove any loose equipment lying around, especially balls and bats.

When practicing throwing, fielding, or other skills with a partner, line up so neither player looks directly into the sun. When inside or when outside near a building, be aware of windows, lights, and people. Do not practice with a window in the ball's line of flight. Be sympathetic to the skill abilities of partners. Do not throw the bat, and do not hit rocks with the bat.

WARM-UP AND COOL-DOWN

Before practicing, you need a 10- to 15-minute warm-up period to increase your heart rate and flexibility. After finishing practice, you should end with a 5-minute cool-down period. If you follow this sequence, you will not only help prepare your body and mind to play softball, but you'll also help prevent injuries.

In the warm-up, your first goal is to get your blood moving. Starting at home plate, jog around the perimeter of the field and return to home plate. Next, you want to prepare yourself for activity by performing a series of dynamic stretches designed to warm up the muscles you will use in the game of softball. Dynamic stretches are stretches that are done while moving and that place less stress on the muscle being stretched.

These stretches take the muscles to their full range of motion in a controlled manner. Do not bounce or perform jerky actions while performing dynamic stretches. Each dynamic stretch should be done in sets of 8 to 12 repetitions. Following is an example of a dynamic stretch sequence:

1. Perform slow and controlled leg swings, front to back and side to side.
2. Perform slow and controlled arm swings, up and down and in large circles.
3. Walk forward, slowly pulling your knee to your chest in a controlled manner. Alternate knees on each step.
4. Walk forward, reaching toward the ground with both hands while slowly raising a leg

behind you in a controlled manner. Alternate legs on each step.

5. Start in a medium squat position. Step sideways with one leg. Bring the other leg back so that you are back in a medium squat position. After a set, repeat, starting with the opposite leg.

6. Perform high-knee skips. Bring your knees as high as you can as you skip.

After completing the dynamic stretch sequence, you need to warm up your legs and throwing arm to get them ready for playing softball. For your arm, begin your warm-up at a medium distance from your throwing partner, exaggerating your throwing motion. Execute more of an outfield throwing motion than an infield throw. Once your arm feels warm, increase the speed of your throw or the distance from your partner.

You need to get your legs ready for the sprinting you will do in the game of softball. One way to warm up your legs and practice baserunning at the same time is to run out a series of hits on the base path. Begin with two home runs, running both at medium speed to warm up your legs. Then run out two singles, two doubles, and two triples, ending with a full-speed home run.

At the end of this, your legs will be warm and you will have worked on the skill of baserunning (see page 108).

At the end of each practice session or game, you should take a few minutes to cool down by stretching out those muscles used the most and by relaxing so that your heart rate returns to a resting rate. This routine should include a combination of dynamic (see previous description) and static-passive stretches. First, you should do light dynamic stretches until your heart rate slows down. Then complete a series of static-passive stretches, which are designed to relax your muscles to help minimize tightness and soreness after a practice or game. The shoulders, arms, torso, back, and legs will typically be used in any softball practice or game. Do your exercises in a relaxed state of mind and body. Move slowly into the stretch position and hold it for 8 to 10 seconds. Do not bounce in the stretch position. During the 8- to 10-second stretch, you should relax. At the end of 10 seconds, try to gently increase the range of the stretch. Be sure to do at least one exercise for each body part. Several books on stretching are available that can give you ideas for specific exercises.

NATIONAL AND INTERNATIONAL ORGANIZATIONS

These resources and organizations will help you learn more about softball rules and programs in your area. (Playing rules can be downloaded from the Web sites of organizations marked with an asterisk.)

Amateur Softball Association of America (ASA)
2801 N.E. 50th Street
Oklahoma City, OK 73111-7203
Phone: 405-424-5266
www.softball.org

International Softball Federation (ISF)*
1900 S. Park Road
Plant City, FL 33563
Phone: 813-864-0100
www.internationalsoftball.com

National Collegiate Athletic Association (NCAA)*
P.O. Box 6222
Indianapolis, IN 46206-6222
Phone: 317-917-6222
www.ncaa.org

National Softball Association (NSA)*
P.O. Box 7
Nicholasville, KY 40340
www.playnsa.com

United States Specialty Sports Association (USSSA)*
611 Line Drive
Kissimmee, FL 34744
Phone: 321-697-3636
www.usssa.com

Key to Diagrams

1,P	Pitcher (fastpitch, slow pitch)
2,C	Catcher (fastpitch, slow pitch)
3,1b	First baseman (fastpitch)
3,1B	First baseman (slow pitch)
4,2b	Second baseman (fastpitch)
4,2B	Second baseman (slow pitch)
5,3b	Third baseman (fastpitch)
5,3B	Third baseman (slow pitch)
6,SS	Shortstop (fastpitch, slow pitch)
7,lf	Left fielder (fastpitch)
7,LF	Left fielder (slow pitch)
8,cf	Center fielder (fastpitch)
8,LCF	Left center fielder (slow pitch)
9,rf	Right fielder (fastpitch)
9,RCF	Right center fielder (slow pitch)
10,RF	right fielder (slow pitch)
B	Baserunner
BR	Batter-runner
H	Hitter
T	Thrower
F	Fielder
∿⟶	Rolled ball
– – –⟶	Hit ball
- - - - -⟶	Thrown ball
⟶	Player movement
◭	Cone
▢	Bucket

Catching and Throwing

Imagine yourself at shortstop. A hard line drive is hit to you. In one fluid motion, you catch the ball and throw it to the first baseman, getting the batter out and doubling up the runner who left first base too soon. Or imagine that you are the left fielder. You race to your right to catch a fly ball, stop, and, stepping in the direction of your throw, throw the ball to second base to prevent the runner on first from advancing.

Softball is a game of catching and throwing. These fundamental defensive skills are keys to your success as a softball player. Every softball player, regardless of position, must master these skills. The related skills of fielding (catching ground balls and fly balls while on defense) and playing catcher behind the plate are addressed in steps 2 and 7. In this step, you will learn how to catch, move the ball and your body into throwing position, and throw the ball—all in one continuous, fluid motion.

Although softball features three general types of throws—overhand, sidearm, and underhand— the overhand throw is the one most often used. The overhand throw is especially useful when the ball must travel a significant distance and when accuracy is important. Because of the major role the overhand throw plays in softball, it is the first throw to learn if you are new to the game and the first skill to review if you are more experienced. The overhand throw is your ticket to being a suc-

cessful defensive player and therefore receives the most attention in this step.

The fastpitch pitcher is the only player who commonly throws the ball with a full underhand motion (see step 3). However, various underhand tosses, including the pitch in slow-pitch softball and the short feed to second base to start the double play, might technically be called underhand throws. The sidearm throw (see step 8) is used for relatively short throws when the ball must travel with speed, parallel to the ground. Highly skilled infielders will occasionally use sidearm throws when, after fielding a ground ball, a quick-release throw is necessary because of the lack of time. The sidearm is the least accurate type of throw and should be used sparingly, even by more experienced players.

Can you imagine someone throwing the ball to you but you do not know what to do to protect yourself? Imagine yourself playing center field, catching a fly ball, and not being able to get the ball to second base—never mind all the way to home plate. For an infielder, the ability to catch and throw the ball quickly helps make plays on baserunners who are attempting to advance to the next base. Outfielders must use the overhand throw because of the great distance the ball has to travel. Throwing and catching are the fundamental defensive skills for all softball players. We begin with catching.

CATCHING THE BALL

Initially, catching a ball coming to you in the air involves tracking the ball—watching the ball and determining the path it is taking—then moving your body, glove, and throwing hand into that path in order to catch the ball. As a fielder, you have no control over the flight of the ball. Therefore, to catch a ball, you must visually pick up the flight of the ball by focusing on it while it is coming toward you and move your body in line with the oncoming ball. Once you are in line with the ball, you should stand squarely, facing the ball with your glove-side foot slightly ahead. Reach your hands out in front of your body to make contact with the ball, and simultaneously shift your weight onto your front foot.

Catching a ball also involves anticipation and a certain amount of decision making on your part. If the ball is arriving above your waist, point the fingers of your glove and of your throwing hand up, as shown in figure 1.1a. If the ball is below your waist, your fingers should point down (figure 1.1b). A ball coming directly at your waist is often the most difficult to catch; to catch it, position your glove hand with the palm facing down, fingers parallel to the ground with the thumb down, and place your throwing hand (palm facing up) under your glove hand, as shown in figure 1.1c. Correct positioning of the hands is crucial to effective catching.

Figure 1.1   Tracking and Anticipation

ABOVE WAIST

1. Point fingers up
2. Focus on ball
3. Align body to ball

BELOW WAIST

1. Point fingers down
2. Focus on ball
3. Align body to ball

AT WAIST

1. Point fingers horizontally
2. Focus on ball
3. Align body to ball

After making the tracking and anticipation decisions about the ball coming toward you, you are now ready to catch the ball. As the ball comes into your glove, squeeze the ball with the thumb and ring finger of your glove hand, and at the same time, cover the ball with your throwing hand. "Give" with the ball (also called *using soft hands*) to cushion its impact by drawing the ball and glove toward your throwing-side shoulder.

As you move the ball and glove to the throwing position, take a two-finger grip on the ball by placing your index and middle fingers on one seam, your thumb on a seam on the opposite side of the ball from your fingers, and your ring finger on the side of the ball (figure 1.2a). If you have a small hand, you can use a three-finger grip (figure 1.2b) by placing your ring finger on the seam with your other two fingers and placing

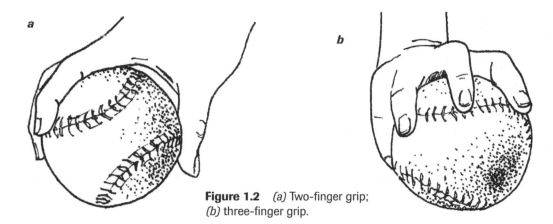

Figure 1.2 *(a)* Two-finger grip; *(b)* three-finger grip.

your pinkie on the side of the ball. At the same time, shift your weight onto your back foot and turn your body so that your glove side is toward the throwing target. With your weight on your back foot, separate your hands and bring the ball in your throwing hand to the throwing position. Your glove-side elbow should point at the throwing target.

This ending position for catching a ball is the same as the ready position for the overhand throw. Ending the catch in this way makes it possible for you to make the transition from the catch to the throw in one continuous motion. Figure 1.3, *a* through *c* shows the catch-to-throw transition leading into the preparation phase for the throw when the ball arrives above your waist.

Figure 1.3   Catching

READY TO CATCH

1. Feet are in forward stride, glove-side foot ahead
2. Focus on ball
3. Fingers are up (for ball arriving above waist)
4. Shift weight forward
5. Meet ball out front

CATCHING

1. Use two hands; squeeze ball
2. Start shifting weight back; begin pivot
3. Give with the ball
4. Use two- or three- finger grip on ball in glove

READY TO THROW

1. Continue to shift weight back
2. Glove side is toward target
3. Glove points to target
4. Weight is on back foot
5. Arms extend; move ball to throwing position
6. Throwing wrist extends

Misstep

You miss the ball, or the ball drops out of your glove.

Correction

Watch the ball. Use two hands and cover the ball in your glove with your throwing hand.

Misstep

The ball stings your hand when you catch it.

Correction

Reach out in front to meet the ball, and give with the ball as you make contact. Draw the ball and glove to your throwing shoulder.

Using two hands to catch the ball not only makes for a surer catch but also makes it easier for you to throw the ball quickly, because you already have the ball in your throwing hand as soon as you catch the ball. Catching the ball one-handed with the glove only makes for a more time-consuming transition from catch to throw and results in a much slower release time. One-handed catches should be used only when the ball is out of your two-hand reach. These types of catches will be discussed later in this step.

Catching Drill 1. *Self-Toss*

For players who are just learning the game or who don't have much experience, this drill will help fine-tune the fundamentals of proper catching.

Without wearing a glove, gently toss a ball up into the air in front of your body so that it goes just above head height. Using both hands, reach up and out to catch the ball, draw it into your throwing shoulder, and then drop your hands and toss it again. You can increase the challenge during the self-toss by tossing the ball ahead so you have to move to catch it. Toss and catch the ball 10 times.

Now, toss the ball onto a high, slanted surface, such as the roof of a shed or garage, so that it will roll off for you to catch. Again, don't wear a glove. Focus on the cue "reach and give" as you concentrate on the catching action. You can increase the challenge on the roof toss by moving back before tossing the ball so you have to move in farther to catch it. Toss and catch the ball 10 times.

Have a coach or an experienced player observe your catching technique and award you points based on the criteria in the success check. For each toss and catch, earn 1 point for each of the three criteria you meet, for a total of 3 points per toss and catch (on 10 self-tosses and 10 roof tosses).

Success Check

- Reach up to meet the ball, and watch it go into your hands.
- Give with the ball as it comes into your hands. Remember, use *soft* hands.
- Bring the ball and hands to the throwing position.

Score Your Success

Self-Toss

25 to 30 points = 5 points

20 to 24 points = 3 points

19 points or fewer = 1 point

Your score _____

Roof Toss

25 to 30 points = 5 points

20 to 24 points = 3 points

19 points or fewer = 1 point

Your score _____

To Increase Difficulty

- Increase the distance you toss the ball ahead of you so you have to move farther to catch it.
- Increase the distance you move back from the roof so you have to move in farther to catch the ball.

- Increase the height you toss the ball so you can work on more difficult tracking skills.

To Decrease Difficulty

- Use a Nerf or Wiffle ball.
- Use a lower toss.

Catching Drill 2. *Partner Toss*

Stand 10 feet (3.0 meters) away from a partner. Both of you should be wearing gloves and facing each other. Using underhand tosses, toss and catch a ball back and forth. For your partner to work on her catching skills, you must make an accurate, soft toss. In the first part of this drill, aim a soft toss directly at your partner. When catching the ball, be sure to stand in a forward stride position with your glove-side foot ahead. As part of the catch, focus on bringing the ball to the throwing position. Remember to focus on "reach, give, and prepare to throw."

For more of a challenge, ask your partner to throw the ball to you at three different heights:

above the waist, at the waist, and below the waist. Catch the ball cleanly, altering your hand position to match the flight of the ball. Complete 10 throws and catches at each height.

Success Check

- Stand with your feet in a forward stride position, with your glove-side foot ahead.
- Reach to meet the ball in front of your body.
- Use two hands to squeeze the ball in your glove.
- Using a two-finger grip, bring the ball to the throwing position.

Score Your Success

Number of consecutive tosses (out of 10) that your partner can reach without taking a step:

    7 to 10 = 5 points

    4 to 6 = 3 points

    1 to 3 = 1 point

    Your score ___

Number of consecutive catches you make on tosses arriving above your waist (out of 10 good tosses):

    7 to 10 = 5 points

    4 to 6 = 3 points

    1 to 3 = 1 point

    Your score ___

Number of consecutive catches you make on tosses arriving at your waist (out of 10 good tosses):

    7 to 10 = 5 points

    4 to 6 = 3 points

    1 to 3 = 1 point

    Your score ___

Number of consecutive catches you make on tosses arriving below your waist (out of 10 good tosses):

    7 to 10 = 5 points

    4 to 6 = 3 points

    1 to 3 = 1 point

    Your score ___

To Increase Difficulty

Ask the tosser to randomly vary the height and distance of the toss to each side of your body.

To Decrease Difficulty

- Use a softer ball.
- Have the tosser use a softer toss.
- Use a larger ball.

THROWING OVERHAND

To initiate the overhand throw, continue from the position described in the "ready to throw" phase of the catch (figure 1.3c, page 3). As you take the ball out of your glove, be sure to grip the ball across the seams with the first two fingers and thumb of your throwing hand. If you have a small hand, you may want to also place your ring finger on the ball for a three-finger grip, with your pinkie on the side of the ball (figure 1.2 on page 3).

Say to yourself, "Turn, step, and throw." These cues will remind you to *turn* your glove side toward the target while extending your throwing hand back (figure 1.4a); to *step* in the direction of the target with your glove-side foot, shifting your weight onto that foot while keeping your hips square to the target (figure 1.4b); and to *throw* the ball by bringing your arm forward and snapping your wrist, leading with the elbow (figure 1.4c). Keep your elbow high and your upper arm parallel to the ground. Rotate your forearm through the vertical, keeping the ball high as it goes by your head. If your forearm drops down to the side instead of staying vertical, the ball will tend to curve and be less accurate, especially when you are making a long throw. On short throws—for example, a throw from third base to first base—the ball should traverse a straight line toward the target. Throws from the outfield should have as flat a trajectory as possible.

After you release the ball, your weight will be forward, your knees will be bent, your throwing shoulder will be forward, and your throwing hand will be low and to the outside of your glove-side knee. Your throwing-side foot will come forward to put you in a balanced position. Figure 1.4, *a* through *c* shows the three phases of the overhand throw, which is the completion of the catch-and-throw combination skill. The full combination skill is described in the next technique section.

Figure 1.4   Overhand Throw

a

b

READY TO THROW

1. Weight is on back foot
2. Glove side is to target
3. Arms are extended; glove is to target
4. Wrist is cocked; ball is to rear

THROWING

1. Step toward target with glove-side foot
2. Push off rear foot
3. Elbow leads throw; hand trails
4. Weight is on front foot
5. Hips are square
6. Forearm rotates through vertical
7. Ball is high
8. Glove hand is low
9. Snap wrist

COMPLETING THE THROW

1. Wrist is snapped
2. Weight is forward
3. Knees are bent
4. Throwing hand is low
5. Throwing shoulder is forward
6. Assume balanced position

c

Misstep

The ball doesn't go very far.

Correction

You may be "pushing" the ball. Extend your arm fully to the rear to initiate the throw. Lead with your elbow as you bring the ball forward.

Misstep

The ball's trajectory is too high.

Correction

Snap your wrist as you release the ball, or release the ball later.

Overhand Throw Drill 1. *Fence Throw*

With a bucket of 10 balls, stand 20 feet (6.1 meters) away from an unobstructed high fence, such as the backstop. (Decrease the distance if using a shorter fence.) Throw each ball directly against the fence. Repeat the phrase "turn, step, and throw" to yourself each time as you go through the complete throwing action. Remember to step with your glove-side foot. Be sure that your arm goes through the full range of motion, and make the entire motion smooth.

After practicing the throwing motion for 10 throws, have a coach or an experienced player observe your performance and evaluate your technique based on the success check criteria. Earn

1 point for each success check you demonstrate per throw.

Success Check

- Turn so your glove side is toward the fence, with your throwing arm extended fully to the rear.
- Step toward the fence with your glove-side foot.
- Throw with your hand and elbow high as the ball passes by your head.
- Follow through to your glove-side knee.

Score Your Success

35 to 40 points = 5 points

25 to 34 points = 3 points

24 or fewer points = 1 point

Your score ___

To Increase Difficulty

- Place a target on the fence and try to hit it.
- Increase the distance of the throws.

To Decrease Difficulty

- Stand with your glove side toward the fence. Step with your glove-side foot toward the fence and throw the ball at the fence.
- From a standing position with your back to the fence, "turn, step, and throw" the ball as far as you can and run after it. Throw it back as far as you can and run to get it. Focus on "turn, step, and throw" each time you throw.

Overhand Throw Drill 2. *Target Accuracy*

When you play softball, you must be able to throw the ball where you want it to go. If you cannot throw the ball to the proper place, you will not be doing your part to help your team get baserunners out.

Mark a target about chest high on a fence or wall. Make the target a rectangle that is big enough for you to hit with a throw from 20 feet (6.1 meters). If you are new to the game, make the target at least 8 feet (2.4 meters) wide; if you are more experienced, make the target narrower.

Stand 20 feet from the target. Using the overhand throwing motion, throw 10 balls at the target. These are practice throws; don't score yourself yet. As you throw, say to yourself, "Turn, step, and throw." Remember to use the full range of the throwing motion. Even though this drill uses a target, you should focus on the "turn, step, and throw" actions of the overhand motion and on the success check criteria, especially stepping with your glove-side foot.

Throw 10 more balls at the same target. This time, concentrate on the target throughout the throwing action. Give yourself 1 point each time you step toward the target with your glove-side foot and hit the target.

Success Check

- Point your glove at the target.
- Step toward the target with your glove-side foot.
- Forcefully rotate your forearm forward.
- Shift your body weight forward as you follow through.

Score Your Success

8 to 10 points = 5 points

5 to 7 points = 3 points

4 points or fewer = 1 point

Your score ___

To Increase Difficulty

- Decrease the size of the target.
- Lengthen the throwing distance.

To Decrease Difficulty

- Increase the size of the target.
- Shorten the distance of the throw.

Overhand Throw Drill 3. *Increase the Distance*

You must be able to throw the ball different distances with accuracy. You may need to throw the ball a long distance, such as from the outfield, or only a short distance, such as from the infield.

On the ground in front of the target you used in the previous drill, mark off distances of 20, 30, 40, 50, and 60 feet (6.1, 9.1, 12.2, 15.2, and 18.3 meters). Stand on the 20-foot mark. Using the overhand throw, deliver 10 consecutive balls toward the target. Count the number of on-target hits. To move back to the next mark, you must hit the target 8 out of 10 times. Each time you meet this goal, move back to the next mark and repeat the drill. You may not move back to a greater distance until you meet the goal for each mark. Try to work your way back to a distance of 60 feet (the distance from home plate to first base).

In a softball game, the target you will throw the ball to is much smaller than the target you have been throwing at in this drill. Your target for a throw

during a game is the glove of the person catching the ball. To practice this skill, make your drill target narrower. Get that bucket of balls again, deliver 10 overhand throws from each distance, and count the number of on-target hits. If you hit the target on 8 out of 10 throws, move back to the next distance. Remember, you cannot move back to the next distance until you meet the goal for each mark.

Success Check

- Focus on the target.
- Force your body weight forward by driving off the back foot.
- On the release, make sure your fingers are directly behind the ball and snap your wrist.
- As you follow through, drive your throwing-side shoulder forward and down.
- Bring your throwing-side foot forward, and assume a balanced position.

Score Your Success

Score yourself based on the greatest distance you were able to reach using two or fewer attempts to meet the goal for each mark:

    Reach 60-foot mark = 5 points

    Reach 50-foot mark = 3 points

    Reach 40-foot mark = 2 points

    Reach 30-foot mark = 1 point

    Your score ___

To Increase Difficulty

- Increase the throwing distance.

- Increase the number of on-target hits required to move back.
- Make the target smaller.

To Decrease Difficulty

- Shorten the throwing distance.
- Decrease the number of on-target hits required to move back.
- Begin the throw with your glove side toward the target (appropriate at shorter distances only).

CATCHING AND THROWING IN GAME SITUATIONS

Playing catch with a partner will help you anticipate how a teammate will work with you as you catch and throw in a game. In a game, the ball is seldom hit or thrown directly at you, so it's difficult to use your basic catching and throwing technique in a stationary position. You must be

able to *adapt* the basic techniques of catching and throwing to the various circumstances that arise when playing the game.

Always try to get your entire body in front of the ball when catching. Catching the ball outside of the midline of your body should be attempted

9

only when it is impossible to get your body in front of the ball.

For most people, the glove-side catch (either two-handed or one-handed) is easier than the catch on the throwing side, because the glove hand is on the same side of the body as the ball. To glove the ball one-handed, you merely extend your arm and body toward the ball, making sure the pocket of your glove is open to receive the ball (figure 1.5a).

Catching the ball on the throwing side involves backhanding the ball (figure 1.5b). This means moving your glove hand across your body to the throwing side and turning the glove over, with the thumb side toward the ground, the fingers paral-

lel to the ground, and the open pocket facing the direction of the ball's flight. Because you must reach across your body to make this catch, you cannot extend as far as when going to the glove side. If necessary, you can increase your reach by turning your back on the ball's origin and stepping toward the ball with your glove-side foot; however, if you do this in order to make the catch, you will probably sacrifice the smooth transition into the throw. Thus, whenever you can, you should get your body in front of the ball so that you will be in a good position to follow up with a throw. Even when the ball is outside the midline of the body, if you can reach the ball with two hands, you should catch it with two hands.

Figure 1.5   Catching Outside the Midline of the Body

a

b

GLOVE-SIDE (FOREHAND) CATCH

1. Move to ball
2. Reach out to catch ball
3. Glove pocket is open to ball
4. Thumb is up; little finger is down
5. Focus on ball

THROWING-SIDE (BACKHAND) CATCH

1. Move to ball
2. Glove hand is across body
3. Turn glove over; thumb is toward ground
4. Glove pocket is open to ball
5. Focus on ball

Misstep

The ball hits the glove but does not stay in it.

Correction

Make sure the glove pocket is open toward the ball. Squeeze your thumb and little finger together in the glove around the ball.

Game Throwing Drill 1. *Throw and Catch*

In a game situation, not every ball is thrown accurately to you so that you can catch it directly in front of your body. In this drill, you will have the opportunity to practice catching balls that are thrown off target to both your glove side and throwing-hand, or nonglove, side. You will also work on throwing accuracy, but you must make the throw to a target that is away from the midline of the receiver's body. Instead of throwing directly at your partner, aim for a spot that will make your partner reach for the ball on the glove side or on the throwing side, away from the body.

You and a partner stand 20 feet (6.1 meters) apart. The catching partner holds the glove chest high away from the body to the glove side. The thrower throws the ball to the glove target. The receiver should catch the ball, move it immediately to the throwing position, and throw it back. Do 10 repetitions and then switch the target to the throwing side. Remember, you must backhand the ball when catching on this side. As you prepare to catch the ball, turn the glove over so that the thumb is toward the ground and the pocket is open for the throw. After 10 repetitions on this side, switch roles and repeat the entire sequence.

Next, challenge each other by setting the glove target in three different positions (chest high): the receiver's glove side, throwing side, and directly in front of the body. After 10 throws and catches at each glove target position, switch roles.

Success Check: Thrower

- Look for the target and step directly toward it.
- Move your arm through the full range of motion for the throw.
- Snap your wrist and follow through as you release the ball.

Success Check: Catcher

- Give a big, open-glove target and watch the ball into the glove.
- Squeeze the ball in your glove with the thumb and ring finger of your glove hand.
- Cover the ball with your throwing hand on all catches except those out of range for a two-handed catch.

Score Your Success

For the first part of the drill, give yourself a score based on the number of combined on-target throws and successful catches out of 20 attempts.

15 to 20 = 5 points

10 to 14 = 3 points

9 points or fewer = 1 point

Your score ___

For the second part of the drill, give yourself a score based on the number of on-target throws as the thrower and successful catches as the receiver (out of 10 attempts for each of the three targets).

8 to 10 = 5 points for each target

4 to 7 = 3 points for each target

1 to 3 = 1 point for each target

Your score (thrower) ___

Your score (receiver) ___

To Increase Difficulty

- Continuously catch and throw the ball to the target rather than stopping after catching and then preparing to throw.
- Extend the possible target positions beyond just chest high, and have the receiver randomly vary the target setup for each throw.
- Have the receiver move the target before the throw is started.

To Decrease Difficulty

- Shorten the throwing distance.
- Make the targets only slightly to the side and in front of the receiver.
- Throw back and forth to chest height using only the amount of force your partner is able to handle when catching.

11

Game Throwing Drill 2. *Line Drives*

Line drives are one of the most difficult types of hits to catch, because they are batted sharply and come at you hard and fast. Getting in front of a line drive in time to catch it can be difficult. You also need to be sure to "give" with the catch to cushion the force so that the ball does not pop out of your glove.

With a partner, stand 40 to 60 feet (12.2 to 18.3 meters) apart, face one another, and play catch. When throwing the ball, snap your wrist forcefully as you release the ball so that it travels with considerable speed in a horizontal path, as a line drive hit would. When receiving the ball, set a target for your throwing partner above and below your waist on both your glove and throwing-arm sides. (Use the backhand catching technique on all line drives to your throwing-arm side.) When you catch the ball, move it directly into the throwing position but do not immediately throw it. Complete 10 throws and 10 catches at each of the receiving positions: above and below the waist on both the glove-hand side and throwing-arm side. Give yourself 1 point for each successful catch and 1 point for each on-target throw.

Success Check

- Whenever possible, get in front of the ball and use two hands.
- Turn your glove to the backhand position for line drives to your throwing-arm side.
- Snap your wrist on the throw.

Score Your Success

30 to 40 points = 5 points
20 to 29 points = 3 points
19 points or fewer = 1 point
Your score ___

To Increase Difficulty

- Increase the distance the ball is thrown to the side of the receiver.
- Increase the force of the throw.

To Decrease Difficulty

- Use less force on the throw, and take more time between throws.
- Reduce the distance of the throw.

CATCHING AND THROWING IN ONE CONTINUOUS MOTION

In a game situation, catching and throwing are typically combined into one skill. The continuous motion from one skill (catching) to the other (throwing) saves time and makes it more likely that you will execute the play successfully. To make the catch and throw continuous, remember that the follow-through phase of the catch becomes the preparation phase for the throw. Figure 1.6, *a* through *c* shows the continuous motion of the catch-to-throw transition.

Figure 1.6   Combined Catching and Throwing

a

CATCH

1. Focus on ball
2. Body is lined up with ball
3. Use two hands
4. Give with the ball

b

TURN

1. Weight is back
2. Glove side is to target
3. Hold ball in two-finger grip
4. Ball is to rear shoulder

c

THROW

1. Step to target
2. Elbow leads
3. Ball is high by head
4. Snap wrist

Misstep

Your catch and release are slow.

Correction

Move into position to catch the ball in front of your throwing side. Catch the ball with two hands and immediately take a two-finger grip on the ball as you take it out of your glove to make the throw.

Catch and Throw Drill 1. *Game Accuracy*

For more experienced players, this is a good time to begin to apply the proper throwing and catching techniques learned in this chapter in simulated game situations. Use the same basic practice setup as in the Throw and Catch drill (page 11). This time, however, imagine yourselves making throws and catches in game situations such as tag plays, force plays, and backhand plays. (Tag and force plays are covered in more detail in step 7.) Take turns with your partner selecting a play to work on. When you are the receiver, toss the ball to the thrower and set an appropriate glove target for the selected play, for example, just below the knees for making a tag play or off to the side for a force play. When you are the thrower, catch the ball from the receiver and make the throw to the set target all in one continuous motion. Continue until each partner has attempted 10 throws and 10 catches for the selected game situation, and then change the simulated game situation. Practice each of these game situations:

- The throw goes just below the knees, as in making a tag play.
- The throw is chest high and out front (the receiver stretches to make the catch out front), as on a force play.
- The throw is chest high and to the receiver's glove side (the receiver stretches to make the catch), as on a force play.
- The throw is knee high and to the receiver's throwing side for a backhanded catch.

Give yourself 1 point for each on-target throw and 1 point for each successful catch you make. Complete 10 throws and 10 catches for each simulated play.

Once you have had consistent success at making throws and catches for various game situations, practice making the plays in random order, changing the selected target after each attempt. The practice opportunity in the first portion of this drill is designed to help you work on using a continuous motion for the catch and throw and also to develop a patterned throwing response to a variety of game situation targets. In a real game, you get only one chance to make an accurate throw and a successful catch on each play. To be successful in this portion of the drill, you must make accurate throws and successful catches on the first attempt. Continue until each partner has attempted 10 throws and 10 catches as thrower and receiver. Give yourself 3 points for each combined on-target throw and successful catch you make.

Success Check

- Focus on the glove target throughout the throw.
- Use a full range of motion for the throw.
- With the glove-side foot, step in the direction of the throw.
- Present a big, open-glove target and watch the ball go into your glove.

Score Your Success

For the first part of the drill, total your points and then determine your score based on the following:

    70 to 80 points = 5 points

    60 to 69 points = 3 points

    50 to 59 points = 1 point

    Your score ___

For the second part of the drill, total your points and then determine your score based on the following:

    50 to 60 points = 5 points

    40 to 49 points = 3 points

    30 to 39 points = 1 point

    Your score ___

To Increase Difficulty

- When in the role of thrower, receive the return throw from the catcher and make your throw to the target all in one continuous motion.
- After returning the ball to the thrower, the catcher quickly moves several steps to one side or the other and sets the glove target. When making the throw, the thrower must step toward the catcher's new position.

To Decrease Difficulty

- Shorten the distance of the throw.
- Decrease the number of targets.
- Have the catcher set the target before you begin your throw.

Catch and Throw Drill 2. *Leaping Line Drives*

The challenge for the receiver in this drill is to catch a ball that requires the receiver to leave the ground in order to make the catch. You must time your jump to catch the ball just as it passes over your head. In addition, this line drive drill again provides accuracy practice for the thrower; however, it is more challenging than previous drills because the target is a point in space above your partner's head. You do not have a physical point at which to aim your line drive throw. You must aim your throw to go above your partner's head so that a leaping catch can be attempted.

To add a gamelike dimension to this drill for more experienced players, the receiver should come down with the ball in the throwing position and immediately throw it back to the thrower. The thrower acts as an infielder covering a base to try to double up a runner who left the base before the catch was made.

Repeat this sequence for 10 catchable leaping line drives and then change roles. As the receiver, count the number of successful catches out of 10 catchable line drives thrown to you. As the thrower, count the number of on-target throws out of the first 10 line drives thrown. You must continue to throw line drives until your partner has received 10 catchable line drives.

Success Check: Thrower

- Aim your throw at a point about a foot (30.4 centimeters) above your partner's head.
- Throw a catchable line drive.
- Step toward your partner with your glove-side foot and shift your body weight forward to increase the force of your throw.

Success Check: Receiver

- Time your jump to receive the ball above and in front of your head.
- Bring the ball to the throwing position as you land.
- Immediately step toward your partner and return the throw.

Score Your Success

As the thrower, give yourself a score based on the number of on-target throws out of your first 10 attempts.

7 to 10 = 5 points

4 to 6 = 3 points

1 to 3 = 1 point

Your score ___

As the receiver, give yourself a score based on the number of successful catches out of 10 catchable line drives.

7 to 10 = 5 points

4 to 6 = 3 points

1 to 3 = 1 point

Your score ___

To Increase Difficulty

- Throw the line drive to the glove side and to the throwing side above your partner's head.
- Throw the line drive higher above your partner's head.

To Decrease Difficulty

Throw the ball directly at your partner and only slightly above the head.

Catch and Throw Drill 3. Continuous Line Drives

You and your partner stand 60 feet (18.3 meters) apart. You throw a line drive to your partner, who catches it and immediately throws a line drive back to you. You should catch the line drive, and, in one motion, throw a line drive back to your partner. Continue this line drive catching and throwing for five minutes. Count the number of consecutive catches you make together. If the ball is dropped by either partner, you must begin counting again at 1. In this drill, the footwork of turning your glove side toward the throwing target and stepping with your glove-side foot as you throw is essential. Work on it! Remember, you are working for a team score in this drill.

Success Check

- Make accurate throws.
- Initiate your turn as you are catching the ball.
- Have the ball back to the throwing position as the turn is completed.

Score Your Success

Give yourself a team score based on the number of consecutive catches between you and your partner during the five-minute trial.

25 or more = 5 points

15 to 24 = 3 points

14 or fewer = 1 point

Your score ___

To Increase Difficulty

- Extend the range in all directions for your partner to catch the ball.
- Increase the force of the throw.
- Decrease the time between throws.

To Decrease Difficulty

- Throw the ball directly at your partner.
- Decrease the force of your throw.

Catch and Throw Drill 4. *Quick-Release Game*

This is a combination of the Partner Accuracy Throw-and-Catch drill and the Line Drives drill, except each partner starts this drill with a softball in hand. Each partner throws a ball to the other partner at the same time. You must catch and immediately release (throw) the ball to your partner. Try to keep the two balls going continuously without a drop or bad throw. Count the number of consecutive catches you make together (count each catch by both partners). If either partner drops a ball, you must begin counting again at 1. Be sure to use correct form, especially the footwork of turning and stepping when throwing. Count the number of successful continuous catches in five minutes of throwing.

Success Check

- Use two hands to catch.
- Bring the ball to the throwing position as you turn and step to throw.
- Make the catch and quick-release throw one continuous movement.

Score Your Success

Give yourself a team score based on the number of consecutive catches between you and your partner during the five-minute trial.

  35 or more = 5 points

  15 to 34 = 3 points

  14 or fewer = 1 point

  Your score ___

To Increase Difficulty

- Move partners farther apart and make the receiver move farther to catch the accurate throw.
- Speed up the rhythm of the catch-and-throw patterns.
- Work on throwing line drives.

To Decrease Difficulty

- Move closer together.
- Slow down the rhythm of the catch-and-throw patterns.
- Use a softer ball.
- Throw the ball with less force.

SUCCESS SUMMARY

The most important skill foundation of a good defensive player is strength in catching and throwing. Softball games are won on solid defensive play. Keep the other team from scoring, get one run, and your team is a winner. The player who can catch the ball and make strong, accurate overhand throws is going to make significant contributions to her team's success, so you should work hard to develop these skills.

Remember, make the catch and throw in one smooth, continuous motion. Track the ball early, and move your body into position in line with the ball. Reach out to catch the ball in front of your body with two hands if possible, and as you draw it to the throwing position, remember "turn, step, and throw." Step in the direction of your throw with the glove-side foot. Use a two-finger grip, move the ball high and forward past your head, and snap your wrist on the release.

In the next step, we will be working on developing fielding skills. Catching is a very important component of fielding, and throwing usually follows a fielding play. Before moving on to step 2, take the time now to look at how you did on the drills in this step. Enter your score for each drill, and then add up your scores to rate your success in the throwing and catching skills.

Catching Drills

1. Self-Toss — ___ out of 10
2. Partner Toss — ___ out of 20

Overhand Throw Drills

1. Fence Throw — ___ out of 5
2. Target Accuracy — ___ out of 5
3. Increase the Distance — ___ out of 5

Game Throwing Drills

1. Throw-and-Catch — ___ out of 35
2. Line Drives — ___ out of 5

Catch and Throw Drills

1. Game Accuracy — ___ out of 10
2. Leaping Line Drives — ___ out of 10
3. Continuous Line Drives — ___ out of 5
4. Quick-Release Game — ___ out of 5

Total — ___ *out of 115*

Your total score will give you an indication of whether or not you have developed your catching and throwing skills to a point that will allow you to be successful in the next steps. If you scored 86 points or more, you have mastered the catching and throwing skills and are ready to move on to the next step. If your total was 70 to 85, you are ready to move on to the next step, although you might benefit from additional practice in selected drills. If you scored fewer than 70 points, you may want to continue practicing the catching and throwing drills to improve your skills and increase your total score before you move to the next step.

Fielding

Defense wins ball games, and a major part of defense is fielding. When the batter hits a ball in a game, it comes to the fielder as a ground ball, line drive, or fly ball. Whatever the situation, the fielder needs to be able to handle all balls hit her way. As indicated in step 1, the specialized technique used to catch such a ball is called *fielding*. In this step, you will learn to field balls that come to you on the ground as well as fly balls that come to you in the air.

When the batter hits a grounder or a fly ball, a defensive player must field the ball before making the play. In the case of a grounder, the fielder must field the ball before throwing to the appropriate base or cutoff player. A fly ball must be caught to make the out. Proper fielding by the infielders is important because fielding a ground ball is the most common play made by an infielder. If the ground ball is not fielded properly, the ball will go through into the outfield, allowing the batter to safely reach first base. Because baserunners need to reach base safely to be in position to score runs, infielders must be consistent in fielding ground balls and making throws to appropriate bases.

Outfielders are the last line of defense; therefore, the skill of fielding ground balls is as important to them as it is for infielders. Ground balls misplayed by outfielders allow the baserunners to advance additional bases, putting them into scoring position and increasing the pressure on the defense.

All fielders playing any form of softball need to know how to field fly balls correctly. Outfielders catch long fly balls; infielders catch pop-ups (fly balls hit in or near the infield).

FIELDING GROUND BALLS

Whenever possible, the fielder should move to a position directly in front of the ground ball before attempting to field it. Fielding the ball on the run makes both catching and throwing the ball very difficult. Being in a stationary position while fielding the ball makes it easy to get down low and watch the ball go directly into the glove, as shown in figure 2.1.

When fielding a ground ball and making a throw to a base to put out a baserunner, you should try to make the fielding action and the throw one continuous motion. Remember the key points for catching and throwing: watch the ball go into the glove, use two hands, turn your glove side toward the target, and step with your glove-side foot in the direction of the target to throw.

When fielding, you need to get rid of the ball quickly to put out the baserunner. Remember, however, that your first priority is to field the ball. You cannot throw anyone out without first having the ball in your possession.

Figure 2.1   Fielding Ground Balls

PREPARING TO FIELD

1. Stagger stride
2. Knees are bent; weight is on balls of feet
3. Back is flat
4. Glove is low

FIELDING

1. Hands are low; glove is open to ball
2. Meet ball out front
3. Use two hands
4. Watch ball into glove
5. Focus on ball

PREPARING TO THROW

1. Shift weight back
2. Glove side is to target
3. Ball is in overhand throwing position
4. Glove-side elbow is to target
5. Throwing hand is on ball

Misstep

The ball goes "through" you and under your glove.

Correction

Remember to keep your glove fingers pointed down, bend your knees, and get your glove low and open to the ball.

Misstep

The ball bounces out of your glove.

Correction

Watch the ball go into your glove, and cover it at once with your throwing hand.

Figure 2.2   Slide step.

During a game, fielders are often required to get into position to field ground balls that are not coming directly toward them. You need to be able to move to your right and left to field balls—that's where hitters are trying to place their hits during a game. The hitter's job is to make it as difficult as possible for you to field the ball coming your way.

To move laterally into position to field a ball hit only a short distance away to the right or left, you should use a *slide step* (figure 2.2). From a ready ground ball fielding position (figure 2.1*a*), take a sideways step with the foot on the ground ball side, then close with the other foot. Repeat these sliding steps until you are directly in front of the ball (usually not more than two or three slide steps), keeping your hands low and glove open to the ball as you watch it go into your glove.

For a ball hit too far to the right or left to reach using the sliding step, you should use the *cross-over step* (figure 2.3). From a ready position (knees

Figure 2.3   Crossover step.

bent and hands at knees), pivot the ball-side foot toward the ball and cross over that foot with the other foot, taking a first step running at a slight angle toward the outfield in the direction of the hit. If possible, run into position directly behind the ball, and field the ball with two hands. If the ball must be fielded on the run, use the glove-side or throwing-side (backhand) stop as shown in figure 1.5 (page 10).

Misstep

You are late getting into position to field the ball.

Correction

Start to move into position as soon as the ball starts coming your way. Use the crossover step and move to the ball at a slight angle.

Ground Ball Drill 1.   *Fielding Thrown Ground Balls*

Stand 30 feet (9.1 meters) away from a partner. The player with the ball throws a ground ball to the fielder so that the ball travels on the ground at least two-thirds of the distance. The fielder fields the ball and returns it with an overhand throw, as if throwing out a baserunner. Practice 10 plays before switching fielder and thrower roles. Field the ball as it is thrown on the ground: directly at you, short in front of you (you must move forward to field the ball), to your glove side, and to your throwing side.

Success Check

- Use appropriate footwork and move quickly to get in position to field the ball.
- Field the ball ahead of your body.
- Make the fielding action and the throw one continuous motion.
- Look for your target and step toward the target to throw.

Score Your Success

Earn 1 point for each success check criteria you demonstrate for 10 plays as the fielder and 10 plays as the thrower.

65 to 80 points = 5 points

50 to 64 points = 3 points

49 points or fewer = 1 point

Your score _____

To Increase Difficulty

- Increase the force of the grounder.
- Increase the distance of lateral grounders.
- Vary the speed of grounders from slow to fast.
- Randomly vary the direction and speed of the grounders.

To Decrease Difficulty

- Continue to practice this drill.
- Reduce the force of the grounder.
- Use a softer ball.
- Increase the distance between partners.
- Reduce the distance of lateral grounders.

Ground Ball Drill 2. *React to the Bouncing Ground Ball*

Softball fields are never perfectly level. Consequently, ground balls may not roll smoothly across the ground. You need to be ready to field ground balls that bounce, sometimes quite erratically, as they approach you. Such grounders can be very difficult to field. For this drill, you should stand 30 feet (9.1 meters) away from a partner, as in the previous drill. The throwing partner throws bouncing ground balls for the fielder to field. Each throw should be directed hard at the ground and at least half of the distance to the fielder so that the ball bounces to the fielder.

First, the thrower sends 10 bouncing grounders directly at the fielder. Then the thrower sends 10 bouncing grounders to the fielder's glove side, followed by 10 bouncing grounders to the fielder's throwing side. Finally, the thrower sends 10 bouncing ground balls randomly to all directions. The partners should switch roles after each type of

ground ball so that each partner gets 10 fielding attempts for each type (in front, glove side, throwing side, and random).

When fielding bouncing grounders, you need to predict the location and height at which the ball will arrive. Get into position and field the ball with both hands. Make the overhand throw back to your partner.

Success Check

- Use appropriate footwork and move quickly to get in position to field the ball.
- Field the ball ahead of your body.
- Watch the bouncing ball into your glove.
- Make the fielding action and the throw one continuous motion.
- Look for your target and step toward the target to throw.

Score Your Success

Earn 1 point for each attempt in which you demonstrate all five success checks. Each player gets 10 attempts to each side (directly in front, glove side, throwing side, random).

　30 to 40 points = 5 points

　20 to 29 points = 3 points

　19 points or fewer = 1 point

　Your score _____

To Increase Difficulty

- Vary the distances of the first bounce from the fielder, beginning far away from the fielder and moving closer and closer.
- Vary the lateral distance, the direction, or the force of the bouncing grounder.
- Begin with the fielder facing away from the thrower. When releasing the ball, the thrower

says, "Turn." The fielder turns, locates the ball, reads its direction, moves into position, fields the ball, and throws it back using an overhand throw.

To Decrease Difficulty

- Continue to practice this drill.
- Repeat the previous ground ball drill.
- Decrease the number of bounces of the grounder.
- Use a softer ball.
- Decrease the lateral distance of the bouncing grounder.
- Set an order for the varying directions of the grounder during the "random" part of the drill (e.g., directly at, glove side, throwing side, repeat).

Ground Ball Drill 3. *Continuous Grounder Fielding*

You and your partner set up 30 feet (9.1 meters) apart. For this drill, you both field and throw ground balls to each other continuously. You throw a ground ball to your partner. Your partner, in one motion, fields the ground ball and throws a ground ball back for you to field.

Mix up the directions, the speeds, and the types of ground balls (rolling or bouncing) you throw to one another. The object is to make each other work hard so that you both will become solid, consistent fielders. However, do not try to throw the ball past your partner.

Repeat two sets of 30 throws (15 per partner). Count the number of successful fielding plays you and your partner make in a row. Each time one of you misses a ground ball, you must begin counting again at 1.

Success Check

- Use appropriate footwork and move quickly to get in position to field the ball.
- Field the ball ahead of your body.
- Watch the ball into your glove.
- Make the fielding action and the throw one continuous motion.
- Look for your target and step toward the target to throw.

Score Your Success

Give yourself a score based on the number of consecutive grounders you and your partner field out of two sets of 30 continuous ground balls.

24 to 30 consecutive grounders = 5 points

15 to 23 consecutive grounders = 3 points

5 to 14 consecutive grounders = 2 points

Fewer than 5 consecutive grounders = 1 point

Your total score ___

To Increase Difficulty

- Decrease the distance between partners.
- Randomly vary the direction, speed, and type of ground ball (rolling or bouncing).

To Decrease Difficulty

- Continue to practice this drill.
- Repeat a previous ground ball drill.
- Reduce the variety of throws.
- Set a pattern of throws (e.g., five rolling alternating with five bouncing throws).

Ground Ball Drill 4. *Wall or Net Rebound Fielding*

Stand 15 feet (4.5 meters) away from a wall or rebound net. When using a rebound net, tip the top of the net frame slightly forward to work on ground balls. Throw the ball against the wall (1 to 2 feet [30.4 to 60.9 centimeters] above the ground) so that it rebounds back to you. Get into fielding position directly in front of the ball. Field the ball and, in one continuous motion, move into the throwing position and throw to the wall for a repeat grounder. Repeat two sets of 20 throws. Count the number of successful fielding plays you make in a row. Each time you miss a ground ball, you must begin counting again at 1.

Success Check

- Use appropriate footwork and move quickly to get in position to field the ball.
- Field the ball ahead of your body.
- Watch the ball into your glove.
- Make the fielding action and the throw one continuous motion.
- Look for your target and step toward the target to throw.

Score Your Success

Give yourself a score based on the number of consecutive grounders you field out of two sets of 20 ground balls.

10 consecutive grounders = 5 points

6 to 9 consecutive grounders = 3 points

3 to 5 consecutive grounders = 2 points

Fewer than 3 consecutive grounders = 1 point

Your total score ___

To Increase Difficulty

• Throw the ball to the wall with more force.

• Increase the speed of fielding and throwing to the wall.

To Decrease Difficulty

• Continue to practice this drill.

• Repeat a previous ground ball drill.

• Use a softer ball.

• Stand farther away from the wall to increase the time you have to see and react to the ball.

• Use a softer throw to the wall.

Ground Ball Drill 5. *Fancy Footwork*

Using a wall or rebound net as in the previous drill, direct your throw at a slight angle to the wall or net so that the rebound goes away from your starting position. Throwing the ball slightly off center to the right causes the rebound to go to your right. Throw the ball to the left of center to cause the ball to go to your left.

Start by directing your throws just off center. Gradually increase the angle of the throws in order to increase the distance you must move to the ball. Use the appropriate footwork–slide step or crossover step–for the distance you must move to the ball. As the angle of the throw increases, move back away from the wall or net to give yourself time to reach the ball. Vary your throws so that you practice going both to your right and to your left to field the ball. Fielding the ball to your throwing-hand side is more difficult because you must travel farther to get into fielding position in front of the ball. Repeat two sets of 10 continuous fielding plays.

Success Check

• Get in front of the ball whenever possible.

• Use the appropriate footwork for the distance you need to travel to the ball.

Score Your Success

Score yourself for each set of fielding plays out of 10 attempts.

7 to 10 successful fielding attempts = 5 points

5 or 6 successful fielding attempts = 3 points

2 to 4 successful fielding attempts = 2 points

Fewer than 2 successful fielding attempts = 1 point

Your total score ___

To Increase Difficulty

• Angle the throw more in order to increase the distance you need to travel to field the ball.

• Move closer to the wall to lessen your reaction time.

To Decrease Difficulty

• Continue to practice this drill.

• Repeat a previous ground ball drill.

• Focus the practice on moving to the glove side.

• Lessen the angle of the rebound to lessen the distance you have to travel.

Fungo Hitting Ground Balls

Figure 2.4 Fungo hitting ground balls.

Fungo hitting is hitting the ball out of your own hand, either onto the ground (ground balls) or into the air (fly balls). This skill is mainly used to facilitate practice of fielding grounders and fly balls or to practice plays that follow fielding, such as tagging up after a caught fly ball. Fungo hitting is not used in a game; however, it does help you develop the eye–hand and eye–bat coordination necessary for hitting.

Players need to practice fielding balls that have come off a bat in order to gain more gamelike experience. If the coach is the only one who can fungo hit the ball toward a fielder, the practice opportunities will be severely limited. On the other hand, if everyone on the team can fungo hit a ball, then a variety of practice opportunities can be set up at the same time—not only to practice fielding ground balls or fly balls but also to work on skills such as tag plays, force plays, and tagging up to advance after a caught fly ball. You need to be able to fungo hit both ground balls and fly balls in order to fully participate in the drills in the remainder of this book. Here we will look at fungo hitting ground balls, a skill necessary for the drill that follows. Later in this step, we will discuss fungo hitting fly balls and using that skill in drills.

To fungo hit a ground ball, begin by holding a ball in the hand you place on the bottom end of the bat. Hold the bat high, back by your rear shoulder, with your top hand gripping the bat as usual. Using a light bat might help. Toss the ball out in front of your front foot so that it will drop to the position in space where it would be if placed on a tee. Once you toss the ball, quickly place your bottom hand on the bat to make your regular two-handed swing and hit the ball. Because you want to hit grounders, let the ball drop just below waist height, as if on a tee, before contacting and swinging through the ball. Be sure to start the bat high so that your swing path is high to low, making the ball go down onto the ground (figure 2.4). Stand so that your tossing shoulder is pointed toward the fielder. Step toward the fielder with your front foot as you begin your swing. Watch the ball until you make contact. If you hit a fly ball instead of a ground ball, start your swing later. Be sure to contact the ball after it drops below your waist.

If you want to practice fungo hitting grounders before you hit to a partner who is working on fielding, you can hit against a wall or fence. Stand far enough away from the wall so that you have plenty of time to field the rebounding ball with your tossing hand. Your other hand continues to hold onto the bat.

Ground Ball Drill 6.   *Fielding Hit (Fungo) Ground Balls*

This drill requires each partner to be able to successfully fungo hit ground balls (see "Fungo Hitting Ground Balls" above) or an additional person who can fungo hit ground balls. This drill is more advanced than the previous drills; therefore, before attempting it, you should have scored a point total that makes you ready to move on in all of the other ground ball drills. Fielding a hit ground ball requires you to remember the principles of fielding ground balls and to recognize that the ball will be coming at you with more force and be less predictable than a thrown ball. You must move quickly to the spot to field the ball, using the appropriate footwork and the appropriate fielding technique.

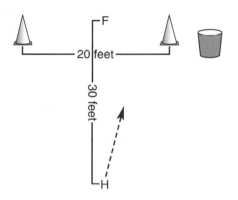

Figure 2.5   Fielding Hit (Fungo) Ground Balls drill.

The fielder is in ready position between two cones that are set up 20 feet (6.1 meters) apart, as shown in figure 2.5. The partner stands 30 feet (9.1 meters) away and fungo hits two sets of 10 ground balls between the cones. The fielder attempts to field each ball, ending in the "preparing to throw" position. The fielder then drops the fielded ball into a bucket that is placed outside the fielding area.

Success Check

- Get in front of the ball whenever possible.
- Use the appropriate footwork to travel the distance to the ball.
- End in the "preparing to throw" position.

Score Your Success

Score yourself for each of the two sets of 10 fielding attempts.

7 to 10 successful fielding attempts = 5 points

5 or 6 successful fielding attempts = 3 points

2 to 4 successful fielding attempts = 2 points

Fewer than 2 successful attempts = 1 point

Your total score ___

To Increase Difficulty

- Increase the distance between cones to increase the lateral distance you must travel to field the ball.

- Ask the hitter to hit the balls with more force, using the original distance or increasing the distance.

To Decrease Difficulty

- Repeat a previous ground ball drill.
- Decrease the distance between cones to decrease the lateral distance you must travel to field the ball.
- Have the hitter hit five balls to your right and then five to your left.
- Have the hitter hit the first set of 10 to your right and the second set of 10 to your left.

FIELDING FLY BALLS

For most players, fielding a fly ball is more difficult than fielding a ground ball. The tracking skill you worked on in step 1 is very important when fielding fly balls. Tracking the ball through the air is difficult because you have little against which to judge the changing position of the ball. Clouds or treetops in your field of vision as you track the ball can help you make the decision on where you must move your body in order to intercept the flight of the ball. Again, many of the principles you learned when working on catching and fielding ground balls will also be applied as you learn to catch a fly ball.

You should field a fly ball above and in front of your throwing shoulder (figure 2.6). As you learned in catching, your fingers should point up. Just as when fielding a ground ball, you want to get in front of the fly ball, but the technique varies a bit. Use the crossover step for all balls hit to the right or left of your starting position. For balls hit over your head, use a drop step. This allows your first step to be back, giving you a good jump on the ball. When using the drop step, your first action is to take a step back with the foot on the side to which the ball is hit. You then cross over with the opposite foot, continuing your run toward the ball.

Figure 2.6 | Fielding Fly Balls

PREPARING TO CATCH

1. When ball is hit, move to get in position to catch ball
2. Move into catch, heading in direction of throw
3. Glove is over throwing shoulder

a

CATCH

1. Catch ball over throwing shoulder
2. Catch ball using two hands
3. Watch ball into glove

b

PREPARING TO THROW *(CROW HOP)*

1. Step toward target with glove-side foot
2. Weight is on glove-side foot
3. Hop on throwing-side foot, closing to glove-side foot
4. Bring ball to throwing position
5. Weight is on throwing-side foot
6. Glove side is toward target
7. Glove elbow is toward target

c

Misstep

You have trouble fielding the ball because you lose it in the sun.

Correction

Use your glove to shield the sun.

Outfielders often must immediately throw the caught ball a great distance. Fielding the ball in front of your throwing shoulder allows you to more easily blend the catch and ensuing throw into one continuous motion. You should also be moving slightly in the direction of the throw as you catch the ball. Using a crow hop as you throw the ball will add increased force to your throw. To execute the crow hop, step toward the target with your glove-side foot, hop on your throwing-side foot to close it to the glove-side foot, and step again toward the target with your glove-side foot as you throw the ball. The footwork rhythm is step-together-step or step-close-step.

Misstep

On a fly ball, you have trouble judging where the ball will come down.

Correction

Track the ball using clouds, treetops, and buildings to help with depth perception.

Misstep

You catch the fly ball as if in a basket below your waist.

Correction

Position your body so you are moving into the ball as you catch it over your throwing shoulder.

Fly Ball Drill 1. *Partner Fly Ball Throws*

Stand 60 feet (18.3 meters) away from your partner, positioned so that neither of you is looking into the sun. The thrower throws balls simulating high fly balls to the fielder. The fielder fields the ball where it is thrown: directly in front, to the glove side, to the throwing side, and slightly behind. The fielder moves under the ball and catches it using proper technique. In a continuous motion, the fielder throws the ball overhand back to the thrower as if throwing out a baserunner who is attempting to advance after the catch. Use the crow hop to increase the force of your throw. Your partner should not have to move more than one step to catch your throw.

Success Check

- Move as soon as you see the thrower release the ball.
- Field the ball in front of your throwing-side shoulder.
- Get behind the ball. Be moving toward the target as you field the ball.
- Use the crow-hop step as you make an overhand throw.
- Make an on-target throw.

Score Your Success

For each type of fly ball (directly in front, glove side, throwing side, and slightly behind), score yourself for 10 attempts.

7 to 10 successful fielding attempts = 5 points

4 to 6 successful fielding attempts = 3 points

Fewer than 4 successful attempts = 1 point

Your total score ___

To Increase Difficulty

- Vary the height, lateral distance, and depth to which the ball is thrown.
- Vary the distance and direction of the throw after the catch by adding a third partner who will change positions to receive the thrown ball from the fielder.

- Increase the speed of the drill by using two balls. As soon as the first ball is caught, the thrower throws the second ball in a different direction.

To Decrease Difficulty

- Continue practicing this drill.
- Ask your partner to throw the ball higher so you have more time to track the ball.
- Use a softer ball.
- Decrease the lateral distance the fielder moves to get under the ball.
- Have the thrower cue the fielder about the throw's direction (when throwing randomly).

Fly Ball Drill 2. *Drop Step*

You and a partner stand 10 feet (3.0 meters) apart. One of you is a tosser, and the other is a fielder. The tosser holds a ball in the throwing hand. The fielder stands in a square stance facing the tosser, with feet shoulder-width apart and the toes of each foot even, equidistant from the tosser.

The tosser fakes a throw to the right or left of the fielder. On this signal, the fielder starts to run back for a fly ball coming to that side, taking the first step back (a drop step) with the foot on the side of the indicated throw while maintaining visual contact with the ball, which is still in the tosser's hand.

Now the tosser throws a fly ball to the side originally signaled. It should be deep and high enough to force the fielder to continue running to catch the ball. After catching the ball, the fielder throws the ball back to the tosser. Change roles after each sequence. Complete two sets of each sequence (10 total attempts for each sequence).

- Fake and throw right five times, consistent distance.
- Fake and throw left five times, consistent distance.
- Fake and throw right five times, varied distance.
- Fake and throw left five times, varied distance.
- Fake and throw a random direction five times, random distance.

Success Check

- Focus on the ball in the tosser's hand.
- Drop step back with the foot on the side that the ball is thrown.
- Cross over with the opposite foot, continuing your run toward the ball.
- Keep your eye on the ball.
- Catch the ball while moving in the direction of your intended throw back to the tosser.
- Throw a catchable ball back to the tosser.

Score Your Success

Score your execution on 10 attempts for each type of fly ball (right side, consistent distance; left side, consistent distance; right side, varied distance; left side, varied distance; random side and distance).

Catch the ball in 9 or 10 attempts = 5 points

Catch the ball in 6 to 8 attempts = 3 points

Catch the ball in fewer than 6 attempts = 1 point

Your total score ___

To Increase Difficulty

- Vary the height of the throw as well as its distance.
- Reduce the arc of the ball's flight so there is less time to track it.

To Decrease Difficulty

- Do not vary the distance of the throws.
- Use a softer ball.
- Make the arc on the ball higher so there is more tracking time.
- Shorten the distance the fielder has to run.
- Practice the drop step first without a thrown ball.

Fly Ball Drill 3. *Zigzag Drill*

This drill allows you to practice your drop step in a continuous manner while working on fielding fly balls on the run. Set up cones in a zigzag pattern approximately 30 feet (9.1 meters) apart to guide the location of each throw (figure 2.8). The tosser starts with three balls. The fielder begins by facing the tosser and standing 3 to 5 feet (91.4 to 152.4 centimeters) in front of the tosser. On the tosser's signal "go," the tosser throws a high fly ball to cone 1, and the fielder uses a drop step to move to catch the ball. As soon as the fielder catches the ball and drops it to the ground (or misses the ball), the

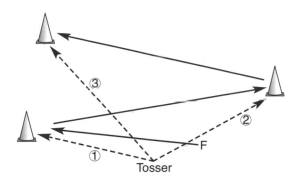

Figure 2.8 Cone setup for the Zigzag drill.

thrower throws another ball to cone 2. The fielder drop steps and moves to catch the second ball. As soon as the fielder catches the ball and then drops it to the ground (or misses the ball), the thrower throws another ball to cone 3. The fielder retrieves the three balls. The tosser and fielder switch roles after each set of three balls. Each person should complete four sets.

- Drop step back with the foot on the side that the ball is thrown.
- Cross over with the opposite foot, continuing your run toward the ball.
- Catch the ball over your throwing shoulder.

Score Your Success

Score yourself for each set of three tosses.

Catch the ball in all three attempts = 5 points

Catch the ball in two attempts = 3 points

Catch the ball in one attempt = 1 point

Your total score ___

To Increase Difficulty

- Vary the height of the throws.
- Increase the distance between cones.

To Decrease Difficulty

- Continue to practice this fly ball drill.
- Repeat a previous fly ball drill.
- Throw the ball higher so there is more tracking time.
- Decrease the number of cones.
- Decrease the distance between cones.

Fly Ball Drill 4. *Net Rebound Fielding*

Stand 15 to 20 feet (4.5 to 6.1 meters) away from a rebound net. Tip the top of the rebound net frame slightly back to work on fly balls. Throw the ball against the net (use the center of the net as a target) so that it rebounds back to you in an arc (fly ball). Get into a fielding position directly in front of the ball. Field the ball and, in one continuous motion, move into the throwing position. Using a crow hop, throw to the net for a repeat fly ball. Repeat two sets of 20 throws. Count the number of successful fielding plays you make in a row. Each time you miss a fly ball, you must begin counting again at 1.

Success Check

- Field the ball in front of your throwing-side shoulder.
- Get behind the ball. Be moving toward the target as you field the ball.
- Use the crow-hop step as you make an overhand throw.

Score Your Success

Score yourself after completing two sets of 20 throws.

Successfully field 15 to 20 consecutive fly balls = 5 points

Successfully 10 to 14 consecutive fly balls = 3 points

Successfully field 6 to 9 consecutive fly balls = 2 points

Successfully field fewer than 6 consecutive fly balls = 1 point

Your score ___

To Increase Difficulty

- Throw the ball to the rebound net with more force.
- Decrease the angle of the rebound net to decrease your reaction time.
- Increase the angle of the rebound net and move closer. This will require you to move back on the ball (drop step).
- Turn the rebound net slightly to the right or left. This will require you to move laterally to field the fly ball.

- Increase the speed of fielding and throwing to the net.

To Decrease Difficulty

- Continue to practice this fly ball drill.
- Repeat a previous fly ball drill.
- Use a softer ball.
- Increase the angle of the rebound net and stand farther away. This will increase the height of the fly ball and increase the time you have to see and react to the ball.
- Use a softer throw to the net.

Fungo Hitting Fly Balls

Figure 2.10   Fungo hitting fly balls.

Fungo hitting a fly ball is the same as fungo hitting a ground ball (see page 24), except the swing path is low to high rather than high to low. Toss the ball a little higher than when tossing for the ground ball, and begin the swing with the bat below your rear shoulder. Shift your weight onto your back foot, and drop your rear shoulder. Swing up at the ball and make contact at about shoulder height (figure 2.10) rather than down at waist height, as is done for the ground ball. Step forward into your hit as you did for the ground ball. Follow through high, with your hands and the bat finishing well above your shoulders.

If you mistakenly fungo hit a ground ball instead of a fly ball, you should toss the ball higher, drop your rear shoulder, swing up at the ball, and contact it at shoulder height. To keep the ball on target, stand with your front shoulder pointing to the target. Toss the ball so the contact point is off your front foot. Step toward the target with your front foot.

You can practice fungo hitting fly balls alone before hitting to a fielding partner, as you did for ground balls. However, rather than using a wall for practice, you should select a high obstacle to hit over, such as the backstop, goalposts, or even a small tree. Use a bucket of balls. Hit all the balls over the obstacle, collect them, and then hit them back. Before long, you will be ready to use your newly learned skill of fungo hitting to provide a partner or teammate with realistic practice in fielding fly balls and ground balls in addition to many combinations of skills.

Fly Ball Drill 5.   *Fielding Hit (Fungo) Fly Balls*

This drill requires each partner to be able to successfully fungo hit fly balls (see "Fungo Hitting Fly Balls" above). This drill is more advanced than previous drills; therefore, before attempting it, you should have scored enough points to move on in all other fly ball drills. If necessary, you can have a coach or someone else who is able to fungo hit assist you in this drill.

Fielding a hit fly ball requires you to remember the principles of fielding fly balls and to recognize that the ball will be coming at you with more force and will be less predictable than a thrown ball. You must move quickly to the spot to field the ball, using the appropriate footwork and the appropriate fielding technique.

This drill requires three people: a fielder, hitter, and catcher. The fielder will begin in ready position at least 30 feet (9.1 meters) away from the hitter (the distance will depend on how far the hitter can hit fly balls). The catcher should stand 5 to 6 feet (1.5 to 1.8 meters) away from the hitter to one side, preferably to the side that the hitter can see. The hitter fungo hits 10 fly balls randomly in front, to the glove side, to the throwing side, and behind the fielder. The fielder attempts to field each ball and throw the ball back to the catcher using good form, including the crow hop. After each set of 10, the fielder becomes the catcher, the catcher becomes the hitter, and the hitter becomes the fielder. Each person should field two sets of 10 fly balls.

Success Check

- Use appropriate footwork for the distance and direction traveled to the ball.
- Field the ball in front of your throwing-side shoulder.
- Get behind the ball. Be moving toward the target as you field the ball.
- Use the crow-hop step as you make an overhand throw.
- Make an on-target throw.

Score Your Success

Score yourself for each set of 10 fielding attempts.

7 to 10 successful fielding attempts = 5 points

5 or 6 successful fielding attempts = 3 points

Fewer than 5 successful fielding attempts = 1 point

Your total score ___

To Increase Difficulty

- Increase the distance and the force of the hit ball to decrease your reaction time, or move closer to the hitter if he is unable to hit the ball with more force at an increased distance.
- Move closer to the hitter, and have the hitter hit longer fly balls. This will increase the distance you need to travel.

To Decrease Difficulty

- Continue practicing this fly ball drill.
- Repeat a previous fly ball drill.
- Have the hitter tell you the direction that the ball will be hit.
- Use a softer ball.
- Move farther away from the hitter, and have the hitter hit high fly balls in the direction indicated. This will increase the time you have to react.

SUCCESS SUMMARY

Second only to pitching (especially in fastpitch), fielding ground balls and fielding fly balls are the two most important defensive skills in softball. When your team is in the field, every player, including the pitcher, must be able to successfully field the ball and make appropriate, accurate throws to put out members of the team at bat. Softball, unlike many other team sports, is very much like an individual sport. You, and you alone, have the chance to make the play on the batter who has hit the ball to you. You are just like the tennis player who must return the serve from the opponent across the net. On the other hand, in basketball, a forward driving past a guard will likely be picked up by another defensive player and be guarded while attempting a shot at the basket. In softball, the fly ball or ground ball that you miss will seldom be playable by another fielder to put the batter out. Good fielding and throwing are critical to you becoming a complete softball player.

Although a fly ball is usually considered a sure out, you know from practice of the skill that catching the fly ball is easier said than done! Ask a skilled observer to watch you field ground balls and fly balls. Ask the person to pay particular attention to your movement to the ball. Do you react quickly to the ball off the bat? Do you get in front of the ball, watch it go into your glove, field it with two hands, and field the ball and throw it in one continuous motion?

To become a skilled fielder, you must field and throw literally hundreds of ground balls and

fly balls that come to you from all directions, at varying speeds, distances, and heights. You must practice fielding a ball in every way a batter could possibly hit it to you. Your success as a fielder depends on your ability to read and react to the ball off the bat, move into position, and field and throw the ball in one continuous motion.

In the next step, we will be discussing the fundamentals of pitching in both fastpitch and slow-pitch softball. Before moving on to step 3, evaluate how you did on the drills in this step. Enter your scores for each drill, and then add up your scores to rate your total success.

Ground Ball Drills

1. Fielding Thrown Ground Balls   ___ out of 5
2. React to the Bouncing Ground Ball   ___ out of 5
3. Continuous Grounder Fielding   ___ out of 10
4. Wall or Net Rebound Fielding   ___ out of 10
5. Fancy Footwork   ___ out of 10
6. Fielding Hit (Fungo) Ground Balls   ___ out of 10

Fly Ball Drills

1. Partner Fly Ball Throws   ___ out of 20
2. Drop Step   ___ out of 25
3. Zigzag   ___ out of 20
4. Net Rebound Fielding   ___ out of 10
5. Fielding Hit (Fungo) Fly Balls   ___ out of 10

Total   ___ *out of 135*

Your total score will give you an indication of whether or not you have developed the skills necessary to be successful in the next steps. If you scored 101 points or more, congratulations! You have mastered the skills of fielding ground balls and fly balls, and you are ready to move on to the next step. If your total score was between

91 and 100 points, you are ready to move on to the next step, although you might benefit from getting additional practice in selected drills. If you scored fewer than 81 points, you should continue to practice the fielding drills to improve your skills and increase your total score before moving on.

Pitching

Pitching is important in all versions of softball. The defense uses the pitch to put the ball in play in a regulation softball game, but the pitch can also be an integral part of defensive strategy.

The softball pitch is delivered with an underhand motion, but the technique varies with the type of game being played. In fastpitch, the windmill is the most common pitching delivery, though the slingshot delivery is still used occasionally. The revolutions of the arm (one or one and a half) in the windmill pitch make it possible for the pitcher to throw the ball very fast. An elite pitcher may pitch the ball at speeds ranging from 60 to 70 miles (96.6 to 112.7 kilometers) per hour. Experienced pitchers may increase the effectiveness of their pitches by putting spin on the ball, which can make the ball break sharply up (a *rise ball*), sharply down (a *drop ball*), to the outside of the plate for a right-handed pitcher (a *curveball*), or to the inside of the plate for a right-handed pitcher (a *screw ball*). In addition, pitchers can throw an off-speed pitch (*change-up*) or can change the speed of most pitches to keep the batter off balance.

The game of modified-pitch softball employs most of the same game rules as fastpitch softball, except for the pitching regulations. The modified pitch is a pendulum-type delivery in which the arm swings down and backward behind the body. As the arm swings forward, the ball must be released to the batter. In the modified pitch, the elbow must be locked as the pitch is released. The modified pitch is very easy to learn.

The slow-pitch game requires a pitch delivered with an arc and without excessive speed. Pitching in slow pitch is a skill that most players can master in a relatively short time, but controlling the height of the arc can be challenging. The arced pitch in slow pitch is a finesse skill and does not require the strength or power of a windmill delivery. However, the modified pitch may be the easiest pitch to learn because the motion is simple and the ball is delivered in a flat trajectory. In addition, for the modified pitch, the pitcher does not need to master the technique of making the ball conform to the required arc in slow pitch and does not need to have the skill to provide the strength and power necessary for fastpitch.

In tennis, volleyball, and racquetball, the serve begins the game. Likewise, in softball, you cannot start or continue the game without the pitch; the batter would never get to hit! In fastpitch softball, pitching can dominate the game, especially in elite-level play. If you want to become an effective fastpitch pitcher, you must be willing to spend many hours developing your technique so that you can put both speed and movement on the ball. Pitching in slow pitch and modified pitch is not as overpowering a factor as it is in fastpitch; however, it is still an important skill, and the pitcher is a vital player on every team.

The slow-pitch and modified-pitch games are designed as hitting games. Pitching regulations ensure that the pitcher gives the hitter a good chance to hit the ball. This makes it possible for the defense to catch or field the ball and make the necessary plays to get baserunners out. However, slow-pitch and modified-pitch pitchers may still challenge the batter. This is done by consistently pitching the ball over the inside or outside corners of the plate and by avoiding pitching a ball over the "fat" part (down the middle) of home plate. A slow-pitch pitcher can also challenge the batter by changing the height of the arc, pitching short or deep, and placing a spin on the ball to cause it to slightly curve or have a backspin, front spin, or knuckle spin.

SLOW-PITCH PITCHING

By rule, the pitching delivery for slow pitch must be underhand. Pitchers can choose to use a two-, three-, or four-finger grip, depending on hand size or the type of spin put on the ball. (Note: In the women's game, the ball is 11 inches; in the men's and coed game, the ball is 12 inches.) The two-finger grip is the same as the two-finger grip for the overhand throw (see figure 1.2a on page 3). For the three-finger grip, place your index, middle, and ring fingers on one long seam and your thumb on a seam on the opposite side of the ball. Your little finger should be bent and placed on the side of the ball. To add additional spin or if your hand is small, you can choose to use a four-finger grip. The four-finger grip (figure 3.1) is basically the same as the three-finger grip except the little finger is wrapped around the ball and placed on a seam if possible.

Before your delivery, your pivot foot (throwing-side foot) must be in contact with the pitching rubber, and you must face the batter squarely and come to a complete stop with the ball in front of your body for a minimum of one second (figure 3.2a). Start your delivery by swinging your arm down, back to the rear, and then forward in the same path in an underhand pendulum motion.

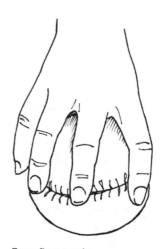

Figure 3.1 Four-finger grip.

Take a step toward the batter with your nonpivot foot as you release the ball (figure 3.2b). (The rules also allow this step to be taken backward or to the side. At the elite level of play, the step backward or to the side protects you more when a ball is hit right back at you.) Your pivot foot must be in contact with the pitching rubber as you release the ball. After releasing the ball, assume your fielding position and be ready for any ball hit back toward you (figure 3.2c).

Misstep

The ball goes too long or falls short of the target.

Correction

The amount of force is incorrect. Adjust the force so that the ball lands just behind the back point of home plate.

Figure 3.2 | Slow Pitch

a   *b*   *c*

PREPARE TO PITCH

1. Stagger stride
2. Pivot foot is on pitching rubber
3. Weight is on back foot
4. Ball is held in front using two-, three-, or four-finger grip
5. Face batter
6. Come to full stop

INITIATE MOTION AND RELEASE

1. Shift weight to pivot foot
2. Arm is down and behind you
3. Step toward batter
4. Arm swings forward; fingers are behind ball
5. Grip ball for intended pitch
6. Release ball in front of hip

FOLLOW THROUGH

1. Step forward with pivot foot
2. Hand is above head
3. Knees are bent; square stance
4. Hands are at ready position to field
5. Watch for and react to hit ball

Misstep

You get hit with the batted ball.

Correction

Be sure to finish in a good fielding position after the release of the pitch.

The rules of slow-pitch softball are governed by two main organizations: the Amateur Softball Association (ASA) and the United States Specialty Sports Association (USSSA). The rules for each vary slightly, mostly in regard to pitching. In the ASA game, the arc of the slow pitch must be between 6 and 12 feet (1.8 and 3.6 meters) from the ground. In the USSSA game, the ball must arc at least 3 feet (1 meter) above the release point and no higher than 10 feet (3.0 meters) from the ground (1.8 and 3.6 meters). Some other versions of the game allow an unlimited arc. Pitching distances also vary by organization. The most common distances are 46 or 50 feet (14 or 15 meters). Since 50 feet is the most often used, it will be used for the drills; however modify the distance to fit your league if necessary.

Misstep

The ball travels in too high an arc.

Correction

You are holding onto the ball too long. Release the ball as your hand passes your hip, and aim at a point 10 to 12 feet (3.0 to 3.6 meters) above the ground, depending on the version of the game, two-thirds of the distance to home plate (about 33 feet [10.1 meters]).

Misstep

The ball travels with no arc.

Correction

You are releasing too soon. Complete the follow-through out and up after you release the pitch.

Although the expectation in the slow-pitch game is for a lot of hitting, the pitcher can challenge batters by putting different spins on the ball and by varying pitch location. The hitter will have difficulty making solid contact with a pitch that is spinning, and the tendency will be for the hitter to pop the ball up or hit it on the ground.

The ball can be made to spin clockwise, counterclockwise, forward, backward, or even curve slightly by either the movement of your hand on the release or the manner in which the ball comes off your fingers. In addition, the pitcher can cause the ball to have no spin by throwing a knuckleball.

For a forward or backward spin, hold the ball across a seam with the two long seams parallel to the ground and perpendicular to the line of direction of the pitch. For a forward spin, hold the ball with the palm up and let the ball roll off the ends of the fingers on the release. You can cause the ball to have a backward spin by releasing the ball one of two ways. One method is to hold the ball with the palm down, the back of the hand toward the batter, and release the ball by pulling up on the seam with the fingers and flicking the hand and wrist up. A second method is to hold the ball with the palm facing your body; you release the ball by pulling up and back on the seam with the fingers and flicking your hand and wrist up and toward your body, ending with the thumb and fingers facing back and with the palm still facing to the side, toward the body.

To make a ball spin clockwise or counterclockwise, hold the ball with your fingers pointing at home plate and resting along one of the four seams. For a clockwise spin, start the release with the palm down, the thumb next to the body, and sharply rotate the wrist so the palm comes up and the thumb rotates up and away from the body. For a counterclockwise spin, start the release with the palm up, the thumb away from the body, and rotate the wrist so the palm goes down and out, ending facing away from the body with the thumb toward the ground. To throw a knuckleball, place the thumb on the front of the ball (on or off the seam). The long seams of the ball should be on the side of the ball. Place the knuckles of the index, middle, and ring finger on the backside of the ball. On the release, the palm is facing the batter, and the ball is pushed away from the hand using the knuckles, with minimal wrist movement. The follow-through for all pitches is out and away from the body, finishing with the hand above the head.

Slow-Pitch Drill 1. *Fence Pitch*

You and a partner stand across from one another on opposite sides of a 6-foot (1.8-meter) high fence. Stand about 25 feet (7.5 meters) from the fence. The distance between you and your partner (50 feet [15.0 meters]) is the regulation slow-pitch pitching distance. Pitch the ball back and forth over the fence, using the fence as a guide to work on the correct arc of the pitch (figure 3.3). Pitch at least 20 balls, trying to get 10 consecutive pitches to clear the fence and go to your partner. Your partner should not have to move to catch the pitch. Your partner will pitch the balls back to you. If you get 10 consecutive pitches before you reach 20 attempts, keep going and see how many times in a row you can pitch a successful pitch.

Figure 3.3
Fence pitch drill.

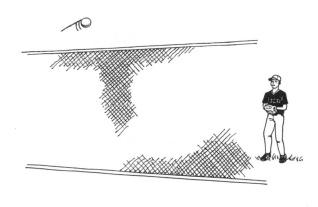

Success Check

- Take one step with the nonpivot foot toward your partner as the pitch is released.
- Use a two-, three-, or four-finger grip with your hand under the ball.

- Release the ball as it passes your hip.
- Follow through with your pitching hand above your head.

Score Your Success

Score yourself based on the number of consecutive pitches that clear the fence and go directly to your partner (out of 20 attempts). Don't count the pitch if your partner has to move to catch it.

10 to 20 consecutive pitches = 5 points

6 to 9 consecutive pitches = 3 points

3 to 5 consecutive pitches = 2 points

1 or 2 consecutive pitches or at least 1 pitch over the fence = 1 point

Your score ___

To Increase Difficulty

- Place spins on the ball.

To Decrease Difficulty

- Shorten the distance of the pitch by moving closer to the fence.
- Pitch over a 4-foot (1.2-meter) fence.

Slow-Pitch Drill 2. *Wall Pitch*

Mark a wall at 1, 6, and 12 feet (30.4, 182.9, and 365.8 centimeters) from the floor. The 6- and 12-foot lines are the pitching height lines. The area between the floor and the 1-foot line is the target for the pitch. Mark the floor 50 feet (15.0 meters) away from the wall; this mark is your pitching rubber.

When pitching in a regulation game, you have a 6- to 12-foot height limitation. For a strike to be called, the pitch, if not hit by the batter or caught by the catcher, must land on the ground just behind the back part of the plate. Aim your pitch to traverse an arc with a peak between the two highest lines marked on the wall (arcing higher than 6 feet, but

not above 12 feet) and to hit the wall between the 1-foot mark and the base of the wall. Hitting the base of the wall in this drill is the same as having the pitch come down just behind the plate.

Stand on the 50-foot floor mark with your throwing-side foot. Pitch the ball using the techniques described in figure 3.2. Remember to follow all three phases. Attempt 10 pitches.

Success Check

- Stagger your stride with the pivot foot on the pitching rubber.
- Hold the ball in a two- or three-finger grip (four fingers if necessary).

- Shift your weight to the pivot foot as your arm swings down and to the rear.
- Step toward the wall target (batter) as the ball is released.
- Follow through out and up.
- Bring your pivot foot to a square stance, with your hands at ready fielding position.

Score Your Success

7 to 10 on-target pitches = 5 points

5 or 6 on-target pitches = 3 points

Demonstrate some success check criteria in at least 2 on-target pitches = 2 points

Fewer than 5 on-target pitches = 1 point

Your score ___

To Increase Difficulty

- Mark the target area the width of the plate. Aim the pitch for the inside and outside corners.

- Place a bucket at the base of the wall. Try to get the pitch to hit the wall and go into the bucket.

To Decrease Difficulty

- Shorten the distance of the pitch.
- Focus mainly on success check criteria by eliminating the 1-foot line as the target area.

Slow-Pitch Drill 3.   Fence Pitch With Target

Stand on one side of a 6-foot (1.8-meter) high fence opposite a partner, about 25 feet (7.0 meters) from the fence. A home plate with a strike mat is in front of each partner. A strike mat can be made of old carpet, vinyl, or plastic. This mat should be the width of home plate, approximately 1 foot (30.4 centimeters) long, and should be cut to fit the back corner of home plate. The distance between you and your partner is the regulation slow-pitch pitching distance (50 feet [14.0 meters]). Pitch the ball back and forth over the fence, using the fence as a guide to work on the correct arc of the pitch. Pitch at least 20 balls, trying to get 10 pitches that clear the fence and land on the strike mat. Your partner will pitch the balls back to you. If you pitch 10 strikes before you reach 20 attempts, keep going and see how many strikes you can pitch.

Success Check

- Take one step toward your partner with your nonpivot foot as you release the pitch.
- Use a two-, three-, or four-finger grip with your hand under the ball.
- Release the ball as it passes your hip.
- Follow through out toward the target and above your head.

Score Your Success

Score yourself based on the number of pitches that clear the fence and land on the strike mat (out of 20 attempts).

10 to 20 strikes = 5 points

6 to 9 strikes = 3 points

3 to 5 strikes = 2 points

1 or 2 strikes or at least 1 pitch over the fence = 1 point

Your score ___

To Increase Difficulty

- Place two ropes, one at 12 feet (3.6 meters) and one at 10 feet (3.0 meters). Pitch the ball the 50-foot distance so that the ball goes between the two ropes.
- Place spins on the ball.

To Decrease Difficulty

- Shorten the distance of the pitch by moving closer to the fence.
- Pitch over a 4-foot (1.2 meter) fence.
- Make the strike mat larger.

Slow-Pitch Drill 4. *Ball in the Bucket*

Place an empty bucket, milk crate, or similar container 50 feet (15.0 meters) away from the pitching rubber. Using correct technique, pitch the ball into the bucket. If you are working alone, use 10 or more balls so that you do not have to retrieve each pitch. If you are working with a partner, stand 50 feet apart, each with a bucket, and pitch one ball back and forth.

Pitch 10 pitches. You earn 2 points if a pitch goes into the bucket (even if it pops out!) and 1 point if a ball hits the bucket on the fly. A pitch must traverse the regulation arc in order for the points to count. Partners should judge for one another. (If you are working without a partner, you can do this drill over the outfield fence to help you judge the regulation height of the pitch.) Your goal is to earn at least 14 points on 10 pitches.

Success Check

- Step in the direction of the target (bucket).
- Bend your knees and use your legs to aid in the lift for the pitch.
- Make sure your hand follows through high, directly in line with the bucket.
- Focus on the target (bucket) throughout the pitch.

Score Your Success

Score yourself based on the number of points you earned in 10 attempts. You earn 2 points if the pitch goes into the bucket and 1 point if the ball hits the bucket on the fly.

14 to 20 points = 5 points

9 to 13 points = 3 points

4 to 8 points = 2 points

1 to 3 points = 1 point

Your score ___

To Increase Difficulty

- Use a smaller bucket.
- Use two buckets placed the width of the plate apart, or use three buckets placed at the width of the plate and at the back corner of the plate. Alternate pitching to each bucket. Vary the size of the bucket to change the difficulty of this option.
- Place a spin on the pitch.
- Place the bucket at a short or long distance to practice increasing the challenge for the batter.

To Decrease Difficulty

- Shorten the distance. Begin at 30 feet (9.1 meters), increasing the distance as your success rate increases.
- Use a bigger bucket, a big cardboard box, or a laundry basket.

MODIFIED-PITCH PITCHING

The technique for pitching the modified pitch is similar to both the slow-pitch and the fastpitch techniques in some aspects. The modified pitch requires an underhand delivery of the ball to the batter, but the pitching motion is limited to a pendulum action only. The arm must come straight back and must go directly back and forward in one smooth motion.

Begin with the heel of your front foot (pivot foot) and the toe of your back foot (nonpivot foot) on the pitching rubber (figure 3.4a). Stand with the pivot foot in a slightly open stance at the front edge of the pitching rubber—the ball of the foot is on the ground in front of the pitching rubber and the heel is fully in contact with the pitching rubber. The toes of your nonpivot foot should be touching the back edge of the pitching rubber and should point toward home plate. Your shoulders should be in line with first and third bases, and your hands should be separated with the ball held in either the hand or the glove.

Bring your hands together and come to a full one-second stop with the ball in front of your body. Because the modified pitch can be thrown with some speed, the two- or three-finger grip (see figure 1.2 on page 3) is preferred. As you begin your delivery, swing your arm backward and open your hips and shoulders so that they face third base (for a right-handed pitcher). As you bring your arm down and forward into the release zone, close your hips and shoulders by driving the hip on your pivot-foot side forward so that your hips and shoulders rotate squarely to face home plate as you release the pitch. The release of the ball is accompanied by a step toward the batter with the nonpivot foot (figure 3.4b). The ball may not be outside your wrist at any point in the delivery, and at the point of release, your elbow must be locked. These rules prevent the pitch from being thrown with excessive speed. After releasing the ball, bring your pivot foot forward and assume a balanced, square fielding stance (figure 3.4c).

Misstep

The pitched ball does not have much speed or lands short of home plate.

Correction

Open your hips and shoulders on the backswing, and drive them closed as you release the pitch. Increase the speed of your arm as it moves in the pendulum motion.

Figure 3.4 — Modified Pitch

PREPARE TO PITCH
1. Heel and toe are on pitching rubber
2. Pivot foot is in front
3. Weight is on back foot
4. Ball is in both hands in front; use two- or three-finger grip
5. Face batter
6. Come to full stop
7. Focus on target

INITIATE MOTION AND RELEASE
1. Shift weight to pivot foot
2. Arm is down and to rear
3. Open hips and shoulders
4. Arm swings forward
5. Step toward batter
6. Close hips and shoulders
7. Release ball at hip
8. Elbow is locked at release

FOLLOW THROUGH
1. Step forward with pivot foot
2. Hand is above head and relaxed
3. Knees are bent; square stance
4. Hands are at ready position
5. Watch for and react to hit ball

Misstep

The pitched ball is consistently too high.

Correction

Release the ball at your hip.

Misstep

As a right-handed pitcher, you consistently pitch the ball outside to a right-handed batter (or as a left-handed pitcher, you consistently pitch the ball outside to a left-handed batter).

Correction

Make sure your arm does not come across your body as you release the ball and follow through. Step in the direction of your pitch.

Modified-Pitch Drill 1. *Fence Target Drill*

On a fence or wall, place a target that is 4 feet (1.2 meters) wide and 4 feet high; position the target 1 foot (30.4 centimeters) from the ground. Stand 15 feet (4.5 meters) from the wall, and pitch 10 pitches to the target. When you can successfully hit the target 10 pitches in a row, move back to 30 feet (9.1 meters) from the wall. Do not score yourself yet; you will begin scoring yourself when you reach the full pitching distance. These first steps are to prepare you for pitching at the full distance. For each attempt, be sure to focus on the success check criteria.

When you are successful at 30 feet, pitch from the full pitching distance (ASA rules: 40' for women and 46' for men). From the full pitching distance, pitch 10 pitches at the target. Count the number of times that you hit the target while demonstrating the success check criteria.

Success Check

- Place your heel and toe on the pitching rubber, use a two- or three-finger grip, and come to a full one-second stop with your hands together.
- Shift your weight to the pivot foot. Make sure your arm travels in the line of direction to the plate (the fence) while moving to the rear and forward.
- Open your hips and shoulders at the top of the backward swing.
- Step in the direction of the target.
- Close your hips and shoulders at the bottom of the swing as the ball is released.
- Snap your wrist as the ball is released.
- Follow through in the direction of the target (fence).
- Assume a fielding position.

Score Your Success

Score yourself based on the number of pitches that hit the target (out of 10 attempts).

8 to 10 successful pitches = 5 points

5 to 7 successful pitches = 3 points

Fewer than 5 successful pitches = 1 point

Your score ___

To Increase Difficulty

- Place a one-foot strip down the middle of the target. This strip becomes a no-pitch zone—the area on the target that you do not want your pitches to hit.

- Attempt to pitch 10 consecutive pitches that hit the target, either the original target or with the one-foot strip.

To Decrease Difficulty

- Continue to practice this drill.
- Practice pitching against the fence without a target.
- Begin at 10 feet (3.0 meters), and increase the pitching distance by 5-foot (1.5-meter) intervals.

Modified-Pitch Drill 2. *Pitching Zone Fence Target*

On a bedsheet or a large piece of heavy cardboard, create a pitching target by drawing a target that is 20 inches (50.8 centimeters) wide and 30 inches (76.2 centimeters) high. On this target, draw five columns. The column down the middle is 8 inches (20.3 centimeters) wide. The two columns on each side are 3 inches (7.6 centimeters) wide. The final zones are created by drawing a 4-inch (10-centimeter) zone that goes across the middle of the two side columns (figure 3.5). Attach the target to a wall or fence approximately 1 foot (30.4 centimeters) off the ground. The middle zone is worth 1 point, the two inside columns are worth 3 points, the two outside columns are worth 5 points, the outside middle is worth 4 points, and the inside middle is worth 2 points.

From the full pitching distance, pitch 10 pitches at the target, attempting to get the highest possible score while demonstrating the success check criteria. The zones with the higher points represent the more ideal pitch locations—high inside, high outside, low inside, and low outside.

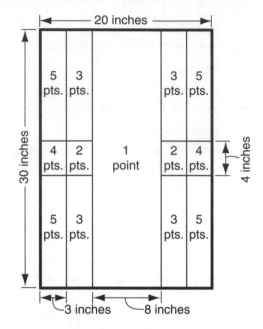

Figure 3.5 Pitching Zone Fence Target drill.

Success Check

- Place your heel and toe on the pitching rubber, use a two- or three-finger grip, and come to a full one-second stop with your hands together.
- Shift your weight to the pivot foot. Make sure your arm travels in the line of direction to the plate (the fence) while moving to the rear and forward.

- Open your hips and shoulders at the top of the backward swing.
- Step in the direction of the target.
- Close your hips and shoulders at the bottom of the swing as the ball is released.
- Snap your wrist as the ball is released.
- Follow through in the direction of the target.
- Assume a fielding position.

Score Your Success

Score yourself based on the number of points you earn after 10 pitching attempts.

35 to 50 points = 5 points

20 to 34 points = 3 points

10 to 19 points = 2 points

19 points or fewer = 1 point

Your score ___

To Increase Difficulty

- Place a 1-foot strip down the middle of the target in the 1-point zone. This strip becomes a no-pitch zone—the area on the target that you do not want your pitches to hit. You receive no points if you hit that area.
- Attempt to pitch 10 consecutive pitches that hit the target, either the original target or with the 1-foot strip.
- Attempt to pitch 5 to 10 consecutive pitches in a particular zone.
- Limit your target to the 5-point zone only.

To Decrease Difficulty

- Continue to practice this drill.
- Repeat the Fence Target drill.
- Decrease the pitching distance.

FASTPITCH PITCHING

Unlike the hitter's game of slow pitch, fastpitch is a pitcher's game. The baseball adage that good pitching will beat good hitting is equally applicable to fastpitch softball. Amateur Softball Association Hall of Fame pitchers Bertha Tickey, Joan Joyce, Donna Lopiano, Lorene Ramsey, and Nancy Welborn dominated women's fastpitch games in the 1960s, 1970s, and 1980s. U.S. women's Olympic team pitchers Lisa Fernandez (1996, 2000, 2004), Michele Granger (1996), Lori Harrigan (1996), Cat Osterman (2004), and Michelle Smith (1996, 2000) continued the dominance of pitching in women's fastpitch. In fact, the 2004 U.S. Olympic team surrendered only one run while earning their second consecutive gold medal! The legendary Harold (Shifty) Gears, Sam (Sambo) Elliot, and Al Linde, in addition to Johnny Spring and Herb Dudley, likewise dominated the men's fastpitch game from the 1950s through the 1980s. The speed of the softball fastpitch is equivalent to that of the overhand baseball pitch based on the decreased distance it is required to travel. Softball pitches thrown 60 to 70 miles per hour (96.6 to 112.6 kilometers per hour) equate to baseballs pitched in the 90-mile-per-hour (145-kilometer-per-hour) range.

The topic of developing and training pitchers for the highest level of fastpitch competition could take an entire book by itself. Even so, the elite pitchers of the world began at some point in their lives to learn the fundamentals of fastpitch pitching. Let's begin with the windmill pitch.

Windmill Pitch

The secret to the windmill pitch is the *perfect circle*. Just as the blades of a windmill rotate in a perfect circle around its axle, the arm of the windmill pitcher traverses a similar circle. In addition, that circle must be in a direct line to the target (home plate).

Imagine a large hoop on its edge at the pitching rubber, with the leading edge pointed at a corner of home plate. If you pushed the hoop, it would roll in a straight line to the target point. During the windmill pitch, the same idea holds true, except the hoop representing the perfect circle is raised above the ground so that the bottom edge is at a height between your hip and knee. The axle is your shoulder. The target point at the plate is also above the ground, somewhere between the batter's armpits and the top of the knees, over home plate. As you begin the pitch, the ball starts at the bottom of that hoop circle, then moves forward, up and over the top, and down the backside. It is released as your arm passes your hip, back where it began—at the bottom of the circle. This then is the perfect circle.

Official fastpitch rules regarding the starting position on the pitching rubber vary according to gender, age, and rule organization (e.g., ASA, federation, NCAA). When you are learning the windmill pitch, we recommend that you "heel and toe" the pitching rubber. Stand with the pivot foot angled in an open stance at the front edge of the pitching rubber so that the ball of the foot is on the ground in front of the pitching rubber and the heel is fully in contact with the pitching rubber. The toes of your nonpivot foot should be touching the back edge of the pitching rubber.

Most pitchers will dig a slight hole in front of the pitching rubber where the ball of the pivot foot contacts the ground. This allows the pivot foot to push off against the front edge of the pitching rubber as the pitch is delivered, thus giving additional force to the pitch. The slightly open stance of the pivot foot enables you to fully open your hips at the top of the circle, making the perfect circle possible.

Align your shoulders with first and third base as you assume your position on the pitching rubber before starting the pitch. When taking a signal from the catcher, you can hold the ball in either your hand or glove, but your hands must be separated. Before starting the pitch, you must bring the hands together (figure 3.6a). Hold the ball so you can take the appropriate grip for the pitch to be thrown. To prevent the batter and the base coaches from seeing the grip you have on the ball (thereby giving the pitch away), cover the ball with your glove so that the back of the glove is toward the batter.

Begin the pitch with a slight bend forward at the waist (your hands are still together). This slight bend provides a negative action that allows for maximum force production. Initiate the pitching motion by starting the ball, still covered by the glove, forward and up the front side of the circle. When the ball is about chest high, separate your hands. At the same time, begin to open your hips and shoulders (if you are a right-handed pitcher, rotate your hips and shoulders so you face third base) and shift your weight onto your pivot foot. Once you separate your hands at any point in the motion, you cannot rejoin them. When your hand is at the top of the circle, your hips and shoulders should be open, your weight should be fully on the pivot foot, and your knees should be slightly bent (figure 3.6b). Your arm should be fully extended with the ball held in a two- or three-finger grip. The hand should be rotated so the back of the hand is toward the batter. The glove hand should be extended up and toward home plate. Your nonpivot foot should begin to step toward the target.

As your hand starts the downswing (down the backside of the circle), your hips and shoulders should begin to close. Begin to shift your weight forward as you complete the step toward home plate with the nonpivot foot. During the down-

swing, your pitching elbow should be relaxed and slightly bent. The knees are still slightly bent, and the front foot begins to plant. Be sure the step does not cross over the ball's line of flight. The toe of the front foot should be turned in slightly. At the same time that the pitching hand is in the downswing, the glove-hand elbow is pulled down into the side.

As your arm goes through the pitching slot, the arm should be bent slightly with the wrist cocked back. As your arm passes your hip, snap your wrist strongly and release the pitch. At the same time, your pivot foot and leg drive hard off the pitching rubber and forward toward your nonpivot foot, causing your hips to close slightly. Transfer your weight to the slightly flexed front leg.

To follow through, bring your pivot foot and leg forward so that you can assume a balanced fielding position (figure 3.6c). Your hand should finish at about chest level (for a fastball), relaxed and away from your body, having followed the path of the front edge of the hoop to complete the perfect circle.

Misstep

The pitch has little speed.

Correction

Open your hips and shoulders at the top of the circle. Forcefully drive your pivot foot leg toward your nonpivot foot leg. Relax your arm and increase its speed as you bring it through the circle. Snap your wrist on the release.

Figure 3.6 | Windmill Pitch

PREPARE TO PITCH

1. Heel and toe pitching rubber
2. Pivot foot is slightly open
3. Weight is on back foot
4. Shoulders are in line with first and third bases
5. Ball is in both hands, with stop in front
6. Start ball forward with both hands, bending slightly forward

b

c

INITIATE MOTION AND RELEASE

1. Shift weight to pivot foot; knees are bent
2. Open hips and shoulders
3. Bring arm back to fully extended position; back of hand is to batter
4. Step toward target; plant foot with flexed front foot
5. Drive off pivot foot
6. Close hips and shoulders by pulling pivot foot toward stride foot
7. Elbow is relaxed
8. Release ball at hip (point of release may vary depending on type of pitch thrown)
9. Keep body in upright position; avoid bending forward at waist
10. Snap wrist on release of pitch

PREPARE TO FIELD

1. Step forward with pivot foot
2. Hand and arm are relaxed out in front of body
3. Knees are bent; square stance
4. Hands are in fielding position
5. Watch for hit ball

Misstep

The pitch is consistently high.

Correction

Release the ball earlier. Keep your body in an upright position.

Misstep

The pitch is off line either inside or outside.

Correction

Have someone stand behind you and check for "the perfect circle" in the line of direction to home plate. Adjust your stride toward the target.

Fastball Drill 1. *Wrist Snap*

The purpose of this drill is to help you develop a strong wrist snap, which will help you throw pitches with maximum speed. Stand with your nonthrowing side facing a target on a net, fence, or wall at

Figure 3.7
Wrist Snap drill.

a distance of 5 feet (1.5 meters). Create the target by placing two parallel lines that are 2 feet (0.6 meters) apart on the net, fence, or wall. The bottom line should be at your mid-thigh level. Your feet should be slightly apart. With your nonpitching hand, hold the forearm of your pitching arm just above the wrist. Cock the wrist back and snap it forward, attempting to pitch the ball between the target lines (figure 3.7).

Success Check

- Cock your wrist back.
- Hold the ball in a two- or three-finger grip.
- With your nonpitching hand, hold your pitching arm just above the wrist to isolate the wrist action.
- Snap your wrist forward and release the pitch.
- Attempt to pitch the ball between the target lines.

Score Your Success

Score yourself based on the number of pitches (out of 10) that hit between the target lines. Complete two sets.

    8 to 10 successful attempts = 5 points
    6 or 7 successful attempts = 3 points
    3 to 5 successful attempts = 2 points
    1 or 2 successful attempts = 1 point
    Your total score ___

To Increase Difficulty

- Increase the distance from the target. (Do not exceed 8 feet [2.4 meters].)
- Decrease the target size.

To Decrease Difficulty

- Decrease the distance from the target. (Do not go less than 2 feet.) At this distance, a soft or cloth ball is recommended.
- Increase the target size.

Fastball Drill 2. *Three-Quarter Stance*

The purpose of this drill is to help you combine a strong wrist snap with the downswing action of the windmill pitch. Stand with your nonthrowing side facing a target on a net, fence, or wall at a distance of 10 feet (3.0 meters). Use the same target as in the Wrist Snap drill. Begin in a three-quarter stance—feet approximately 18 inches (45.7 centimeters) apart with the front foot facing slightly to the right (right-handed pitcher). Start with your pitching arm at the top of the circle, ready for the downswing

with the wrist cocked back. The nonthrowing arm should be extended out, facing the target. Begin the pitching action by lifting and replacing your front foot and beginning your downswing action. Pull your nonthrowing elbow into your side, and snap your wrist and release the pitch as the ball passes your hip.

Success Check

- Cock your wrist back.

- Hold the ball in a two- or three-finger grip.
- Start with your pitching arm at the top of the circle, with your wrist cocked.
- At the beginning of the downswing action, lift and replace your front foot.

- Pull your nonthrowing elbow into your side.
- Snap your wrist as the ball passes your hip, and release the pitch.
- Attempt to pitch the ball between the target lines.

Score Your Success

Score yourself based on the number of pitches (out of 10) that hit between the target lines.

8 to 10 successful attempts = 5 points

6 or 7 successful attempts = 3 points

3 to 5 successful attempts = 2 points

1 or 2 successful attempts = 1 point

Your score ___

To Increase Difficulty

- Increase the distance from the target. (Do not exceed 15 feet [4.5 meters].)
- Decrease the target size.

To Decrease Difficulty

- Decrease the distance from the target. (Do not go less than 6 feet [1.8 meters]). At this distance, a soft or cloth ball is recommended.
- Increase the target size.
- Repeat the Wrist Snap drill.

Fastball Drill 3. *Speed and Accuracy*

The purpose of this drill is to work on developing speed and accuracy at the same time. This will help you develop a consistent technique and avoid getting into the habit of aiming pitches, which can decrease your speed.

For this drill, you can use the same target that was used in the Pitching Zone Fence Target drill (modified-pitch drill 2, see page 42). In addition, place five pitching rubbers (or lines) at distances of 15, 20, 25, 30, and 43 (or 40 or 46) feet (4.5, 6.1, 7.6, 9.1, and 13.0 (or 12.0 or 14.0) meters from the target. Begin from a pitching distance of 15 feet. Pitch 10 pitches at the target, attempting to get the highest possible score while demonstrating the success check criteria. The zones with the higher points represent the more ideal pitch locations—high inside, high outside, low inside, and low outside.

Success Check

- Heel and toe the rubber. Use a two- or three-finger grip. Make a full one-second stop with your hands together.
- Shift your weight to your pivot foot. Make sure your arm travels in line to the plate (the fence) while moving to the rear and forward.
- Open your hips and shoulders at the top of the backward swing.
- Step in the direction of the target.
- Close your hips and shoulders at the bottom of the swing as the ball is released.
- Snap your wrist as the ball is released.
- Follow through in the direction of the target.
- Maintain a consistent pitch speed.
- Assume a fielding position.

Score Your Success

Score yourself based on the number of points you earn in 10 pitching attempts from each distance. Do not move on to the next distance unless you score 5 points at 15, 20, and 25 feet and at least 3 points at 30 feet. Your final score is the score you achieve at the regulation distance for your league.

35 to 50 points = 5 points

20 to 34 points = 3 points

19 points or fewer = 1 point

Your final score (regulation distance) ___

To Increase Difficulty

- Place a 1-foot (30.4-centimeter) strip down the middle of the target (the 1-point zone). This strip becomes a no-pitch zone—the area on the target that you do not want your pitches to hit. You receive no points if you hit that area.

- Attempt to pitch 10 consecutive pitches that hit the target (either the original target or a target with the 1-foot strip).
- Attempt to pitch 5 to 10 consecutive pitches to a particular zone.
- Limit your target to the 5-point zone only.

To Decrease Difficulty

- Continue to practice this drill at the distances you are having difficulty with.
- Enlarge the target areas.
- Decrease the incremental distances that you move back.

Fastball Drill 4. *Four Corners*

The purpose of this drill is to help you consistently hit the four corners of the strike zone—high inside, high outside, low inside, and low outside. Pitch from 40, 43, or 46 feet, depending on your age and league rules, and attempt to pitch 10 strikes in a row to each corner. You should work with a catcher for this drill, but if one is not available, a target could be used instead. If you have been successful enough on the previous drills to be attempting this drill, it is assumed that you are able to perform the windmill pitch while consistently demonstrating the success check criteria of the previous drills. Therefore, the focus of this drill is the result—hitting the glove.

You earn 1 point for each pitch that hits the catcher's glove. Pitch two sets of 10 pitches to each corner: high inside, low inside, high outside, low outside.

Success Check

- Execute the windmill pitch correctly.
- Maintain a consistent pitch speed.
- Consistently pitch the ball to the catcher's glove.

Score Your Success

Score yourself based on the number of points you earn after two sets of 10 pitching attempts to each corner.

56 to 80 points = 5 points

40 to 55 points = 3 points

39 points or fewer = 1 point

Your score ___

To Increase Difficulty

Attempt to pitch to the corners in sequence (high inside, low inside, high outside, low outside), hitting the glove four consecutive times. Each sequence of four pitches is a set. Attempt 10 sets.

To Decrease Difficulty

- Repeat previous drills.
- Decrease the pitching distance.
- Continue practicing this drill.

The technique described for the basic windmill delivery is the foundation from which various types of pitches can be thrown. Each pitch requires a slight variation on the grip, the release point, and the direction and height of the arm on the follow-through. The following sections describe the variations used to throw the change-up, drop ball, curveball, and rise ball pitches.

Change-Up

For a beginning pitcher, a good companion pitch to the fastball is the change-up. For an elite pitcher, the change-up can be a very effective pitch because the change of speed keeps even the best hitter off balance.

The two most common grips for throwing the change-up are the knuckle and palm grips; the palm grip is easier to use. Instead of holding the ball in the fingertips, force the ball into the palm of the hand and grip it with all four fingers and the thumb (figure 3.8a). Use your regular fastball motion and delivery, eliminating the wrist snap on release. The friction caused by the ball coming off your palm and fingers will slow the speed of the pitch and provide an effective change-up.

The knuckleball grip is especially difficult if you have a small hand and you are throwing a 12-inch softball. Hold the ball with your knuckles across a seam (figure 3.8b). Again use your regular fastball motion and delivery, releasing the ball from your knuckles rather than your fingertips. This slows the speed of the pitch and results in an effective change-up.

Another option for throwing the change-up is to use a backhand delivery. Using a four-finger palm grip, release the ball with the back of yo[u]r hand facing the batter. Flick your wrist toward t[he] batter and up after releasing the ball. The moti[on] is the same as for the fastball, except that duri[ng] the downward motion of the circle, you rotate t[he] arm to allow for the backhanded release of t[he] pitch (figure 3.9). The follow-through is out a[nd] up with the palm facing the batter.

The change-up is effective because it disrup[ts] the batter's timing. That is why the motion a[nd] delivery of the change-up must be the same [as] for the fastball. The batter's timing is keyed [to] the motion. If you try to throw a change-up or [an] off-speed pitch by slowing your arm speed, t[he] batter is immediately able to pick that up a[nd] adjust the timing of the swing.

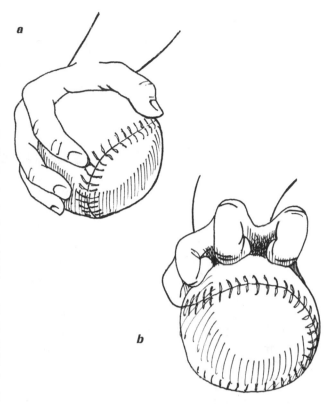

Figure 3.8 Change-up grips: *(a)* four-finger palm grip; *(b)* knuckle grip.

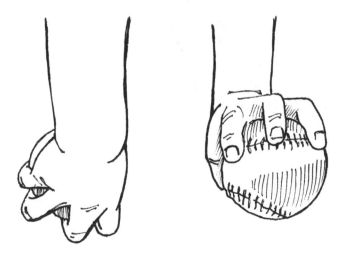

Figure 3.9 Backhand delivery for a change-up.

Misstep

The pitch has too much speed.

Correction

Place the ball farther into the palm. Release the pitch with a firm wrist.

Misstep

The pitch does not reach home plate.

Correction

Increase the speed of the windmill motion.

Change-Up Drill 1. *Three-Quarter Stance*

The purpose of this drill is to help you develop the change-up release with the downswing action of the windmill pitch. Stand with your nonthrowing side facing a target on a net, fence, or wall at a distance of 10 feet (3.0 meters). Use the same target as in the Wrist Snap drill (see page 46). Begin in a three-quarter stance—feet approximately 18 inches (45.7 centimeters) apart with the front foot facing slightly to the right (right-handed pitcher). Start with your pitching arm at the top of the circle, ready for the downswing with the wrist cocked back. The nonthrowing arm should be extended out, facing the target. Begin the pitching action by lifting and replacing your front foot and beginning your downswing action. Pull your nonthrowing elbow into your side, and release the pitch using the selected change-up grip.

Success Check

- Begin with your pitching arm at the top of the circle, with your wrist cocked.
- At the beginning of the downswing, lift and replace your front foot.
- Pull your nonthrowing elbow into your side.
- On the release, use the appropriate wrist action for your selected grip.
- Attempt to pitch the ball between the target lines.

Score Your Success

Score yourself based on the number of pitches (out of 10) that hit between the target lines:

    8 to 10 successful attempts = 5 points

    6 or 7 successful attempts = 3 points

    3 to 5 successful attempts = 2 points

    1 or 2 successful attempts = 1 point

    Your score ___

To Increase Difficulty

- Increase the distance from the target. (Do not exceed 15 feet [4.5 meters].)
- Decrease the target size.

To Decrease Difficulty

- Decrease the distance from the target (no closer than 6 feet [1.8 meters]). At this distance, a soft or cloth ball is recommended.
- Repeat the drill.
- Increase the target size.

Change-Up Drill 2. *Barrier Drill*

This drill enables you to work on delivering the pitch into the strike zone while minimizing the arc. Attach a rope to two standards so that you can stretch it across the path of your pitch. The rope should be set at a height of 5 to 5 1/2 feet (1.5 to 1.7 meters) and positioned approximately halfway between the pitcher and catcher. (You need to have a catcher for this drill.) The pitch should cross under the rope and be caught by the catcher after it crosses over the plate. Complete two sets of 10 pitches.

Success Check

- Use a windmill delivery.
- If you use a palm or knuckleball grip, make sure your wrist is firm on the release. Follow through up and away from your body.

- If you use a backhand release, make sure the back of your hand faces the batter, and flick your wrist up. Follow through out and up with the palm facing the batter.

Score Your Success

Score yourself for each set based on the number of change-up pitches (out of 10) that go under the rope and over home plate:

8 to 10 successful attempts = 5 points

6 or 7 successful attempts = 3 points

3 to 5 successful attempts = 2 points

1 or 2 successful attempts = 1 point

Your total score ___

To Increase Difficulty

- Lower the rope to 4 to 4 1/2 feet (1.2 to 1.4 meters).

- Pitch to the inside and outside corners.
- Alternate fastballs and change-ups.
- Alternate fastballs and change-ups while working the corners.
- Attempt the drill using a different grip.

To Decrease Difficulty

- Raise the rope to 6 feet (1.8 meters).
- Move the rope closer to home plate.
- Attempt a different grip to find the one that is most successful.

Change-Up Drill 3. *Alternating Fastballs & Change-Ups*

The purpose of this drill is to practice adjusting the release of the pitch to throw the fastball or change-up. To use the change-up effectively, you must be able to move from a pitch with speed to an off-speed pitch seamlessly. You can practice this drill using any of the speed pitches, but it will be described using the fastball and change-up.

For this drill, you should work with a catcher in full catching gear. (If you use a target instead, you will not get the feedback about the speed of the pitch that a catcher can give you.) Pitch from a pitching rubber at a distance of 40, 43, or 46 feet.

Beginning with a fastball, throw 20 pitches, alternating between fastball and change-up. The object is for you to be able to effectively change speeds and make the necessary adjustments to throw the appropriate pitch in sequence. The focus is on the change of speeds, not the accuracy of the pitch.

Success Check

- Use a windmill delivery.
- Notice a distinct change of speeds.

Score Your Success

You earn points based on the number of pitches (out of 20) on which you successfully alternated speeds:

14 to 20 pitches = 10 points

10 to 13 pitches = 7 points

4 to 9 pitches = 3 points

1 to 3 pitches = 1 point

Your score ___

To Increase Difficulty

- Add accuracy by having the catcher give you a target that you must hit. The target should move to the different points of the strike zone—high inside, low inside, high outside, low outside.
- Once you have practiced the drop and rise ball pitches, you can add those pitches to this drill and alternate those with the change-up.

To Decrease Difficulty

- Instead of alternating every other pitch, pitch two fastballs, then two change-ups.

- Repeat change-up drills 1 and 2.

Drop Ball

Batters can more easily adjust the timing of their swing to hit fast, straight pitching than they can to hit a ball that is moving up or down as it approaches the plate. The drop ball, as the name implies, approaches the plate straight and flat like a fastball, but as it gets to the plate, it breaks sharply down, or drops. A good drop ball will break just before reaching the batter, causing the batter to swing over the ball for a strike or causing the batter to top the ball, inducing a ground ball.

The two most common drop ball pitches are the peel drop and the turnover drop. Both pitches drop down, but the turnover drop also breaks away from a right-handed batter when thrown by a right-handed pitcher. As with the change-up, the drop ball fools the batter only if it looks like a fastball as the pitcher releases it and if the pitch approaches the plate like a fastball. A ball that "dies a natural death"—dropping to the ground in a slow arc all the way from the pitcher's hand to the plate—is not going to fool any batter!

The peel drop ball has a top-to-bottom forward spin. Grip the ball with two or three fingers held close together across one of four seams (figure 3.10). The thumb should be on a seam on the side of the ball opposite the fingers. On the release, the fingers are under the ball, and the thumb is on top.

Take a shorter stride, release the thumb first, and let the ball roll off the fingertips with a slight lifting action so that you start the ball spinning forward and your fingers come over the top of the ball as it is released (figure 3.11). The follow-through of the arm is low, just above the waist and slightly across the body.

The turnover drop ball has a counterclockwise spin, with the key being the spin placed on the pitch at release. The grip and stride length are the same as for the peel drop. Release the thumb first and then turn the hand over, letting the ball roll off the fingertips and forcing a counterclockwise spin. Just before release, drive your shoulder over the ball and force your thumb down to cause the counterclockwise spin to drop down (figure 3.12). The follow-through of the arm is low, tight to the body, with the hand finishing at the midline of the body just below the waist.

Try each pitch and initially use the release that is most successful for you. Once you have mastered a particular drop pitch, you can always add a second drop pitch to your repertoire.

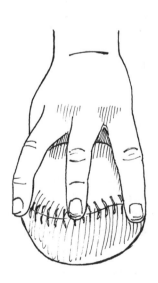

Figure 3.10 Peel drop grip.

Figure 3.11 Peel drop release.

Figure 3.12 Turnover drop release.

Misstep

The ball does not break down.

Correction

Focus on producing the spin on the pitch. Focus on ending the pitch with the appropriate follow-through.

Misstep

The ball breaks late so the batter has the opportunity to hit the ball before it breaks.

Correction

The problem could be your stride, your driving shoulder, or both. Shorten your stride, or drive your shoulder over the ball on release.

The following drills are designed to allow you to work on the specific drop release that you have selected. Complete either the Peel Drop Football drill or the Turnover Drop Football drill, and then attempt the Barrier drill. If you want to try both releases to determine the one that you have the most success with, perform the other football drill (peel drop or turnover drop) and then repeat the Barrier drill using that release. Your score for only one of the football drills will count toward your total score.

Drop Ball Drill 1. *Peel Drop Football Drill*

The purpose of this drill is to help you get the feel of imparting the appropriate spin on the ball for the peel drop. Grip a small to medium-size football lengthwise by placing two or three fingers on the seam of the ball and placing your thumb on the top side of the ball. Begin in a three-quarter stance approximately 5 feet (1.5 meters) from a net or wall. Take a short stride toward the wall or net, and attempt to impart the appropriate spin on the ball. The ball should land at the base of the wall or net, and the seam of the ball should be rotating away from you.

Success Check

- Pitch the football so that it lands at the base of the wall or net.
- Pitch the football so that it rotates away from you.
- Pitch the football so that it stays straight and does not wobble after release.
- Take a short stride.
- Drive your throwing-side shoulder over the ball.

Score Your Success

Score yourself based on how well you demonstrated all the success check criteria on 10 football spin pitches.

7 to 10 pitches = 15 points

5 or 6 pitches = 3 points

4 pitches or fewer = 1 point

Your score ___

To Increase Difficulty

- Begin with your arm at the top of the windmill motion.
- Do a full windmill motion.

To Decrease Difficulty

- Hold the football in one hand and attempt to spin the ball into your other hand.
- Start in the short-stride position and attempt to spin the ball to the base of the wall or net.

Drop Pitch Drill 2.   *Turnover Drop Football Drill*

The purpose of this drill is to help you get the feel of imparting the appropriate spin on the ball for the turnover drop. Grip a small to medium-size football lengthwise by placing two or three fingers on the seam of the ball and placing your thumb on the top side of the ball. Begin in a three-quarter stance approximately 5 feet (1.5 meters) from a net or wall. Take a short stride toward the wall or net, and attempt to impart the appropriate spin on the ball. The ball should land 2 or 3 feet (.6 or .9 meters) in front of your stride foot, spinning like a helicopter blade.

Success Check

- Pitch the football so that it lands 2 to 3 feet in front of your stride foot.
- Pitch the football so that it rotates like a helicopter blade.
- Take a short stride.
- Drive your throwing-side shoulder over the ball.
- Make sure your pitching hand finishes at the midline of your body, just below your waist.

Score Your Success

Score yourself based on how well you demonstrated all the success check criteria on 10 football spin pitches.

   7 to 10 pitches = 5 points

   5 or 6 pitches = 3 points

   4 pitches or fewer = 1 point

   Your score ___

To Increase Difficulty

- Begin with your arm at the top of the windmill motion.
- Do a full windmill motion.

To Decrease Difficulty

- Hold the football in one hand and attempt to spin the ball into your other hand.
- Start in the short-stride position and attempt to spin the ball so that it lands 2 to 3 feet in front of the stride leg.

Drop Ball Drill 3.   *Barrier Drill*

The purpose of this drill is to help you work on the break of the drop pitch. Stretch a rope across the path of the pitch approximately 4 feet (1.2 meters) high and 6 feet (1.8 meters) in front of home plate (figure 3.13). Pitching from a distance of 40, 43, or 46 feet, release the pitch using one of the drop releases. The ball should pass over the rope and hit a target on the ground that is placed no farther than 12 inches (30.4 centimeters) behind home plate. Complete two sets of 10 pitches.

Figure 3.13   Barrier drill.

Success Check

- Use the correct pitching technique for the selected release (peel or turnover).
- Pitch the ball so that it goes over the rope at a fairly level trajectory (no arc).
- Pitch the ball so that it lands on the target.

Score Your Success

Earn 1 point for each pitch that goes over the rope at a level trajectory and hits the target.

15 to 20 points = 5 points

10 to 14 points = 3 points

9 points or fewer = 1 point

Your total score ___

To Increase Difficulty

• Move the rope closer to home plate.

• Pitch to the corners—inside and outside for the peel drop; outside (right-handed batter) for the turnover drop.

To Decrease Difficulty

• Lower the rope to 3 feet (.9 meters).

• Move the rope farther away from home plate.

• Remove the rope.

Curveball

In baseball, the curveball has a 12:00 to 6:00 sweeping action, while in softball the ball breaks on a horizontal plane with a 3:00 to 9:00 action for a right-handed pitcher. Unlike the drop ball, the curve does not change planes; this makes the curve somewhat easier to hit, especially if it does not have a sharp break.

The most common grip for the curveball is accomplished by holding the ball so that the seams form an upside-down C. Place your index and middle finger on the top seams and your thumb on the seam on the bottom part of the C (figure 3.14a). If you use a three-finger grip, place your ring finger on the seam and your middle finger between the seams (figure 3.14b). The ball is released by pulling the index finger across the ball and releasing the ball slightly out in front of the hip. This is a later release point than all the other pitches. The arm follows through across the body, finishing at about waist height (figure 3.15).

The most effective curveball is one that starts on the outside corner of the plate and then breaks sharply outside, causing the batter to reach to make contact. An elite pitcher with excellent control can make the curveball appear to be going at a batter and then break sharply over the plate for a strike.

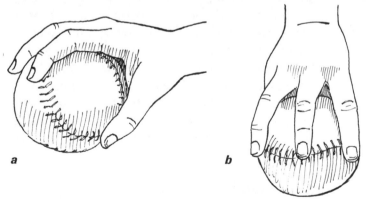

Figure 3.14 Curveball grips: *(a)* upside-down C; *(b)* three-finger grip.

Figure 3.15 Curveball follow-through.

Misstep

The ball breaks late or not at all.

Correction

The problem could be the stride or the throwing shoulder. Shorten the stride or exaggerate the pulling action across the ball.

Curveball Drill 1.   *Spin Drill*

The purpose of this drill is to practice the spin of the pitch. Draw a line on the ball that intersects two seams (figure 3.16). Stand about 3 feet (.9 meters) from a net. If a net is not available, move farther away, use a soft cloth ball, and pitch into a wall.

Figure 3.16   Spin drill.

Using a full windmill pitching motion, throw the curveball into the net, trying to make the ball spin in a counterclockwise direction while keeping the line on the ball parallel to the ground.

Success Check

- Grip the ball using the upside-down C grip.
- Release the ball a little in front of the hip.
- Follow through across the body, finishing at waist height.
- Pitch the ball so that it spins in a counter-clockwise direction.
- Pitch the ball so that the line on the ball stays parallel to the ground.

Score Your Success

Score yourself based on how well you demonstrated all the success check criteria on 10 pitches.

   8 to 10 pitches = 5 points

6 or 7 pitches = 3 points

5 pitches or fewer = 1 point

Your score ___

Curveball Drill 2.   *Barrier Drill*

For this drill, you will need to work with a catcher in full catching gear. The purpose of the drill is to work on producing a sharp break, making the pitch look as if it is coming in straight and then having it break at the last second.

Figure 3.17   Barrier drill.

Place a batting tee or a soccer corner flag approximately 10 feet (3.0 meters) in front of home plate (figure 3.17). The barrier should be placed so that it is in line with the outside (right-handed pitcher) or inside (left-handed pitcher) corner of home plate. You should strive to get the pitch to go as close as possible to the inside edge of the barrier, without touching it. The pitch should end up behind and on the other side of the barrier when the catcher catches it after the ball crosses over the outside corner (right-handed pitcher) or inside corner (left-handed pitcher) of home plate. Pitch two sets of 10 pitches.

Success Check

- Use the appropriate release and follow-through for the type of curve selected.
- Get the pitch to pass close to the barrier and to break so that it is caught behind and on the other side of the barrier.
- Pitch the ball so that it crosses over the outside edge (right-handed pitcher) of home plate.

Score Your Success

Give yourself a score based on the number of pitches (out of 10) that pass by the barrier and are caught behind and on the other side of the barrier as the pitch crosses over the outside edge (right-handed pitcher) of home plate. Complete two sets.

8 to 10 successful pitches = 5 points

6 or 7 successful pitches = 3 points

3 to 5 successful pitches = 2 points

1 or 2 successful pitches = 1 point

Your total score ___

To Increase Difficulty

- Move the barrier so that it lines up with the middle of home plate.
- Move the barrier so that it lines up with the opposite side of home plate (inside or outside).
- Move the barrier so that it is closer to home plate.

To Decrease Difficulty

- Repeat the previous drill.
- Move the barrier farther away from home plate.
- Remove the barrier.

Rise Ball

The rise ball is one of the most difficult spin pitches to learn to throw effectively. The key to an effective rise ball is to make it look like a high fastball until it breaks up sharply just in front of home plate. The movement should not be a gradual rise; rather, the pitch should appear to be coming in straight and then jump up. At that point, the batter has already committed to the swing path for the high fastball, and the pitch jumps over the bat. The rise ball is typically a strikeout pitch. Experienced pitchers seldom throw the rise ball in the strike zone.

For the rise ball to jump, it must have a reverse (or backward) spin. Grip the ball with the middle finger along the length of one of the four seams, on the raised part of the seam. Place the index finger next to the middle finger, either flat or with

the tip of the finger on the ball (figure 3.18). The thumb is on a seam opposite the fingers.

Your stride should be slightly longer. Increase the lateral lean of the trunk to get the throwing-side hip out of the way of the arm and get low and under the ball. Release the ball with the hand under the ball and away from the body. Rotate the wrist outward so the thumb goes up and to the rear and the middle finger pulls up against the seam, causing the backward rotation of the ball. The follow-through is high, toward the target and out in front of the body (figure 3.19).

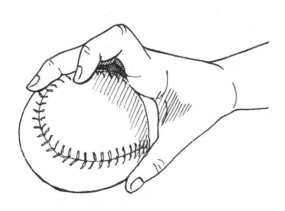

Figure 3.18   Rise ball grip.

Figure 3.19   Rise ball follow-through.

Rise Ball Drill 1. *One-Knee Football*

The purpose of this drill is to help you get the feel of imparting the appropriate spin on the ball for the rise. Using a small to medium-size football, you can work on the spin and easily see whether or not you were successful. This drill can be done with a partner or by using a target area on a wall or fence (two parallel lines approximately 3 feet [.9 meters] apart with the bottom line 4 feet [1.2 meters] off the ground). Kneel on your throwing-side knee parallel to the target, and extend the other leg at a 90-degree angle facing the target (figure 3.20). Grip the football across the seams. Begin with the ball at the top of the pitching motion. Attempt to throw the football in a spiral with an upward action so that it is caught above your partner's waist or hits the target zone.

Success Check

• Throw the football so that it travels in an upward trajectory in a spiral.

• Throw the football so that it is caught above the waist or hits the target.

Figure 3.20
One-Knee Football drill.

Score Your Success

Give yourself a score based on the number of successful attempts out of 10:

    8 to 10 pitches = 5 points

    5 to 7 pitches = 3 points

    4 pitches or fewer = 1 point

    Your score ___

To Increase Difficulty

• Use a softball instead of a football.

• Repeat the drill from a standing position. Start in a three-quarter stance, and stride toward the target.

To Decrease Difficulty

• Use a smaller football.

• Repeat the drill.

Rise Ball Drill 2. *Barrier Drill*

The purpose of this drill is to help you work on the break of the rise ball. Stretch a rope across the path of the pitch approximately 4 feet (1.2 meters) high and 10 to 12 feet (3.0 to 3.6 meters) in front of home plate (figure 3.21). Pitching from a distance of 40, 43, or 46 feet, throw a rise ball that passes under the rope, goes over home plate, and is caught by the catcher (in full catcher's gear) above the height of the rope. Complete two sets of 10 pitches.

Success Check

• Use the correct pitching technique for the rise ball.

• Get the pitch to go under the rope and then rise so that the catcher catches it above the height of the rope.

• Pitch the ball in the strike zone.

Figure 3.21   Barrier drill.

Score Your Success

Score yourself based on how well you demonstrated all the success checks in each set of 10 pitches.

8 to 10 pitches = 5 points

6 or 7 pitches = 3 points

5 pitches or fewer = 1 point

Your total score ___

To Increase Difficulty

- Move the rope closer to home plate.

- Pitch to the inside and outside corners. Do not give yourself a point if the ball goes over the middle of home plate.

To Decrease Difficulty

- Lower the rope to 3 feet (.9 meters).
- Increase the strike zone or remove home plate.
- Move the rope farther away from home plate.
- Remove the rope.

The following drill can be used with slow-, modified-, or fastpitch pitching, and it is intended to help you practice combining pitches or working the different areas of the strike zone in a gamelike setting.

Combination Drill. *Innings*

The purpose of this drill is to simulate pitching in a gamelike setting. There is no batter, but the pitcher throws to a catcher in full gear at the appropriate pitching distance (40, 43, or 46 feet for fastpitch; 50 feet for slow pitch). The catcher calls the pitches and location. The catcher should only call pitches that the pitcher has demonstrated success on in the previous drills. For example, in slow pitch, the catcher might only call location, but in fastpitch, the catcher might call for a rise ball on the outside of the plate.

The catcher calls pitches for each imaginary batter and determines if the pitch is a ball or a strike. Three strikes for an out; four balls for a walk. If a pitcher throws a pitch down the middle of the plate, it is a home run. The pitcher throws three innings of work, keeping track of the score.

The pitcher earns 1 point for a strikeout; minus 1 point for a walk; minus 1 point for a run scored; and minus 1 point for a home run. The pitcher earns a 1-point bonus for each inning without any walks or home runs.

Success Check

- Throw the pitches—and throw to the location—that the catcher calls.
- Avoid throwing the pitch down the middle of the plate.

Score Your Success

Give yourself a score based on the number of points earned in three innings:

9 to 12 points = 5 points

6 to 8 points = 3 points

3 to 5 points = 2 points

1 or 2 points = 1 point

Your score ___

To Increase Difficulty

- Increase the point values for walks, runs, and home runs.
- Decrease the size of the strike zone.

To Decrease Difficulty

- Repeat one or more of the previous drills designed to develop pitching accuracy.
- Increase the size of the strike zone.
- Count pitches down the middle of the plate as a base hit rather than a home run.

Additional drills that call for pitching in simulated game situations can be found in step 4. Pitchers can also practice their skills in the games in steps 10 and 11. Your development as a pitcher, whether for slow pitch, modified pitch, or fastpitch, depends on the various opportunities you have to develop correct form and technique. These opportunities include drills and simulated game situations. You should take advantage of as many of these opportunities as possible.

SUCCESS SUMMARY

In softball, the pitcher is the boss! In fastpitch softball, pitching is considered by most experts to be at least 85 percent of the game. No-hitters and one-hitters with one or two runs determining the winner of the game are common in elite-level fastpitch softball games. If you have ever experienced a game in which the pitcher walks batter after batter, walking in run after run, you know the frustration that every person, including the pitcher, feels in this situation. The old baseball adage "good pitching will beat good hitting any day" is also applicable for slow-, modified-, and fastpitch softball games. Although the slow- and modified-pitch games are more of a hitter's game, pitchers contribute to the winning effort of the team in a way similar to that of a fastpitch pitcher. They do so by putting spin on the ball and by placing the ball so that the batter is forced to hit a pitch that is out of his strength area of the strike zone.

Becoming a consistent and effective pitcher will take considerable practice and is only attainable if you are willing to put in many hours of work. Going from pitching at targets to practicing in simulated game situations is a very important practice progression for pitchers to make before pitching in a real game.

As you practice your pitching skills, ask an experienced observer to use the success checks to evaluate you and help you make appropriate corrections in your pitching motion. Continue to practice the drills until you are consistently successful. Do not be afraid of revisiting a particular drill to refine a pitch or correct a problem.

This step covers pitching for three different versions of softball, and you are not expected to master the pitching techniques for each type of game. But before you move on to step 4, you should evaluate how you did on the drills for the pitching skills that you chose to develop based on the game that you play. Enter your score for each drill that you performed, and add up your scores to rate your total success. Your total score provides an indication of whether or not you have developed the skills necessary to be effective in the selected game.

Slow-Pitch Drills

1. Fence Pitch		___ out of 5
2. Wall Pitch		___ out of 5
3. Fence Pitch With Target		___ out of 5
4. Ball in the Bucket		___ out of 5
Total for slow-pitch drills		___ *out of 20*

Modified-Pitch Drills

1. Fence Target Drill		___ out of 5
2. Pitching Zone Fence Target Drill		___ out of 5
Total for modified-pitch drills		___ *out of 10*

Fastball Drills

1. Wrist Snap		___ out of 5
2. Three-Quarter Stance		___ out of 5
3. Speed and Accuracy		___ out of 5
4. Four Corners		___ out of 5
Total for fastball drills		___ *out of 20*

Change-Up Drills

1. Three-Quarter Stance   ___ out of 5
2. Barrier Drill   ___ out of 10
3. Alternating Fastballs & Change-Ups   ___ out of 10

Total for change-up drills   ___ ***out of 25***

Drop Ball Drills

1. Peel Drop Football Drill   ___ out of 5
2. Turnover Drop Football Drill   ___ out of 5
3. Barrier Drill   ___ out of 5

Total for drop ball drills   ___ ***out of 10****

Curveball Drills

1. Spin Drill   ___ out of 5
2. Barrier Drill   ___ out of 10

Total for curveball drills   ___ ***out of 15***

Rise Ball Drills

1. One-Knee Football   ___ out of 5
2. Barrier Drill   out of 10

Total for rise ball drills   ___ ***out of 15***

Combination Drill

1. Innings   ___ out of 5

---

* Your score for only one of the football drills counts toward your total score.

If you are a slow-pitch pitcher, total up your points for the slow-pitch drills and add your score for the combination drill. If you scored a minimum of 18 points, you have mastered the skills necessary to pitch in a slow-pitch game. If your total was 15 to 17 points, you would benefit from additional practice in selected drills. If you scored fewer than 15 points, you should continue to practice the slow-pitch drills to improve your skills and increase your total score.

If you are a modified-pitch pitcher, total up your points for the modified-pitch drills and add your score for the combination drill. If you scored a minimum of 11 points, you have mastered the skills necessary to pitch in a modified-pitch game. If your total score was 9 to 10 points, you would benefit from additional practice in selected drills. If you scored fewer than 9 points, you should continue to practice the modified-pitch drills to improve your skills and increase your score.

If you are a fastpitch pitcher, you are not expected to master all of the different pitches in fastpitch softball. A reasonable goal is to have three good pitches (including the fastball) in your repertoire, and then work to add a fourth pitch. Score yourself on all the pitches, and then select the two pitches (in addition to the fastball) with the top point totals. Add your scores in those three pitches plus your score for the combination drill to determine your final score. If you scored a minimum of 15 points in the fastball drills and a minimum of 30 total points, you have developed adequate pitching skills. If you scored fewer than 30 total points, you should continue to practice the fastpitch pitching drills to improve your skills and increase your total score.

Hitting

Hitting is the first offensive softball skill to learn. The *batter* is the player from the offensive team who is up at bat. Every offensive play in a game starts with a player being at bat and attempting to hit a pitched ball. Imagine you are up to bat, the score is tied, there are two outs, and a runner is on third base. If you get a base hit, the run will score, and your team will take the lead or maybe even win the game. Hitting is a fun part of the game, but it is a complex skill—in a very short period of time, you must make many judgments about contacting a moving object (the ball) with another moving object (the bat).

If you are just learning to hit, you can simplify the hitting process by breaking it down into components. Begin by eliminating the movement of the ball as a factor—use a batting tee, which is a device that allows you to practice the hitting technique with a stationary ball. Then, when you have developed some confidence and skill in contacting the ball with the bat, you are ready to hit a pitched ball

or a soft toss, which allows you to practice hitting a ball tossed from a short distance. More experienced hitters may want to begin hitting practice with the soft toss (instead of the tee).

The goal of offensive play in softball is to score runs. As explained in "The Sport of Softball" (page viii), the winner of an official game of softball is the team that scores the greater number of runs in seven innings of play. A run can be scored only when a batter gets on base, progresses around the bases, and crosses home plate safely before three outs are made. Although there are several ways for a batter to get on base, hitting the ball is the most fun. Once runners are on base, hitting the ball is an important technique for advancing the runners (causing them to move to a base closer to home plate) and, eventually, scoring runs. Probably the most fun of all is to hit the ball to a place that allows you (and any runners on base) to advance more than one base at a time—a double, a triple, or a home run.

TAKING A FULL SWING

Hitting involves moving the bat from a stationary position behind the back shoulder into the path of the ball, making contact with the ball somewhere between the midline of the batter's body and just out in front of the front foot. The batter completes the swing by wrapping the bat around

the front shoulder while keeping the body in a balanced position. The exact contact point in hitting depends on where the ball is pitched and where the batter wants the ball to go. A right-handed batter wanting to hit an inside pitch to left field needs to contact the ball well out in front of the front foot. On the other hand, the same batter intending to hit an outside pitch to right field will contact the ball just after it passes the midline of her body. Our initial instruction will focus on the contact point being at your front foot.

There are many different theories about hitting: swing level, swing down on the ball, swing up at the ball, keep two hands on the bat during the follow-through, take the top hand off the bat on the follow-through, and so on. In addition, you will use many different hitting adaptations or skills, depending on the game situation and the type of pitching you are facing. Slap or punch hitting against fast pitching, place hitting to take advantage of gaps in defensive positioning, and hitting behind the runner to advance that person to the next base are examples of hitting adaptations that are used in specific game situations; they will be covered in steps 5 and 9. The hitting techniques discussed in this step are fundamental to all hitting; therefore, these techniques should be mastered before attempting any of the adaptations for specific game situations. As you strive to develop your hitting skill using the various hitting drills that follow in this step, you will have an understanding of the complete technique and a mental picture of what hitting a ball entails.

In an official game, hitting is done from the batter's box. The *batter's box* is the marked area on either side of home plate in which the batter must stand when making contact with the ball.

When learning to hit, you should stand in a square stance with your feet shoulder-width apart and your knees and hips slightly bent. A *square stance* is one in which the toes of both feet are equidistant from the edge of home plate or the line of the batter's box that is parallel to home plate. As you develop your hitting skills, you may want to use different stances. An *open stance* is one in which the front foot is farther back from the edge of home plate than the back foot. In a *closed stance,* the front foot is closer to home plate than the back foot. If you are using a batting tee, stand so that your front foot is opposite the post of the tee.

Grip the bat so that the middle row (second row) of knuckles of both of your hands line up. To achieve this grip, bend over, put the barrel end of the bat on the ground, and place your hands on the grip end of the bat so that it angles across the fingers of both hands—from the tip (end joint) of your index fingers to the crease formed by your

Figure 4.1
Proper grip.

palm and your pinkie fingers (figure 4.1). Lift the bat up, maintaining this hand position on the bat, and check the alignment of the middle (second) knuckles of both hands.

If you are just learning to hit, do not try to mimic a professional hitter's batting stance. Begin with the fundamentals; then, as you gain more experience as a hitter, you can find the style that works for you.

Grip the bat as shown in figure 4.1, and raise the bat to your back shoulder with your hands at the top of your strike zone (figure 4.2a). Hold the bat at a 45-degree angle. Raise your back elbow slightly so that it is almost parallel to the ground. Extend your front arm comfortably; it should also be parallel to the ground. Your front shoulder is slightly lower than your back shoulder; your head is up, with your chin resting on your front shoulder; and both eyes are focused on the pitcher's pitching hand. Your initial swing movement is forward.

A more experienced hitter may choose to use a preswing motion and cock her hips. For this type of hitting, hold the bat with the proper grip, but hold it 4 to 6 inches (10.2 to 15.2 centimeters) away from your body between the midline of your body and your back shoulder. Keep your elbows down. Your forearms should form an upside-down V, and your front arm should form an L (figure 4.2a).

Hitting a ball involves swinging the bat into the path of the ball and making contact with the ball. However, two very important movements of your body must occur before starting to swing the bat. As the pitch leaves the pitcher's hand (timing will vary depending on the speed of the pitcher), you should take a short step—no longer than 6 inches—toward the pitcher with your front foot, pointing your toes in the direction of first base. This step is often called the *stride.*

Next, begin to turn your hips toward the pitcher by pivoting on the ball of your back foot, keeping the front foot in contact with the ground. As the hips turn, start the bat swing. Leading with your front elbow and hands, bring the bat into the swing path or the path of the ball. Keep the wrists cocked so that the barrel end of the bat trails the hands while you begin to extend your arms and move your hands forward into the contact zone. Keep your head still and both eyes focused on the ball. Two eyes see the ball.

A more experienced player who is using a pre-swing motion would move the bat back slightly and cock her hips, closing the front hip slightly, before the stride. If using this technique, during the swing, you should think of yourself unwinding or uncorking from your feet up.

Your position at the contact point (figure 4.2b) is the major determining factor for your effectiveness as a hitter. At the point of contact, when the bat meets the ball, your hips should be square to the ball (belly button to the ball), your arms should be slightly flexed, and your head should be down with your eyes focused on seeing the ball hit the bat. Your front leg is straight, your back leg is bent slightly, and your weight is centered over your back knee. Your shoulder, hip, and knee should form a straight line. Swing the bat through the path of the ball. A good cue is "swing short to the ball, long through the contact or hitting zone." Do not shift your weight onto your front foot during contact unless you are using a punch or slap swing against extremely fast pitching. (Note: Your weight

shifts forward onto the front foot at the end of the follow-through so that you can take your first step out of the batter's box toward first base with your back foot.)

Fully extend your arms and continue the swing after the bat contacts the ball. Stopping the swing on contact is like trying to run out an infield hit and stopping on first base rather than running over the base. To stop on the base, you must slow down before getting to the base. This usually results in the ball beating you to the base, thereby putting you out. When hitting, stopping your swing on contact means you have had to slow down your swing before contacting the ball, resulting in a less forceful hit.

To complete your swing, roll your wrists so that the thumb of your top hand points to the ground as you force the bat to wrap around your body. The exact position will depend on the location of the pitch at contact but will usually be between your waist and front shoulder. For example, when hitting a low pitch, you should go down to get the ball and then follow through high. Chin position is a good indication of proper head-on-the-ball position throughout the swing. In the starting position, as you wait for the pitcher to begin the pitch, your chin should be in contact with your front shoulder. On the follow-through or completion of the swing, your chin should be in contact with your back shoulder, which has rotated forward (figure 4.2c). A good swing allows you to maintain balance while at the same time having proper plate coverage. Finally, hold onto the bat!

Figure 4.2 Hitting the Ball

INITIATING THE SWING

1. Stance is square
2. Middle knuckles are aligned
3. Knees are bent
4. Hands are back; back elbow is up
5. Focus on ball
6. Chin is on front shoulder
7. Take short step with front foot; point toes toward first base
8. Initiate hip turn
9. Lead swing with front elbow

b

c

MAKING CONTACT

1. Hips are square to ball
2. Arms are extending
3. Front leg is straight
4. Back leg is bent
5. Weight is centered over back knee
6. Focus on ball
7. Hands are firm; thumbs are on top

COMPLETING THE SWING

1. Weight is moving over front leg
2. Swing through ball
3. Complete wrist roll
4. Hips rotate
5. Hands wrap around shoulder
6. Chin is on back shoulder

Misstep

You consistently top the ball, hitting it on the ground.

Correction

Check for a high-to-low swing path. Lower your starting hand position to a height at the top of your strike zone.

Misstep

You consistently pop the ball up.

Correction

Shorten your stride by taking a shorter step with your front foot. Eliminate any loop in your swing; don't drop the barrel of the bat below the horizontal swing path before contact. This will cause a low-to-high swing path on contact.

HITTING THE BALL OFF THE TEE

Hitting the ball off the batting tee is one of the easiest ways to work on achieving some of the important components of proper hitting technique—specifically the hip turn, including the footwork and the total body position at the contact point. Because the ball is stationary as you attempt to make contact, you do not have to adjust your swing to the changing positions a tossed or pitched ball would have as it approaches. This allows you to focus on those aspects of the complex act of hitting that need the most work.

Because the contact point is opposite your front foot when hitting up the middle (figure 4.2b), you should take your initial batting stance with

Figure 4.3 Proper distance from the batting tee.

your front foot directly opposite the post of the tee. Stand at a distance from the tee that allows the center of the barrel of the bat to go over the post of the tee as you swing the bat to the contact point (figure 4.3).

Adjust your position at the tee by taking a few practice swings without a ball on the tee. When you are ready to add a ball, follow the key points shown in figure 4.2, and practice hitting using the batting tee hitting drills.

In addition to providing an initial method for inexperienced players to practice their hitting technique, the batting tee allows experienced players to effectively work on problem areas in their swings. For the batter who lets the head "fly" during the swing, focusing on the ball while it is on the tee will help the batter keep his head down and steady, thereby achieving good focus on the ball at the contact point. A player who is having difficulty hitting an inside pitch can set up at the batting tee so the contact point is out in front of the plate, which is appropriate for an inside pitch. This provides effective practice for hitting that type of pitch.

If you feel comfortable with the bat in your hands, and you know the key points about the swing and can consistently execute them, you can bypass the batting tee practice and move on to practicing hitting using a soft toss or a pitched ball.

Misstep

You cannot reach the ball when you swing, or you hit the ball on the handle of the bat.

Correction

Stand with your front foot opposite the tee, and adjust your position so the barrel of the bat goes over the tee.

Misstep

You hit the tee instead of the ball.

Correction

Keep your back shoulder up; do not drop your back elbow as you swing. Make sure your hands take a direct line to the ball; do not drop your hands.

The following drills are used to practice your hitting techniques with a batting tee. Other drills in this step involve working on hitting a soft-tossed ball and hitting a pitched ball; these drills follow their respective sections. Although the drills are in a progressive order within each section, you do not necessarily have to start with the first batting tee drill and progress in order through the last pitched-ball drill. You can select drills from the various categories that meet your specific needs for practice.

If you are just beginning to develop your hitting technique, you will find it helpful to move back and forth between practicing with the batting tee (or with a soft-tossed ball) and practicing against live pitching, perhaps at a modified distance. Hitting is an extremely complex action. Using the variety of practice opportunities in these drills will help you develop into an effective hitter.

Batting Tee Drill 1. *Using a Net or Fence*

Position the batting tee 10 feet (3.0 meters) from a hanging net or a fence. Stand beside the tee so that the line of flight of the batted ball is toward the net or fence. Place a bucket of 10 regulation balls next to you. Place a ball on the tee, assume your correct batting stance beside the tee, and hit the ball off the tee into the net or fence. Hit 10 balls.

If you are working with a partner, the ball feeder should stand with the bucket of balls on the side of the tee opposite the hitter and place the ball on the tee. *Caution:* The hitter needs to wait until the feeder removes her hand from the ball and steps back from the tee before swinging at the ball. The feeder should watch the hitter hit the ball and provide feedback. Use the technique points from figure 4.2. Switch roles after hitting 10 balls. Repeat the drill so that each of you hits the ball 20 times.

Success Check

- Stand in a square stance with your front foot opposite the tee.
- Focus on the ball.
- Initiate the hip turn, and pivot your feet.
- Swing through the ball.

Score Your Success

Earn 1 point each time the ball hits the fence or net.

15 to 20 hits = 5 points

10 to 14 hits = 3 points

9 hits or fewer = 1 point

Your score ___

To Increase Difficulty

Use the bottom hand only to make the swing.

To Decrease Difficulty

Practice going through the full swing motion with no ball on the tee. Once you feel comfortable with the swing motion, repeat the drill.

Batting Tee Drill 2. *Target Practice*

Mark three lines on the net or fence. The first line should be 2 feet (.6 meters) from the ground, the second line should be 4 feet (1.2 meters) from the ground, and the third line should be 8 feet (2.4 meters) from the ground (figure 4.4). These lines mark the ground ball target area, the line drive target area, and the fly ball target area.

Using the same procedures as in the previous drill, hit 10 balls below the 2-foot line, 10 between the 4- and the 8-foot lines, and 10 above the 8-foot line. To hit the low target, use a high-to- low swing path (as if you were attempting to hit a ground ball). To hit the middle target, use a horizontal swing path (as if you were attempting to hit a line drive). To hit the high target, use a low-to-high swing path (as if you were attempting to hit a fly ball).

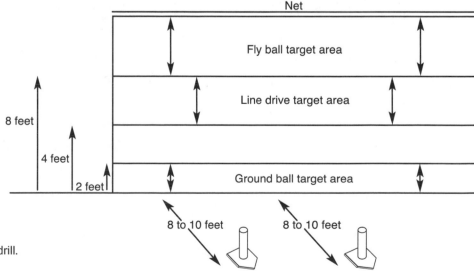

Figure 4.4 Target Practice drill.

Success Check

- Use a high-to-low swing for the low target.
- Use a horizontal swing for the middle target.
- Use a low-to-high swing for the high target.

Score Your Success

Give yourself a score for each of the target areas (low, middle, and high) based on the number of on-target hits out of 10 attempts:

8 to 10 on-target hits = 5 points

5 to 7 on-target hits = 3 points

4 or fewer on-target hits = 1 point

Your total score ___

To Increase Difficulty

- Randomly vary the target on each hit.
- Have a partner call the target.

To Decrease Difficulty

- Close your eyes and practice the three swing paths.
- Focus on only one target area.

Batting Tee Drill 3.   *Bottom Hand Only Swing*

Use the target from the previous drill (figure 4.4). Put the tee at the center height setting. Stand with your regular grip on the bat. As you swing at the ball, let go of the bat with your top hand and make contact with the ball while holding the bat with your bottom hand only. Be sure to complete the full swing with the one hand. Try to hit the ball at line drive height or lower. Hit 10 balls to the net. Collect the balls and repeat (or switch roles with your partner if you have a partner setting balls on the tee). Count the number of balls that go line drive height or lower from swings in which the bat does not hit the tee.

Success Check

- Hit the middle of the ball (make full contact).
- Swing through the ball; do not stop your swing on contact.
- Take a full turn on the ball.
- Do not hit the tee.

Score Your Success

Give yourself a score based on the number of on-target hits (out of 10 swing attempts) in which the bat doesn't hit the tee.

8 to 10 on-target hits = 5 points

5 to 7 on-target hits = 3 points

4 or fewer on-target hits = 1 points

Your score ___

To Increase Difficulty

- Hit to the fly ball target only.
- Hit to the line drive target only.
- Hit to the ground ball target only.

To Decrease Difficulty

- Use a shortie bat.
- Use a very light bat.
- Keep your top hand on the bat with a loose grip to help guide the bat through the swing path.

Batting Tee Drill 4. *Low Ball/High Ball*

Use the net or fence as in the previous drills, but do not use target areas. Adjust the height of the batting tee to work on the low pitch, then the high pitch. Hit 10 balls at each height. Change roles if a partner is setting balls on the tee for you, or go collect the balls if you are working alone. Strive for clean hits—no bat contact with the tee.

Success Check

- Keep your head down and focus on the ball on the tee at contact, then on the top of the post that held the ball at the completion of your swing.
- Use a high-to-low or low-to-high swing path depending on the tee setting.
- Execute a good hip turn. Your hips should be square and your arms extended at the point of contact.
- Make clean hits—no bat contact with the tee.

Score Your Success

Give yourself a score based on the number of cleanly hit balls out of 10 attempts at each height.

   8 to 10 clean hits = 5 points

   5 to 7 clean hits = 3 points

   4 or fewer clean hits = 1 points

   Your total score ___

To Increase Difficulty

- If you are using an adjustable tee, challenge yourself by setting the tee for high inside, high outside, low inside, and low outside balls.
- If you are using a fixed tee, adjust your stance at the tee to hit high inside, high outside, low inside, and low outside balls.

To Decrease Difficulty

Adjust the tee so that the ball is only slightly lower or higher than the middle of the strike zone position, and repeat the drill.

Batting Tee Drill 5. *Hip Turn With Partner*

Position the tee 10 feet (3.0 meters) in front of a net or fence. Set the tee so the ball is at waist height, and stand at the tee as if you were hitting the ball up the middle. Hold the bat parallel to the ground behind your back by bending both arms at the elbow and placing the knob end of the bat in the crook of your front elbow and the barrel end in the crook of your back elbow (figure 4.5). Use the longest bat you can find. If the bat is not long enough for the barrel to contact the ball on the tee as you rotate your hips into the contact position, try using a stickball bat or a long, large dowel.

Your partner stands on the far side of the tee with a bucket of 10 balls. The partner places a ball on the tee, removes her hand from the tee, and signals you to swing. Hit the ball off the tee by taking a short step with your front foot, pointing your toes toward first base, rotating your hips into the hitting contact position (making sure to pivot on the ball of your back foot), and watching the bat contact

Figure 4.5
Hip Turn With Partner drill.

the ball on the tee. Concentrate on the hip turn, maintaining your balance throughout the swing and seeing the ball with two eyes. After 10 hits, collect the balls and switch roles with your partner.

Success Check

- Pivot on the ball of your back foot.
- Bring your hips square to the ball at contact.

- Keep your front leg straight and your back leg bent.
- Keep your weight centered and your shoulder, hip, and knee in alignment.
- See the ball with two eyes.
- Maintain your balance.

Score Your Success

Give yourself a score based on the number of times (out of 10 attempts) you successfully demonstrate all the success check criteria and the hit ball reaches the net or fence.

8 to 10 times = 5 points

5 to 7 times = 3 points

4 times or fewer = 1 point

Your score ___

HITTING THE SOFT TOSS

You can practice your hitting stroke and work on its timing by swinging at a moving ball that is tossed to you from the side and slightly in back of your contact point. This is called a *soft toss*. To hit a soft toss, you must judge the path of a ball that is tossed to you by a person at your side a short distance away. You must also judge the timing of your swing so that the bat arrives at the contact point at the same time as the tossed ball. Making these judgments on a ball tossed a short distance is viewed by many as a preliminary step to being able to make the necessary judgments when hitting a pitched ball.

The toss is made from the side and slightly to the rear of the hitter for the safety of the tosser. Because the ball is coming at you from the side and slightly behind, you may find the soft toss more difficult to hit than a softly pitched ball from someone standing behind a protective screen about 10 to 12 feet (3.0 to 3.6 meters) in front of you. This method of delivering a short-distance moving ball to a hitter is called a *front toss*. If a more experienced player or coach is available for the front toss, you should practice hitting that toss before attempting the soft-toss drills. Soft-toss drills provide an opportunity for a lot of swings at the ball because the accuracy of the pitcher is

not a factor in your opportunity to practice your hitting technique.

The soft toss really involves skills for two people: one tossing the ball and one hitting the ball. Your ability to toss the ball properly is extremely important for two reasons. The batter cannot hit the ball unless it is tossed correctly; the ball must come down ahead of the front foot of the hitter. In addition, your own safety as the tosser requires proper execution; if you toss the ball too far toward the hitter's back foot, the batted ball could be hit back at you.

The tosser and hitter face each other with the hitter in a batting stance and the tosser kneeling on the ground about 8 to 10 feet (2.4 to 3.0 meters) away from the hitter; the tosser should be positioned well back of the hitter's rear foot (figure 4.6). When tossing, you should toss the ball with a gentle down-up motion of your hand and arm. This should make the ball loop toward the batter, coming down into the hitter's contact zone and about 2 feet (60.9 centimeters) from the front foot. Toss the ball as if you wanted it to land on an imaginary batting tee positioned opposite the batter's front foot. A more experienced tosser working with an experienced hitter could take a kneeling position 8 to 10 feet away from the hitter directly opposite the hitter's back foot.

When hitting a soft toss, stand with your feet shoulder-width apart in the same batting stance as when hitting off the tee (figure 4.7a). After your partner tosses the ball, take the same swing at the ball as you did at the ball on the tee. Initiate your swing with a slight step with your front foot. Time your swing so that you contact the ball about waist high and opposite your front foot (figure 4.7b). To protect the tosser, you must only hit balls tossed into the hitting contact zone, which is in front of and opposite your front foot. Do not swing if the toss does not drop to a position opposite your front foot. Hitting a ball tossed toward the midline of your body, despite the fact that it might be in the strike zone, could result in the ball hitting the tosser. After contacting the ball, complete your swing by wrapping your hands, still holding the bat, around your shoulders (figure 4.7c).

When you are the tosser, you can assist the hitter by observing the techniques used during all three phases of her swing. At the completion of the swing, you can reinforce correct techniques used and make suggestions where needed.

Figure 4.6 Correct positions for the tosser and hitter during the soft toss.

Figure 4.7   Hitting the Soft Toss

a

Initiating the Swing

TOSSER

1. Kneel to rear of hitter's back foot
2. Ball is in throwing hand
3. Focus on target opposite hitter's front foot

HITTER

1. Stance is square
2. Knees are bent
3. Middle knuckles are aligned in grip
4. Hands and bat are back
5. Weight is on back foot
6. Head is still; focus on ball

b

c

Contact Point

TOSSER

1. Lift hand and arm
2. Release ball up and forward
3. Watch ball drop to target area
4. Watch hitter make contact

HITTER

1. Step with front foot; point toes to first base
2. Hips start pivot; rotate on ball of back foot
3. Hips are square at contact; belly button is to ball
4. Back knee is bent; front leg is straight
5. Weight is over back knee
6. Arms and wrists are extending
7. Head is down; two eyes are on ball
8. Back shoulder is to chin

Completing the Swing

TOSSER

1. Relax arm
2. Watch hitter's technique

HITTER

1. Arms are extended; roll wrists
2. Hands wrap around shoulder
3. Chin is on back shoulder
4. Weight is shifting to front leg
5. Hips are fully rotated

Misstep

When you toss the ball to the hitter, the ball goes in a straight line toward the batter.

Correction

Make the ball traverse an arc to get to the target spot in the hitter's contact zone. Make your tossing motion down and up, not back and forward.

Misstep

When you swing to hit the ball, you miss the ball completely.

Correction

Watch the ball go from the tosser's hand to your bat. Try to contact the middle of the ball.

The tosser will not be scored in the following drills. However, the role of the tosser is extremely important. The hitter will not be able to practice unless the toss is on target. As the tosser, remember to release the ball up and forward so that it drops down into the hitter's contact zone. If you are having trouble tossing the ball to the hitter's target area, you should practice your tosses without a hitter. Place a target, such as a glove or a bucket, on the ground where a ball tossed into the contact zone for the hitter would drop if not hit. The ball must drop straight down into the target from at least 5 feet (1.5 meters) high.

Note: Using the backstop or outfield fence and regulation softballs for the soft-toss drill was an accepted practice for years. Recently, though, there has been litigation against teachers and coaches because of the ball's rebounding off the fence and hitting a participant. Consequently, using the bare fence for this drill is not recommended. However, you can hang a large, thick gymnastic-type mat (not crash pad type) on the fence so that the mat will absorb much of the force of the hit ball, thereby dramatically limiting the rebound. Another option is to use fleece balls or some other nonrebounding type of ball for this drill. The fence option is then performed in the same manner as when using a net.

Soft-Toss Drill 1. *Using a Net or Fence*

With a partner, position yourselves as hitter and tosser 10 feet (3.0 meters) from a hanging net (or blanket). You should be positioned so that the batted ball hits the net. The tosser has a bucket of 10 fleece, cloth-covered, or regulation balls. More experienced hitters can use 10 to 20 old tennis balls. Tennis balls are smaller and therefore more difficult to track and hit. Be sure the net's hole size will restrict tennis balls before you try this drill with them.

Conduct the drill using the technique points for both the tosser and the hitter as described in figure 4.7 for each of the three phases of hitting a soft toss.

The hitter switches places with the tosser after hitting 10 balls. Repeat the drill two times, for a total of 20 hits for each partner.

Success Check

- Make sure your hips are square at contact.
- Keep two eyes on the ball.
- Extend your arms and wrists into the hit.
- Only hit balls that are tossed opposite your front foot.

Score Your Success

Give yourself a score based on the number of hits (out of 20 tosses in your contact zone) that go directly into the net.

15 to 20 hits = 5 points
10 to 14 hits = 3 points
9 hits or fewer = 1 point
Your score ___

To Increase Difficulty
Use a smaller ball.

To Decrease Difficulty
Use a larger ball.

Soft-Toss Drill 2. *Tracking the Ball*

Your ability to track the ball is a very important part of your development as a hitter. This drill will give you practice in this all-important aspect. Set this drill up as in the previous drill, but be sure to use a net rather than a fence. Put numbers on tennis balls. Before tossing the ball, the tosser calls a number, and the hitter must recognize the correct number and hit only that numbered ball. If a different numbered ball is tossed, the hitter must recognize the wrong number and not swing.

In a variation of this drill, you use white and yellow softball-size Wiffle balls. The tosser calls the color rather than the number, and again, the hitter must only hit the ball if it is the called color. Continue until 10 balls have been tossed accurately into the hitter's hitting zone. Switch roles and repeat the drill. Continue the drill until each player has had the opportunity to hit 20 tossed balls.

The tosser must make accurate tosses to the hitter's contact zone. As the tosser, remember to call the number or color clearly and in a timely manner. If you have a difficult time tossing the ball to the hitter's target area, practice without a hitter and use a target for your tosses.

Success Check

- Keep two eyes on the ball.
- Extend your arms and wrists into the hit.
- Only hit balls of the called number or color.
- When hitting the called ball, make contact with the ball.

Score Your Success

Give yourself a score based on the number of attempts (out of 20) in which you made the correct decision and made contact with the ball of the correct number or color.

18 to 20 = 5 points

15 to 17 = 3 points

14 or fewer = 1 point

Your score ___

To Increase Difficulty

- Use baseball-size colored Wiffle balls.
- Have the tosser vary the position of the toss within the hitting zone.

To Decrease Difficulty

Use a Wiffle-ball bat and colored Wiffle balls.

Soft-Toss Drill 3. *Bat–Eye Coordination*

For this drill, you need 15 to 20 golf-ball-size Wiffle balls. You also need a wooden wand or dowel, a broom handle that has been cut to bat length, or a stickball bat. *Caution:* Be sure that anything you use to hit with has a taped hand grip that enables you to securely hold onto it. If you are making your own bat, do not use plastic tape or any other slick or slippery material for the grip. Cloth-backed adhesive tape works well.

This drill is similar to soft-toss drill 1, but for safety reasons, this drill should be performed in an unobstructed area without a net or fence. You may want to do the drill in groups of three; the third player retrieves the Wiffle balls and puts them in a container as they are hit. Rotate roles after the hitter has had a minimum of 15 swings.

The key to hitting a smaller ball is to track it carefully into the contact zone. Do not overswing (swing too hard); just try to make solid contact with the ball. This is a difficult skill and one you should practice often, especially if you find you are swinging and missing the ball in games.

As the tosser, remember to toss the ball so that it drops down waist high opposite the hitter's front foot. If you still have a difficult time tossing the ball to the hitter's target area, go back and review the technique points in figure 4.7 and continue to practice tossing without a hitter.

Success Check

- Keep your head down, and, with both eyes, watch the ball into the contact zone.
- Make solid contact.
- Don't overswing.

Score Your Success

Give yourself a score based on the number of full-contact hits (ball goes forward) out of 15 swings.

12 to 15 = 5 points

8 to 11 = 3 points

7 or fewer = 1 point

Your score ___

To Increase Difficulty

Have the tosser vary the position of the tosses within the hitter's contact zone.

To Decrease Difficulty

Use a Wiffle-ball bat to work on improving your skill.

Soft-Toss Drill 4. Hit the Ball Where It's Tossed

This drill requires three people. It is set up like the previous drill, except that you use regulation softballs and a real bat. The hitter and tosser position themselves as they did for all other soft-toss drills. The tosser should have a bucket with at least 25 balls. The third player takes an empty bucket to the field to retrieve the hit balls.

The tosser must now adjust the height of the tosses for the hitter. Toss the ball into the contact zone above the hitter's waist for fly ball attempts and below the waist for ground ball attempts. The hitter practices hitting fly balls using a low-to-high swing path. Next, the hitter practices hitting ground balls using a high-to-low swing path.

The fielder should use proper ground ball and fly ball fielding techniques. Refer back to step 2 to refresh your memory on the correct techniques.

Put the fielded balls into the bucket. After a set of 10 tosses at each height to the hitter, rotate roles. The fielder brings the full bucket in to the tosser position. The hitter takes the empty bucket out to the fielding position. The tosser moves to the hitting position. Continue the rotation until each partner has had a turn at each position.

Although only the hitter will score points, you should use the practice opportunity in the other two positions to continue to work on improving your skill as a tosser and a fielder.

Success Check

- Make solid contact using a low-to-high swing path for a fly ball.
- Make solid contact using a high-to-low swing path for a ground ball.

Score Your Success

Give yourself a score based on the number of successful hits out of 10 intended fly ball swings and 10 intended ground ball swings.

    7 to 10 = 5 points

    5 or 6 = 3 points

    4 or fewer = 1 point

    Your total score _____

To Increase Difficulty

Have the tosser use a random order on 10 tosses for fly ball and ground ball attempts.

To Decrease Difficulty

Repeat the drill focusing only on that swing path.

HITTING A PITCHED BALL

Your challenge in hitting a pitched ball is to predict the flight of the pitched ball and then time your swing to make contact with the ball in your hitting contact zone. All of the hitting techniques discussed previously are applicable to hitting the pitched ball: the grip with the middle knuckles aligned, the proper step and hip turn, the arms extending at the point of contact, and an appropriate follow-through that completes the swing.

The swing must be executed without a lot of thought as you work on hitting a pitched ball. When hitting a pitched ball, focus on tracking the ball's path and timing your swing to intercept the ball at the contact point, which is out in front of your front foot if hitting up the middle but will vary depending on the location of the pitch. Another judgment you must now make is to determine whether the pitched ball will be a ball (outside the strike zone) or a strike (in the strike zone). For the more experienced player, game strategy decisions—such as hitting behind the runner, placing the ball into a gap area in the defense, or hitting a long sacrifice fly ball to score a runner from third base—are added to the mix during a game. These judgments of tracking, reading, and reacting are much like those you had to make when fielding a ground ball and especially when fielding a fly ball. The following drills will provide you with more gamelike opportunities to work on your hitting skill. So pick up your favorite bat and go have some fun!

Any of the following drills that involve hitting the pitched ball can be done as combination drills, with fielders practicing the skills of fielding ground balls and fly balls, throwing, and catching. Many of the drills also require a pitcher who can pitch with accuracy or a mechanical pitching machine. If drills are done in groups of two or three players, you must make a provision for collecting the hit balls. Use a large plastic bucket with a handle for ease in carrying the retrieved balls. You can also use a plastic milk crate, but it is more difficult for one person to carry.

If throwing is not one of the practice tasks when fielders are used, you should use two buckets. Start with a full one by the pitcher and an empty one in the field. Collect the fielded balls in the bucket in the field. The players who are rotating into and out of the hitting role should carry the buckets in and out.

Misstep

You have no power in your swing.

Correction

Swing through the entire range of motion—short to the ball, long through the hitting zone. Start your hands well back by your back shoulder, not in front of your body.

Pitched-Ball Drill 1. *Bleacher Ball Drop*

Mark a target area with cones or some other marking device in the field 100 feet (30.5 meters) from the bleachers. You need a partner for this drill. The hitter places a glove on the ground (to simulate home plate) approximately 2 feet (.6 meters) away from the end of a set of bleachers. The hitter stands at "home plate" facing the bleachers with the front

Figure 4.8 Bleacher Ball Drop drill.

foot opposite the plate. The hitter takes a couple of practice swings to make sure the bat covers home plate but will not contact the bleachers during the swing. The partner stands at the end of the bleacher, slightly in front of and above the head of the hitter. The partner in the bleachers should have a bucket of 20 balls. If you are outside, use regulation softballs; if you are inside, use Wiffle or fleece balls.

The partner drops the ball so that it angles down toward the back edge of the plate, simulating the slow-pitch pitch, or drops it straight down on the front edge of the plate, simulating a modified pitch or fastpitch (figure 4.8). The hitter swings, hitting the ball as it comes into the contact zone. Hit 10 balls, then change roles. Collect the balls after both partners hit. Repeat the sequence.

This drill can also be set up to include fielders. Fielders should have an empty bucket in the field to collect the balls. Fielders should concentrate on the hitter, see the ball as it leaves the bat, and quickly move into position to field the ball with two hands. Scoring for this drill is only for the hitter.

Success Check

- Time the swing so that you hit the ball in the contact zone by your front foot.

- Keep your head down. With two eyes, see the bat hit the ball.

Score Your Success

Give yourself a score based on the number of hits that reach the 100-foot target area out of 10 swings:

8 to 10 = 5 points

6 or 7 = 3 points

Fewer than 6 = 1 point

Your score ___

To Increase Difficulty

- Ask your partner to specify the type of hit that must be executed (fly ball or ground ball) before dropping the ball.

- Use specific targets at varying distances and directions.

To Decrease Difficulty

Repeat the drill without using a target distance.

Pitched-Ball Drill 2. *Call Balls and Strikes*

Game play requires that hitters be able to read the pitch that is being delivered. A hitter must not waste an at-bat by standing and watching three strikes go by or swinging at pitches that are not in the strike zone. Hitters need to practice watching the ball as it comes from the pitcher into the hitting zone so they can tell a strike from a ball.

This drill requires a group of three—a hitter, a pitcher, and a catcher. The pitcher stands at an appropriate regulation pitching distance from home plate. The catcher is in the catcher's position behind home plate (in full gear). The hitter takes her regular batting stance at the plate with a bat.

The pitcher focuses on proper pitching technique and attempts to throw strikes. For an increased challenge, the pitcher can try to hit the corners with her pitches. Using a regulation softball, the pitcher delivers 10 pitches to the hitter. The hitter strides and initiates the hip turn and shoulder turn only. The hitter keeps her hands and arms still and does not swing at the ball. The hitter watches the ball pass over (or by) the plate and calls a ball if the pitch is outside the strike zone or a strike if the pitch goes into the strike zone. The catcher verifies the call of the pitch. Remember, the strike zone is the area over home plate, between the batter's back shoulder and the front knee for slow pitch, and between the top of the forward armpit and the

Figure 4.9 Fastpitch and modified-pitch strike zone.

top of the knees for fastpitch and modified pitch (figure 4.9). Rotate roles after 10 pitches.

Success Check

- Take the stride and initiate the hip and shoulder turn only. Do not swing the bat at the ball.

- Watch the ball from the pitcher's hand to the catcher's glove, and accurately call a ball or a strike.

Score Your Success

Give yourself a score based on the number of calls that the hitter and catcher agreed on (out of 10 pitches):

8 to 10 = 5 points

5 to 7 = 3 points

Fewer than 5 = 1 point

Your score ___

To Increase Difficulty

• Have the hitter call the position of the pitch (e.g., high outside, low inside) in addition to calling a ball or strike.

• Have the hitter call the type of hit that is dictated by the pitch (see step 9)—for example, if the pitch is inside, pull the ball; if the pitch is outside, hit to the opposite field; if the pitch is low, hit the ball on the ground; if the pitch is high, go for the home run. This applies only to strikes.

To Decrease Difficulty

If you are having trouble with the drill, use an umpire to verify the batter's and catcher's ball and strike calls.

Pitched-Ball Drill 3. *Making Contact*

This drill requires a group of three, with additional fielders as an option. Set up as in the previous drill. The catcher must wear complete catching gear. The hitter takes a full swing at each strike pitch and attempts to make contact with the ball. Focus on contacting the ball in your hitting zone and using correct technique. See the ball with two eyes. Take a smooth, fluid swing at the ball. Just make contact; do not try to hit the ball hard. Hit the middle of the ball. Hit the ball where it is pitched. The pitcher should throw strikes, try to hit the corners, and vary the location. The batter has a maximum of 10 strike pitches to score points. A strike pitch that is not swung at counts as 1 of the 10 and scores no points. The catcher calls balls and strikes. Score each hit according to the ball's path as shown in table 4.1 and figure 4.10.

Success Check

• Hit strikes.
• Meet the ball out front.
• Just make solid contact.

Table 4.1   Scoring the Making Contact Drill

Landing zone	Settle zone	Contact points		Hits		Points scored
Foul	Foul	1	×		=	
Infield A	Infield A or B	2	×		=	
Infield B	Infield B	3	×		=	
Infield A or B	Outfield	4	×		=	
Outfield	Outfield	5	×		=	
					Total points	

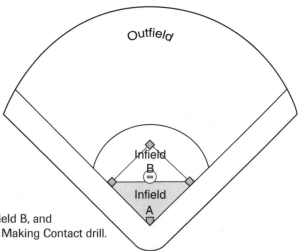

Figure 4.10   Infield A, infield B, and outfield boundaries for the Making Contact drill.

Score Your Success

Give yourself a score based on the number of points you score on 10 strike pitches.

    45 to 50 points = 5 points

    35 to 44 points = 3 points

    25 to 34 points = 2 points

    24 points or fewer = 1 point

    Your score ___

To Increase Difficulty

Hitt the outside pitch to the opposite field and pulling the inside pitch.

To Decrease Difficulty

Repeat the drill but do not use the scoring chart. Instead, count 1 point for every hit that goes anywhere in fair territory. Try to score at least 7 points in 10 hits.

Pitched-Ball Drill 4. *Between the White Lines*

Hitting between the white lines means putting the ball in play in fair territory (the area between the white foul lines). It is not always the home run that wins the game. In fastpitch softball, the home run is difficult to hit and occurs less frequently than in slow pitch. Consequently, hitters must be able to hit the ball and keep it in play. When the ball is hit into the field of play (fair territory), baserunners have the chance to advance and either score or become threats to score.

This drill is set up as in the previous drill. The hitter attempts to hit a fair ball into the outfield, but distance is not the focus. Instead, you should focus on making contact and putting the ball in play.

As the hitter in this drill, you should make up game situations for yourself—for example, you need a base hit with two outs and a runner on third; or with no outs and a runner on second, you must hit the ball to right field to advance the runner to third base; or with one out and a runner on third, a long fly ball will score the run.

The batter has a maximum of 10 strike pitches to score points. A strike pitch that is not swung at counts as 1 of the 10 and scores no points. The catcher calls balls and strikes.

Success Check

- Use a smooth, fluid swing.
- Keep your head down, watch the ball to the bat, and see the ball with two eyes.
- Make solid contact; hit the middle of the ball.

Score Your Success

Give yourself a score based on the number of balls hit that successfully accomplish the 10 game situations you set:

    7 to 10 = 5 points

    4 to 6 = 3 points

    Fewer than 4 = 1 point

    Your score ___

To Increase Difficulty

Place hit the ball for each situation.

To Decrease Difficulty

Repeat the drill but don't use imaginary game situations. Just try to make solid contact and hit the ball between the white lines.

Pitched-Ball Drill 5.   *Hitting Line Drives*

Mark the outfield with two curved lines going from foul line to foul line, one 100 feet (30.5 meters) and the other 130 feet (39.6 meters) from home plate (figure 4.11). The area between the lines is the target landing area for line drives.

The hitter attempts to hit a line drive that would clear the infield but land in front of the outfielders. In addition to landing in the target area, a successful hit must be judged to be a line drive (it must traverse a relatively horizontal path) and not a fly ball. If available, a trained observer can make the judgment, or participants in the drill can judge.

Timing of the swing is critical for success in this drill if hitting against an arc-trajectory pitch such as in slow pitch. The ball must be contacted above the waist as it drops through the strike zone. The swing must be horizontal, and the middle of the ball should be contacted. If practicing with a pitcher using a flat pitch, ask the pitcher to keep the pitches above the waist. The batter has a maximum of 10 strike pitches to score points. A strike pitch that is not swung at counts as 1 of the 10 and scores no points. The catcher calls balls and strikes.

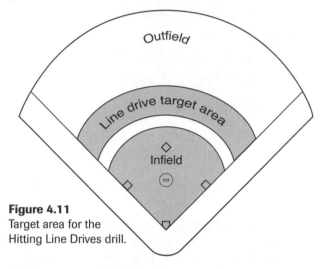

Figure 4.11
Target area for the
Hitting Line Drives drill.

Success Check

- Use a horizontal swing path.
- Make contact in the middle of the ball.

Score Your Success

Give yourself a score based on the number of line drive hits that land in the target area (out of 10 strike pitches):

7 to 10 = 5 points

4 to 6 = 3 points

Fewer than 4 = 1 point

Your score ___

To Increase Difficulty

Hit the line drives to selected spots within the target area (e.g., to right field).

To Decrease Difficulty

Increase the depth of the target area and repeat the drill.

Pitched-Ball Drill 6.   *Hitting the Gap*

From home plate, mark two fan-shaped alleys to the outfield. One alley goes through the shortstop position to the left center-field fence, and the other goes through the second baseman's position to the right center-field fence (figure 4.12). The hitter attempts to hit the ball into these alley target areas and preferably all the way to the fence. A line drive or long fly ball hit into these alleys in the outfield (gaps in coverage by the defensive outfielders) will most often result in a single, double, or triple, advancing any baserunners one or more bases.

Because the accurate placement of each pitch is key to a hitter's opportunity for success in this drill, the use of a pitching machine is recommended. If live pitching is used, the hitter must receive 10 pitches to hit that are waist high or above and in the strike zone.

Score each on-target hit according to the ball's path as shown in table 4.2.

Success Check

- Use a full hip turn, with your arms extending at contact, to hit line drives or long fly balls.
- Adjust your stance and swing in order to hit to the opposite-field alley.

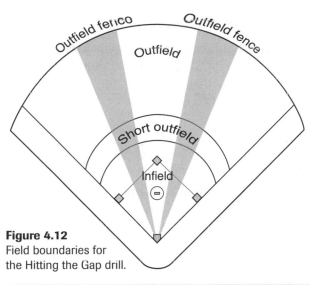

Figure 4.12
Field boundaries for
the Hitting the Gap drill.

Table 4.2   Scoring the Hitting the Gap Drill

Landing zone	Settle zone	Contact points		Hits		Points scored
Infield alley	Short outfield	1	×		=	
Outfield alley	Outfield	3	×		=	
Outfield alley	Outfield fence	5	×		=	
					Total points	

Score Your Success

Give yourself a score based on the number of points scored on 10 hit balls:

40 or more = 5 points

30 to 39 = 3 points

20 to 29 = 2 points

Fewer than 20 = 1 point

Your score ___

To Increase Difficulty

- Based on the pitch location, hit the ball to the appropriate alley.
- Alternate hitting to the left-field and right-field alleys.

To Decrease Difficulty

- Increase the size of the alley.
- Don't use the point system. Just attempt to hit the ball in the alleys.

Pitched-Ball Drill 7.   *Hitting Behind the Runner*

Use the alley marking to right center field from the previous drill as the beginning of a new target area. Extend that area all the way to the right-field foul line to complete the full target area for this drill (figure 4.13). The hitter attempts to hit the ball to this right-side target. In a game situation, a runner on first or second base could advance to third or beyond when you hit behind the runner into this alley.

To hit to the right side, the right-handed hitter should close the batting stance slightly—so the left foot is closer to home plate than the right foot—and delay the swing, making contact when the ball is toward the back of the plate. The left-handed hitter should open the stance slightly—drawing the front foot back away from the plate—and should hit the ball when it is out in front of the plate, attempting to pull the ball.

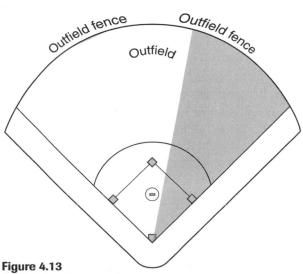

Figure 4.13
Right-field alley for
the Hitting Behind the Runner drill.

81

As in the previous drill, the use of a pitching machine to accurately deliver hittable pitches is recommended. If using live pitching, the pitcher can help facilitate this drill by pitching the ball to the outside part of the plate for a right-handed batter, and to the inside for a left-handed batter.

Success Check

- Adjust your stance and the timing of your swing to hit to the right-field target.
- Swing through the ball. Hit line drives or ground balls.

Score Your Success

Give yourself a score based on the number of times (out of 10 strike pitches) you hit the ball into the outfield target area.

7 to 10 times = 5 points

4 to 6 times = 3 points

Fewer than 4 times = 1 point

Your score ___

To Increase Difficulty

Score points only if the ball goes all the way to the outfield fence.

To Decrease Difficulty

Use a batting tee and repeat the drill.

Pitched-Ball Drill 8. *Situation Play*

Because live pitching is used in this drill, the drill is more appropriate for more experienced players. Although all players involved do not have to be varsity-level pitchers, each must have enough pitching skill to throw strikes to the batter on a majority of the pitches.

As in previous drills, a pitcher, catcher, and hitter are needed. The pitcher and hitter alternate setting hypothetical game situations. For example, one player says, "There's a runner on third base and no one out in the bottom of the seventh inning with the score tied." The batter attempts to execute a hit or out that would produce positive offensive results for the situation described. The pitcher attempts to get the batter out. Using the regulation three strikes (an out) and four balls (a base on balls), the batter has one turn at bat to accomplish the given task. Because a full defensive team is not used in the field, participants must make judgments on hit balls as to whether they would be base hits or outs of various kinds, and whether catchable fly balls would be deep enough to advance a runner, and so on.

The batter scores 1 point for each turn at bat that produces a positive offensive result for the specified situation. A base on balls is always 1 point for the batter. The pitcher scores 1 point when the batter fails to produce a positive result, that is, the

batter makes an out that doesn't advance a runner. A strikeout is always 1 point for the pitcher. The pitcher and hitter each set three situations for the batter. All three players rotate roles after six situations have been completed. Only the pitcher and hitter score points.

Facilitate this drill by having a bucket of balls at the pitching station and an additional three players with an empty bucket in the field retrieving the hit balls. At the completion of the rotation of the original three players, they move to the field, the fielders move into the pitcher, catcher, and hitter roles, and the drill continues.

To modify the drill for intermediate players, or if some groups of more experienced players do not have enough pitching expertise, use a pitching machine. The catcher and hitter set the situations and earn the points. Because game situations are used in this drill, there is no need to increase or decrease the difficulty.

Success Check

- When pitching, throw accurately enough for a "game" to occur.
- When batting, make appropriate offensive choices to address the situations. Execute the required skills.

Score Your Success

Give yourself a score based on the number of points scored in set situations (six as hitter and six as pitcher).

5 or 6 points = 5 points
3 or 4 points = 3 points
1 or 2 points = 1 point
Your total score ___

SUCCESS SUMMARY

Stepping up to the plate with runners in scoring position and advancing the runners with a base hit is the epitome of fun in offensive fundamentals. Another aspect of the fun in hitting is the opportunity you have as the hitter to match wits with the pitcher. In a game situation, the pitcher is trying to prevent you from successfully accomplishing your task. The pitcher will try to pitch to your weakness and stay away from your strength.

To match wits with the pitcher, you need to know your strengths and weaknesses as a hitter. And, especially in fastpitch, you need to know the strengths and weaknesses of the pitcher. Learn the tendencies pitchers have in pitching to batters, particularly to you, in certain game situations. With two strikes on you, is the pitcher's out pitch a rise ball, a drop, a high-inside fastball, or a change-up? Does the pitcher repeat the same pattern of pitch placement for each batter? Does the defense play you to pull the ball? The mental aspect of hitting—so important if you are going to be a strong and successful hitter—is also a fun part of the game for the offensive player.

The individual nature of the sport of softball is just as apparent in the offensive phase of the game as it is in the defensive phase. When you are in the batter's box facing the pitcher and attempting to accomplish the offensive task at hand, no one else can help you. You, and you alone, must make the judgments and execute the technique to produce the desired result.

Remember the importance of the correct contact position: Your hips are square to the ball, your arms and wrists are extending at the point of contact, your bat contacts the ball at a point off the front foot (if hitting up the middle), your head is kept still, and both your eyes see the ball hit the bat. Use the appropriate swing path for the pitched ball and for the task to be accomplished. Be a relaxed hitter. Be aggressive, want to hit, outguess the pitcher. Hitting is fun!

At the beginning of this step, you were told that although the drills are in a progressive order within each category, they should not be viewed as being presented in a natural progression from batting tee drill 1 to the last of the pitched-ball drills. Rather, you were advised to select drills from the various categories that would give you the best opportunity to improve your hitting technique—based on your level of experience, hitting ability, and specific hitting problems you want to work on.

Enter your score for each drill you completed. Add them to rate your hitting success at this point in time. At the end of the chart, you will find instructions on how to interpret your total score in relation to the maximum possible.

Batting Tee Drills

1. Using a Net or Fence   ___ out of 5
2. Target Practice   ___ out of 15
3. Bottom Hand Only Swing   ___ out of 5
4. Low Ball/High Ball   ___ out of 10
5. Hip Turn With Partner   ___ out of 5

Soft-Toss Drills

1. Using a Net or Fence   ___ out of 5
2. Tracking the Ball   ___ out of 5
3. Bat–Eye Coordination   ___ out of 5
4. Hit the Ball Where It's Tossed ___ out of 10

Pitched-Ball Drills

1. Bleacher Ball Drop   ___ out of 5
2. Call Balls and Strikes   ___ out of 5
3. Making Contact   ___ out of 5
4. Between the White Lines   ___ out of 5
5. Hitting Line Drives   ___ out of 5
6. Hitting the Gap   ___ out of 5
7. Hitting Behind the Runner   ___ out of 5
8. Situation Play   ___ out of 10

Total score   ___ *out of 110*

If you participated in all of the drills and scored 83 points or more, congratulations! You have mastered the basic techniques for hitting. Now would be a good time to go back and try some of the variations described for increasing the difficulty of the drills in order to further develop your hitting skill. If your score was 66 to 82 points, you have done well but could benefit from getting additional practice on those drills in which you had difficulty. If your score was 65 points or fewer, you need additional practice on the drills in order to develop your basic hitting technique before moving on to the more difficult variations.

If you are a more experienced player and you participated in selected drills, add your scores for the drills that you participated in. Next, add the total possible number of points for those drills. If your score was 75 percent of the total possible points, you are ready to move on. If your score was between 60 and 74 percent of the total possible points, you could benefit from additional practice. If your score was less than 60 percent of the total possible points, you need additional practice in order to develop the hitting skills needed to move on to the next steps.

Bunting and Slap Hitting

In fastpitch softball, getting on base or moving runners into scoring position by use of the short game can be exciting and can challenge the defense. The short game includes the sacrifice bunt, the bunt for a hit (surprise bunt), the push bunt, the slash bunt, the running slap, and the drag bunt. Each of these skills, with minor exceptions, is designed to place the ball in front of or between infielders, with the ball typically not hit with enough force to get out of the infield.

These skills are usually used when the batter or baserunner has good speed and the bunt will create confusion for the defense. The short game can be used as a means to manufacture runs, particularly for teams that have good speed and limited power. This step will introduce you to the skill techniques of short-game hitting. No matter your foot speed, being skilled in short-game hitting will improve your ability to see the pitch and make contact with the ball.

SACRIFICE BUNT

As the name implies, in executing the sacrifice bunt, the batter sacrifices her opportunity to get on base with a base hit in exchange for moving a baserunner. The batter bunts the ball so that the defense, in order to get an out, makes the force play at first, and the baserunner moves to the next base and into scoring position.

The most important part of executing the sacrifice bunt is to move from your normal batting stance (figure 5.1a) into the bunting position as the pitcher begins the windup. You should begin your pivot as the pitcher begins the windup, and you should be in the sacrifice bunting position when the pitcher's arm is at the top of the windup.

The fact that you are going to lay down a bunt need not be kept a secret from the opposing team; everyone in the ballpark knows when a situation calls for a sacrifice bunt. The defense will be in the preliminary bunt-defense position to defend against the possibility of the bunt before you make any move in the batter's box. Your responsibility is to put the ball on the ground! To have the greatest possibility of success in this endeavor, you must be in a stationary position with a good view of the oncoming ball as you make contact. Pivoting into your bunting position before the pitch will ensure that you have a good view of the ball. Successfully laying down a bunt on a pitch traveling at excessive speed while you are in the process of moving into your bunting position is difficult.

Both feet must be in or touching the batter's box when you make contact with the ball on any hit, or you will be called out. To accomplish this while assuming the bunting position, you must pivot on the balls of both feet so that your feet are staggered and facing the pitcher (figure 5.1*b*).

Keep your knees slightly bent, and hold your bat parallel to the ground (or at a slight angle) at the top of your strike zone. Your arms should be slightly bent and away from your body, with your elbows relaxed and down. Grip the bat loosely with the bottom hand in its regular starting position at the knob end of the bat.

Figure 5.1   Sacrifice Bunt

PREPARE TO SACRIFICE BUNT

1. Assume batting position
2. Hands and bat are back
3. Focus on pitcher

SACRIFICE BUNT

1. As pitcher begins windup, pivot to staggered stance with feet facing and shoulders square to pitcher
2. Bat is parallel to ground at top of strike zone; arms are away from body and relaxed
3. Bottom hand uses hitting grip
4. Top hand is outside grip area, perpendicular to ground
5. Bat rests on index finger; thumb is on top
6. Give with the bat as you contact top half of ball

RUN TO FIRST

1. Take first step toward first base with back foot
2. Get into foul territory as quickly as possible
3. Run through first base

As you pivot your feet and raise the bat to the top of the strike zone, slide the top hand down the throat of the bat to a position just outside the grip area. As you slide your hand down the bat, release the bottom three fingers from the bat, maintaining grip contact with the index finger and the thumb. Rotate your hand so that it is perpendicular to the ground and the back of your hand faces the plate. Make an open fist with your hand in this position, and grip the bat loosely with the edge of the index finger under the bat and the thumb at the back and slightly on top of the throat. Do not maintain your regular top-hand grip on the bat with all fingers wrapped around the bat as you prepare to bunt the ball. An inside pitch could hit the fingers of your top hand, which is very painful and could end your season!

Once you are in position, focus on the pitcher and her release point. Keep your eyes focused on the ball as it leaves the pitcher's hand. Because the purpose of the sacrifice bunt is to advance the runner, bunt only strikes. If you work the pitcher for a walk, you have been successful because by advancing to first base yourself, you advance the other runner. In addition, you have become another baserunner with the potential to score.

Know your strike zone, and do not bunt at a pitch that is outside that zone. With no strikes in your count, you can be very picky and only bunt the perfect pitch. Once you have a strike on you, you must expand your bunting zone, but the pitch should still be a strike. When you do bunt the ball, remember that it must be put on the ground—no pop-ups allowed! To keep the ball down, remember to hold your bat at the top of the strike zone. Then any pitch that is over the bat is a ball that you should let go. Any pitch in the strike zone will be below your bat; therefore, to contact the ball, you have to bring the bat down on top of the ball, which makes it easier to direct the ball down to the ground.

Misstep

The ball is popped up on the bunt attempt.

Correction

Remember to keep the bat at the top of the strike zone and only bunt pitches that are below that point. Work on seeing and contacting the top half of the ball.

Bunt the ball down either the first- or third-base line, not directly at the pitcher. In a sacrifice bunt, you are actually allowing the ball to make contact with the bat while your primary bat movement is down. When the ball contacts the bat, your arms and grip should be relaxed so that the bat cushions (or catches) the ball, resulting in a soft

bunt that drops down and rolls 10 to 12 feet (3.0 to 3.6 meters) from the plate and forces a fielder to move to field it. Direct the bunt by pushing your bottom or top hand slightly forward so that the ball is directed to the right or left side of the infield. Place the bunt so that the best (or only) play that the defense has is to throw to first.

Misstep

The ball is bunted with too much force.

Correction

Remember to keep your grip and arms loose so that they are soft on contact and you deaden the pitch on contact.

After you bunt the ball, take your first step out of the batter's box with your back foot (figure 5.1c). Be careful not to run into the bunted ball in fair territory; you will be called out. Get into foul territory as quickly as possible and try to

beat the throw to first. A sacrifice bunt does not mean you bunt the ball, give yourself up, and go back to the dugout! If you advance the runner and reach first base safely, your team has increased its opportunity to score runs.

Misstep

The ball is bunted foul.

Correction

Be sure to keep the bat parallel to the front of home plate or very slightly angled. Increased bat angle will cause the ball to go foul.

SURPRISE BUNT

The surprise bunt—a bunt for a base hit—is a skill typically used by a batter who has good speed and tries to catch the defense off guard by putting down a bunt and beating it out to first base. Unlike the sacrifice bunt, the batter's intent is to get on base and move baserunners, if there are any, to the next base without causing an out.

When performing the surprise bunt, the batter waits to initiate the movement as long as possible in order to surprise the defense. Instead of pivoting to a position facing the pitcher, as in the sacrifice bunt, the foot action is much more subtle. The batter begins in a normal batting stance (figure 5.2a). The batter drops the back foot slightly back and slides the top hand up the bat (thumb and index finger behind the bat). With the bottom hand the batter pulls the knob of the bat toward the front hip, putting the bat in a slightly angled position, square to the pitcher, at the top of the strike zone (figure 5.2a). The batter should look for a good pitch to bunt, remembering that a pitch higher than the bat will be a ball and, if bunted, will likely be popped up. The batter should try to place the ball down the third- or first-base line, forcing the fielders to move forward or to the side to field the ball. After making contact, the hitter begins toward first base by stepping with the back foot and getting into foul territory as soon as possible (figure 5.2c).

Misstep

You show bunt too early.

Correction

Remember to wait until just before the release of the pitch to move into bunting position.

Figure 5.2 **Surprise Bunt**

PREPARE TO SURPRISE BUNT

1. Assume batting position
2. Hands and bat are back
3. Focus on pitcher

BUNT

1. As pitcher begins windup, drop back foot slightly back to allow hips to open toward pitcher just before release of pitch
2. Hold bat in slightly angled position, square to pitcher, and at top of strike zone
3. Bottom hand is in hitting grip, pulling knob of bat to front hip
4. Top hand is outside grip area
5. Bat head rests on index finger; thumb is on top
6. Give with the bat as you contact ball

RUN TO FIRST

1. Take first step toward first base with back foot
2. Get into foul territory as quickly as possible
3. Run through first base

Misstep

The ball is bunted directly to the fielder.

Correction

Try to place the ball in the alleys between the fielders.

Misstep

The bunter watches to see where the bunted ball lands rather than running immediately to first base.

Correction

Remember to take your first step toward first base with your back foot immediately after bunting the ball. Run straight through first base.

The following bunting drills can be used for either the sacrifice or surprise bunt. Be sure to refer to the success checks for the appropriate type of bunt as you attempt each drill. Keep your score for either the sacrifice or surprise bunt, and record your score in the space provided.

Sacrifice or Surprise Bunt Drill 1. *Mimetic Bunts*

You and a partner set up as hitter and pitcher in your respective positions in the batter's box and at the pitching rubber. The hitter has a bat; the pitcher does not have a ball. The hitter assumes his regular hitting position. The pitcher starts behind the pitching rubber. As the pitcher steps onto the pitching rubber to "take the signal from the catcher" and then begins the pitching motion, the hitter uses the technique illustrated in figure 5.1 (sacrifice) or 5.2 (surprise) to assume the appropriate bunting position. The pitcher continues the motion through release and follow-through. When you are the hitter, ask your partner to critique your technique of moving from the hitting to the bunting position. After 10 repetitions, switch roles. Complete two sets of 10 repetitions for each type of bunt.

Success Check: Sacrifice Bunt

- Pivot on the balls of your feet.
- Stand in a staggered stance with your feet facing and shoulders square to the pitcher.

- Hold the bat at the top of the strike zone, parallel to the ground.
- Hold the bat with the top hand outside the grip; the bat should rest on the index finger, with the thumb on top.
- Stop in the bunting position before the release of the pitch.

Success Check: Surprise Bunt

- Drop your back foot slightly back.
- Hold the bat in a slightly angled position, square to the pitcher, at the top of the strike zone.
- Pull the knob of the bat to the front hip.
- Rest the bat head on the index finger, thumb on top.
- Give with the ball on contact.
- Direct the ball down to the ground.

Score Your Success

As the hitter, score yourself for two sets of 10 attempts as the hitter (for each type of bunt) in which you demonstrate all success check criteria.

8 to 10 attempts = 5 points

5 to 7 attempts = 3 points

4 or fewer attempts = 1 point

Your total score ____

To Decrease Difficulty

- Continue to practice this drill.
- Practice each of the success check criteria separately.
- Have your partner call out each of the success check criteria one at a time. Perform each of the criteria in the order that they are called.

Sacrifice or Surprise Bunt Drill 2. *Front-Toss Bunt*

You and a partner set up as hitter (bunter) and tosser. The tosser has a bucket of 10 regulation balls and is positioned 10 feet (3.0 meters) from the bunter. Place a screen in front of and just to the nonthrowing side of the tosser. After the ball is released, the tosser can step behind the screen for protection. Before tossing the ball for the bunter, the tosser needs to give a signal to the hitter (e.g., raise an arm above the head) so that the bunter can square around to be in correct position to bunt the ball as it is tossed. Remember, the timing is different for the sacrifice and surprise bunts. Switch places after 10 attempts. Complete two sets of 10 repetitions for each type of bunt.

Success Check: Sacrifice Bunt

- Pivot on the balls of your feet.
- Stand in a staggered stance with your feet facing and shoulders square to the pitcher.

- Hold the bat at the top of the strike zone, parallel to the ground.
- Hold the bat with the top hand outside the grip; the bat should rest on the index finger, with the thumb on top.
- Stop in the bunting position before the release of the pitch.
- Direct the ball down to the ground.

Success Check: Surprise Bunt

- Drop your back foot slightly back.
- Hold the bat in a slightly angled position, square to the pitcher, at the top of the strike zone.
- Pull the knob of the bat to the front hip.
- Rest the bat head on the index finger, thumb on top.
- Give with the ball on contact.
- Direct the ball down to the ground.

Score Your Success

Score yourself for two sets of 10 attempts (for each type of bunt) in which you demonstrate all the success check criteria.

8 to 10 attempts = 5 points

5 to 7 attempts = 3 points

4 attempts or fewer = 1 point

Your total score ___

To Increase Difficulty

- Decrease the distance between the tosser and bunter.
- Increase the speed of the toss.
- Use smaller balls.

To Decrease Difficulty

- Decrease the speed of the toss.
- Use larger balls.
- Use softer balls (softees).

Sacrifice or Surprise Bunt Drill 3. *Bunt the Pitched Ball*

Set up in groups of three—pitcher, catcher, and batter. The catcher must wear full catching gear. (The catcher could be eliminated; instead use a catch net with a target behind the batter. Work in pairs or make the third person the on-deck batter.) The batter takes a position in the batter's box. The catcher is behind the plate. The pitcher has a bucket of 10 balls and takes a position 20 to 46 feet (6.1 to 14 meters) from the batter, depending on the pitcher's pitching skill, in line with the pitching rubber. Before pitching the ball, the pitcher must signal the batter so that the batter can pivot into the sacrifice or surprise bunting position at the appropriate time in the delivery of the pitch. The pitcher attempts to deliver a flat, moderate-speed pitch into the strike zone for the batter. (If available, a pitching machine could be used.) The batter squares around into the sacrifice bunting position or pivots into the surprise bunting position and attempts to bunt the ball down on the ground. After 10 balls are pitched, collect the balls, return them to the bucket, and rotate positions—hitter to catcher, catcher to pitcher, and pitcher to hitter. Complete two sets of 10 repetitions for each type of bunt.

Success Check: Sacrifice Bunt

- Pivot on the balls of your feet.
- Stand in a staggered stance with your feet facing and shoulders square to the pitcher.
- Hold the bat at the top of the strike zone, parallel to the ground.
- Hold the bat with the top hand outside the grip; the bat should rest on the index finger, with the thumb on top.

- Stop in the bunting position before the release of the pitch.
- Direct the ball down to the ground.

Success Check: Surprise Bunt

- Drop your back foot slightly back.
- Hold the bat in a slightly angled position, square to the pitcher, at the top of the strike zone.
- Pull the knob of the bat to the front hip.
- Rest the bat head on the index finger, thumb on top.
- Give with the ball on contact.
- Direct the ball down to the ground.

Score Your Success

Score yourself for two sets of 10 attempts, varying the type of bunt. Earn 1 point for each successful bunt.

Your total score ___

To Increase Difficulty

- Decrease the distance between the tosser and bunter.
- Increase the speed of the pitch.
- Use smaller balls.

To Decrease Difficulty

- Decrease the speed of the pitch.
- Use larger balls.
- Use softer balls (softees).
- Perform a set of 10 sacrifice bunts and a set of 10 surprise bunts.

Sacrifice or Surprise Bunt Drill 4. *Placing the Bunt*

Set up in groups of three—pitcher, catcher, and batter. The catcher must wear full catching gear. (The catcher could be eliminated. Instead use a catch net with a target behind the batter. Work in pairs or make the third person the on-deck batter.) The batter takes a position in the batter's box. The catcher is behind the plate. The pitcher has a bucket of 10 balls and takes a position 15 to 20 feet (4.5 to 6.1 meters) from the batter in line with the pitching rubber. Before pitching the ball, the pitcher signals the batter so that the batter can pivot into the sacrifice or surprise bunting position at the

appropriate time during the delivery of the pitch. The pitcher attempts to deliver a flat, moderate-speed pitch into the strike zone for the batter. (If available, a pitching machine could be used.) The batter moves into the appropriate bunting position and attempts to bunt the ball down on the ground. The batter tries to place the bunt in target areas down the first- or third-base line. Each target area is marked by five cones that are placed approximately 4 feet (1.2 meters) from the foul lines. The last cone is 15 feet (4.5 meters) from home plate. Each batter has five attempts to bunt the ball down the baseline on the right-field side and five attempts to bunt the ball down the baseline on the left-field side. After 10 balls are pitched, collect the balls, return them to the bucket, and rotate positions—hitter to catcher, catcher to pitcher, and pitcher to hitter. Complete two sets of 10 repetitions (5 down each baseline) for each type of bunt.

Success Check: Sacrifice Bunt

- Pivot on the balls of your feet.
- Stand in a staggered stance with your feet facing and shoulders square to the pitcher.
- Hold the bat at the top of the strike zone, parallel to the ground.
- Hold the bat with the top hand outside the grip; the bat should rest on the index finger, with the thumb on top.

- Stop in the bunting position before the release of the pitch.
- Direct the ball down to the ground, and place it in one of the designated areas.

Success Check: Surprise Bunt

- Drop your back foot slightly back.
- Hold the bat in a slightly angled position, square to the pitcher, at the top of the strike zone.
- Pull the knob of the bat to the front hip.
- Rest the bat head on the index finger, thumb on top.
- Give with the ball on contact.
- Direct the ball down to the ground, and place it in one of the designated areas.

Score Your Success

Score yourself for each set of 5 attempts down the first-base line and 5 attempts down the third-base line (for each type of bunt). Earn 1 point for each successful bunt.

Your total score ___

To Increase Difficulty

- Decrease the distance between the tosser and bunter.
- Increase the speed of the pitch.

- Decrease the size of the designated target area.
- Vary the bunt selected within each set.

To Decrease Difficulty

- Decrease the speed of the pitch.
- Use larger balls.
- Increase the size of the designated target area.

PUSH BUNT

Typically, the push bunt (figure 5.3) is an option used from the sacrifice bunting stance, but more advanced players can perform the push bunt from a surprise bunt position. The push bunt is a good alternative if the defense is charging in as you attempt to bunt. The object of the push bunt is to get the ball by the fielders at first or third base. Instead of "giving" with the bat as it contacts the ball to drop the ball down, the bunter pushes the bat into the ball on contact to direct it by the defense.

Misstep

The ball is bunted with too little force to get by the fielders, either in the air or on the ground.

Correction

Remember to keep your grip and arms tight and push the bat out on contact.

Once the batter decides to push bunt and reads the defense, she has two basic choices: push the ball in the air over the rushing defensive player at third or push the ball on the ground between the third or first baseman and the pitcher. Attempting to push the ball over the fielder's head does not work down the first-base line because typically the second baseman is going into that area to cover first on a bunt. Pushing the ball on the ground past the fielders has a fairly high success rate if the ball is placed out of the reach of the first and third basemen, who are in close to home plate. Once the ball gets past these players, the pitcher is the only possible fielder.

| **Figure 5.3** | **Push Bunt From Sacrifice Bunt Position** |

PREPARE TO PUSH BUNT

1. Assume sacrifice bunting position

BUNT

1. As defense charges, tighten arms and wrist
2. At contact, push bat out and down (ground ball) or at a slight angle up (pop-up)

RUN

1. Take first step toward first base with back foot
2. Get into foul territory as quickly as possible
3. Run through first base

Misstep

The ball is pushed on the ground directly to the fielder.

Correction

Angle the bat so that it faces the space where you are trying to bunt the ball.

Misstep

The ball is bunted foul.

Correction

Adjust the angle of the bat.

Push Bunt Drill 1. *Front-Toss Push Bunt*

You and a partner set up as hitter (bunter) and tosser. Place two cones down the first-base line and two cones down the third-base line, approximately 10 feet (3.0 meters) from home plate. The cones represent the charging defenders from first and third. The tosser has a bucket of 10 regulation balls and is positioned 10 feet from the bunter. Place a screen in front of and just to the nonthrowing side of the tosser. Before tossing the ball, the tosser signals the hitter (e.g., raises an arm above the head) so that the hitter can correctly time when to move into the sacrifice bunting position. The bunter attempts to push the ball between and past the cones and the pitcher. Switch places after 10 attempts. Complete two sets of 10 repetitions.

Success Check

• Move into sacrifice bunting position.

• At contact, push the bat out and down for a ground ball or at a slight angle up for a pop-up.
• Direct the ball down to the ground between the cones and the pitcher and past the cones, unless you are attempting to push the ball over the fielder's head to increase your challenge.

Score Your Success

Score yourself for two sets of 10 attempts. Earn 1 point for each successful bunt.

Your total score ___

To Increase Difficulty

• Add a third cone and decrease the distance between home plate and the cones.
• Increase the speed of the pitch.
• Attempt to pop the ball over the cones on the third-base line.

• Attempt a push bunt from the surprise bunt position.

To Decrease Difficulty

• Decrease the speed of the pitch.
• Start with your feet and bat in bunting position.
• Use larger balls.
• Eliminate one cone from each side to enlarge the target area.

Push Bunt Drill 2. *Push Bunt the Pitched Ball*

Set up in groups of three—pitcher, catcher, and batter. The catcher must wear full catching gear. (The catcher can be eliminated. Instead use a catch net with a target behind the batter. Work in pairs or make the third person the on-deck batter.) The batter takes a position in the batter's box. The catcher is behind the plate. The pitcher has a bucket of 10 balls and takes a position 20 to 40 feet (6.1 to 12.2 meters) from the batter, depending on the pitcher's skill, in line with the pitching rubber. Place two cones down the first-base line and two cones down the third-base line, approximately 10 feet (3.0 meters) from home plate. The cones represent the charging defenders from first and third. Before pitching the ball, the pitcher signals the batter so that the batter can prepare to move into the sacrifice bunting position. The pitcher attempts to

deliver a flat, moderate-speed pitch into the strike zone for the batter. (If available, a pitching machine could be used.) The bunter attempts to push the ball between and past the cones and the pitcher. After 10 balls are pitched, collect the balls, return them to the bucket, and rotate positions—hitter to catcher, catcher to pitcher, and pitcher to hitter. Complete two sets of 10 repetitions.

Success Check

• Move into sacrifice bunting position.
• At contact, push the bat out and down for a ground ball or at a slight angle up to push the ball over the fielder's head.
• Direct the ball down to the ground between and past the cones and the pitcher, or direct the ball over the fielder's head.

Score Your Success

Score yourself for two sets of 10 attempts.

Your total score ___

To Increase Difficulty

• Add a third cone and decrease the distance

between home plate and the cones, thus decreasing the target area.
• Increase the speed of the pitch.
• Attempt to push the ball in the air over the cones on the third-base line.

- Attempt a push bunt from the surprise bunt position.

To Decrease Difficulty

- Decrease the speed of the pitch.
- Start with your feet and bat in bunting position.

- Use larger balls.
- Eliminate one cone from each side to enlarge the target area.
- Eliminate all of the cones and work on pushing the ball forward.

SLASH BUNT

The slash bunt (figure 5.4) is used in similar situations to the push bunt, but for the slash bunt, the batter swings at the ball. It is another technique to use when the defense takes away the sacrifice bunt by virtue of their aggressive play. The slash bunt is hit with more force than the push bunt and has the potential to get out of the infield. The resulting hit, especially if executed to the first-base side, could send the advancing runner from first base all the way to third base.

From sacrifice bunting position (staggered stance with feet facing and shoulders square to pitcher, hands separated on bat), simply slide your hands back together, meeting at the midpoint or top of the grip. Rotate your torso and bat slightly back, and take a three-quarter swing at the ball.

The target for the placement of the slash bunt is based on the same factors described for the push bunt. Keeping your feet facing the pitcher will help you keep your head still and enable you to better maintain your focus on the incoming pitch. If you attempt to move your feet back into your hitting stance, you will find it difficult to keep the pitch in focus and initiate your swing in the time it takes for the pitch to come to the plate. Another benefit of the slash bunt is that by feigning a slash, you may stop the charge of the third and first basemen toward the plate, making it possible to go through with the sacrifice bunt.

| Figure 5.4 | **Slash Bunt** |

a *b* *c*

PREPARE TO SLASH BUNT

1. Assume sacrifice bunting position

BUNT

1. As defense charges, slide hands together and rotate torso and bat slightly back
2. Take a three-quarter swing at the ball
3. Attempt to place ball past charging first and third basemen

RUN

1. Take first step toward first base with back foot
2. Get into foul territory as quickly as possible
3. Run through first base

Misstep

You miss the pitch because you overrotate your torso, move your feet back to hitting position, and attempt to take a full swing at the ball.

Correction

Keep your feet facing the pitcher in a staggered position, and only slightly rotate your torso and bat back. Keep your eyes focused on the pitcher and take a three-quarter swing.

Misstep

You hit the ball foul.

Correction

You are swinging either too early or too late. Bring the bat back as soon as you see the defense charge. Using a three-quarter swing, slap the ball down into fair territory.

Slash Bunt Drill 1. *Front-Toss Slash Bunt*

You and a partner set up as hitter (slasher) and tosser. Place two cones down the first-base line and two cones down the third-base line, approximately 10 feet (3.0 meters) from home plate. The cones represent the charging defenders from first and third. The tosser has a bucket of 10 regulation balls and is positioned 10 feet from the slasher. Place a screen in front of and just to the nonthrowing side of the tosser. Before tossing the ball, the tosser signals the slasher (e.g., raises an arm above the head) so that the slasher can correctly time when to move into the sacrifice bunting position. When the pitch is about halfway to the batter, the batter pulls the bat back, preparing to slash the ball. The slasher attempts to slap the ball between and past the cones and the pitcher. Switch places after 10 attempts. Complete two sets of 10 repetitions.

Success Check

- Move into sacrifice bunting position.
- When the pitch is about halfway to home plate, slide your hands together and rotate your torso and bat slightly back. (In this drill, it is assumed that the defense is charging.)
- Take a three-quarter swing at the ball.
- Attempt to place the ball between and past the cones and the pitcher.

Score Your Success

Score yourself for two sets of 10 attempts. Earn 1 point for each successful bunt.

Your total score ___

To Increase Difficulty

- Increase the speed of the pitch.
- Attempt to hit the ball in the air over the cones on the third-base line.
- Alternate a sacrifice bunt with a slash bunt.

To Decrease Difficulty

- Decrease the speed of the pitch.
- Start with your feet and bat in sacrifice bunting position.
- Use larger balls.
- Eliminate one or more cones from each side to enlarge the target area.
- Use a batting tee.

Slash Bunt Drill 2. *Slash Bunt the Pitched Ball*

Set up in groups of three—pitcher, catcher, and batter. The catcher must wear full catching gear. (The catcher can be eliminated. Instead use a catch net with a target behind the batter. Work in pairs or make the third person the on-deck batter.) The batter takes a position in the batter's box.

The catcher is behind the plate. The pitcher has a bucket of 10 balls and takes a position 20 to 40 feet (6.1 to 12.2 meters) from the batter, depending on the pitcher's skill, in line with the pitching rubber. Place a screen in front of and just to the nonthrowing side of the pitcher. Place two cones down the first-base line and two cones down the third-base line, approximately 10 feet (3.0 meters) from home plate. The cones represent the charging defenders from first and third. Before pitching the ball, the pitcher signals the batter so that the batter can prepare to move into the sacrifice bunting position. The pitcher attempts to deliver a flat, moderate-speed pitch into the strike zone for the batter. (If available, a pitching machine could be used.) The bunter attempts to slash the ball between and past the cones and the pitcher. After 10 balls are pitched, collect the balls, return them to the bucket, and rotate positions—hitter to catcher, catcher to pitcher, and pitcher to hitter. Complete two sets of 10 repetitions.

Success Check

- Move into sacrifice bunting position.
- When the pitch is about halfway to home plate, slide your hands together and rotate your torso and bat slightly back. (In this drill, it is assumed that the defense is charging.)
- Take a three-quarter swing at the ball.
- Attempt to place the ball between and past the cones and the pitcher.

Score Your Success

Score yourself on two sets of 10 attempts. Earn 1 point for each successful bunt.

Your total score ___

To Increase Difficulty

- Add a third cone and decrease the distance between home plate and the cones, thus decreasing the target area.
- Increase the speed of the pitch.
- Attempt to hit the ball in the air over the cones on the third-base line.

- Add fielders at first and third. The fielders alternate charging and staying back, forcing the batter to make decisions regarding whether to sacrifice bunt or slash bunt.

To Decrease Difficulty

- Repeat the previous drill.
- Decrease the speed of the pitch.
- Start with your feet and bat in bunting position.
- Use larger balls.
- Eliminate one or more of the cones from each side to enlarge the target area.

RUNNING SLAP

The running slap is used more as a means of getting on base by hitting the ball rather than as a form of bunting. Right- or left-handed players who have very good speed and may have difficulty making good contact from a normal hitting stance typically use this skill. The running slap is executed from the left side of the batter's box, with the objective of slapping a medium to slow rolling ground ball to the shortstop or slapping a fly ball over a drawn-in infield.

Assume a normal batting stance in the left side of the batter's box (figure 5.5a). The first step is a short jab-type step with the right foot. The second step is a crossover step with the left foot; this step should be aggressive and in the direction of the pitcher (figure 5.5b). If the step is toward first base, this will cause the slapper to pull the bat away from home plate, often resulting in a swinging strike or a foul ball to the left side. This crossover step must land inside or in contact with the front line of the batter's box; otherwise, the batter will be out if she makes contact with the ball.

Misstep

The crossover step results in the batter running toward first rather than toward the pitcher.

Correction

Execute the crossover step so that it is in the direction of the pitcher.

Misstep

The step with the left foot ends up outside of the batter's box.

Correction

If contact is made with the pitch, the batter is out. Adjust the step so that it lands inside of or on the front line of the batter's box.

Use an inside-out swing. Keep your hands close to your body and high in the strike zone. The head of the bat should not drop below the hands; the knob of the bat should point to the pitcher. Contact the ball deep in the hitting zone with your weight on your left foot to ensure proper alignment for running to first (figure 5.5c).

A good hitter who can hit from the left side and has good speed can use this skill very effectively. The hitter can switch back and forth from the running slap to taking a full regular swing at the ball, keeping the defense back on their heels and unsure of the batter's intent.

Misstep

The batter pulls his head before contact, missing or mis-hitting the ball.

Correction

Keep the head still and the eyes on the ball on contact.

Figure 5.5   Running Slap

RUNNING SLAP

1. Take first step, a short jab-type step, with right foot
2. Take second step, an aggressive crossover step toward pitcher, with left foot
3. Keep left foot inside or on front line of batter's box during second step
4. Use inside-out swing
5. Keep head of bat above hands, and point knob of bat toward pitcher
6. Keep front side closed
7. Contact pitch deep in hitting zone
8. Keep eyes on ball on contact; keep head still

PREPARATION

1. Assume normal batting stance in left side of batter's box

c

RUN

1. Make contact with ball with weight on left foot as you run toward pitcher
2. Take first step after contact with right foot, running toward first base
3. Get into foul territory as quickly as possible
4. Run through first base

Misstep

The batter opens the front side, pulling the bat away from the contact zone and resulting in a swinging strike or a foul ball to the left side.

Correction

Keep the front side closed.

Misstep

The batter drops the hands and pops the ball up.

Correction

Keep the hands at the top of the strike zone.

Running Slap Drill 1. *Fence Swing*

This drill helps you develop the feel of the inside-out swinging motion that is such a critical component of successful execution of the running slap.

Stand facing a fence, net, or curtain. To determine how far away from the fence you should stand, place the knob of the bat against your hip; the bat head should just barely touch the fence. Begin in your normal batting stance, with the fence in front of you. Place a bucket or cone where the pitcher would be between you and the fence. Take the initial jab step and then cross over with your left foot straight toward the pitcher. When your weight is on your left foot, do a self-check. Look back at the position of your bat. The knob of the bat should be facing the pitcher, and the head of the bat should be higher than the handle. Continue with the swing, working on the inside-out bat ac-

tion. If you are executing the swing correctly, the bat head will not hit the fence. Do the self-check one or two times and then take 10 swings without the self-check. Repeat this drill twice.

Success Check

- Take a short jab step with the right foot, and cross over with the left foot toward the "pitcher."
- Turn the knob of the bat to face the pitcher, and keep the bat head higher than the handle.
- Swing using an inside-out action.
- Keep your front shoulder in and your head still.
- Do not make contact with the fence on the swing.

99

Score Your Success

Score yourself on two sets of 10 attempts. Do not count the self-check. Earn 1 point each time you do not hit the fence.

Your total score ___

To Increase Difficulty

Place the front line of the batter's box in the appropriate spot based on your normal batting stance and position. Repeat the drill while attempting to land with your left foot within or on the front line of the batter's box.

To Decrease Difficulty

- Repeat this drill.
- Do a self-check on every swing.
- Walk through the swing slowly.

Running Slap Drill 2. *Catching the Ball From a Front Toss*

This drill gives you the sense of how deep in the zone you should make contact with the ball when performing the running slap. This drill requires a slapper and a pitcher. The slapper stands in the left side of the batter's box in a normal hitting stance with a fielding glove on the left hand (the slapper does not have a bat). The pitcher has a bucket of 10 to 15 balls and stands 15 to 20 feet (4.5 to 6.1 meters) from the batter in line with the pitching rubber. A second bucket is placed beside home plate opposite the slapper. The pitcher signals for the slapper to take the initial jab step and then tosses the ball in a flat trajectory over the plate at waist level. The slapper attempts to catch the ball off the back hip while the slapper's weight is on the left foot (contact position; see figure 5.6). Each slapper gets 10 attempts to catch a catchable pitched ball. All caught balls are placed in the second bucket. If the pitch is not in the strike zone or is too high or too low, it does not count as an attempt. After 10 catchable balls are pitched, collect the balls, return them to the bucket, and rotate positions—slapper to pitcher and pitcher to slapper. Complete two sets of 10 repetitions.

Figure 5.6
Catching the ball from a Front Toss drill.

Success Check

- Take a short jab step with the right foot on the pitcher's signal.
- Cross over with your left foot toward the pitcher.
- Keep your front shoulder in and your head still.
- Catch the tossed ball off your back hip, with your weight on your left foot.
- Run through the catch and take one or two steps toward first base.

Score Your Success

Score yourself for two sets of 10 attempts. Earn 1 point for each catch, counting only catchable pitches.

Your total score ___

To Increase Difficulty

- Increase the speed of the pitch.
- Use a pitching machine.
- Have a pitcher throw from the regulation pitching distance.

To Decrease Difficulty

- Repeat this drill or the previous drill.
- Decrease the speed of the pitch.
- Hang a Wiffle ball on a string from above so that it is positioned in the spot that you would catch the ball off of your back hip. Walk through the slapping motion, and catch the Wiffle ball with your weight on your left foot.

Running Slap Drill 3. *Slapping Off a Tee*

This drill gives you the opportunity to execute the running slap while keeping the ball stationary until contact is made. You can do this drill by yourself or with one or more fielders. You need a home plate and a batter's box, a batting tee, and a bucket of 10 balls.

Begin in your normal batting stance in the left side of the batter's box. Place a tee on the back third of home plate. Begin the running slap motion by taking a jab step with your right foot and crossing over with your left foot, stepping toward a cone representing the pitcher. Use the inside-out swing and contact the ball on the tee, back in the zone, attempting to place the ball in the direction of the shortstop. You could also set up this drill so that you hit into a net that has a target that identifies the intended direction of the slap. Take a new ball from the bucket after each attempt. After completing 10 attempts, collect all of the hit balls. Complete two sets of 10 repetitions.

Success Check

- Take a short jab step with your right foot, and cross over with your left foot toward the "pitcher."
- Turn the knob of the bat to face the pitcher, and keep the bat head higher than the handle.
- Swing using an inside-out action.
- Keep your front shoulder in and your head still.
- Make contact with the ball with your weight on the left foot.
- Land with your left foot on or within the front line of the batter's box.
- Slap the ball in the direction of the shortstop.

Score Your Success

Score yourself for two sets of 10 attempts.

Your total score ___

To Increase Difficulty

Increase the speed of your running steps.

To Decrease Difficulty

- Repeat this drill.
- Slowly walk through the swing.
- Use a larger ball.
- Begin in the contact position (weight on left foot) and use an inside-out swing to make contact with the ball on the tee.

Running Slap Drill 4. *Slapping a Pitched Ball*

This drill gives you the opportunity to perform the running slap with a pitch coming at you. Set up in groups of three—pitcher, catcher, and batter. The catcher must wear full catching gear. (The catcher can be eliminated. Instead use a catch net with a target behind the batter. Work in pairs or make the third person the on-deck batter.) The batter takes a position in the batter's box. The catcher is behind the plate. The pitcher has a bucket of 10 balls and takes a position 15 to 20 feet (4.5 to 6.1 meters) from the batter; the pitcher should be in line with the pitching rubber behind a protective pitching screen. (If a screen is not available, the tosser should be closer and should use Wiffle balls.) Before pitching the ball, the pitcher signals the batter so that the batter can time when to take the initial jab step before the delivery of the pitch. The pitcher attempts to deliver a flat, moderate-speed pitch into the strike zone for the batter. (If available, a pitching machine could be used.) The slapper moves into contact position and attempts to slap the ball in the shortstop's direction, taking two or three steps toward first base. After 10 balls are pitched, collect the balls, return them to the bucket, and rotate positions—slapper to catcher, catcher to pitcher, and pitcher to slapper. Complete two sets of 10 repetitions.

Success Check

- Take a short jab step with your right foot, and cross over with your left foot toward the pitcher.
- Turn the knob of the bat to face the pitcher, and keep the bat head higher than the handle.
- Swing using an inside-out action.

- Keep your front shoulder in and your head still.
- Make contact deep in the zone, with your weight on your left foot.
- Land with your left foot on or within the front line of the batter's box.
- Slap the ball in the shortstop's direction.

Score Your Success

Score yourself on two sets of 10 attempts. Earn 1 point for each successful slap.

Your total score ___

To Increase Difficulty

- Increase the speed of your running steps.
- Increase the speed of the pitch.
- Alternate between a running slap and a full swing (if you are a natural left-handed hitter).

- Add defense and attempt to pop the ball over the defense.

To Decrease Difficulty

- Repeat this drill.
- Repeat previous drills.
- Use a larger ball.
- Decrease the speed of the pitch, or perform this drill with a front toss rather than a pitched ball (see sacrifice and surprise bunt drill 2).

DRAG BUNT

The hitter executing the drag bunt (figure 5.7) also uses the element of surprise to be successful, with the intent of getting on base rather than simply advancing the runner. The term *drag bunt* comes from the fact that the technique, when used by a left-handed batter, causes the ball to be dragged with the batter-runner down the first-base line (figure 5.7b). Batting from the left side is an advantage because the batter is much closer to first base when contact is made and, therefore, has a shorter distance to run than a right-handed batter. If the left-handed batter also has good foot speed and has a good eye for the ball, the drag bunt is an excellent alternative to swinging away for a hit or executing the running slap. A batter who can use both the running slap and the drag bunt effectively is very difficult to defend.

The foot action for the drag bunt is similar to that for the running slap, making it difficult for the defense to initially pick up the batter's intent. However, the bat action and contact zone are different. To execute the drag bunt, as you take the step with your left foot toward the pitcher, you should slide your top hand up the bat into a bunting position and get the bat out in front and slightly ahead of the left foot. Open your hips to get the bat in a slight angle toward the first-base line. Make contact with the ball in front of home plate but slightly back in the zone. Your intent is to bunt (drag) the ball down the first-base line, so you do not want to contact the ball too far out in front. As contact is made, give slightly so the ball is not pushed out too far, which would create an easy play for the defense.

Misstep

The batter squares the bat to the pitcher or angles it toward third, causing the ball to be bunted at the pitcher or down the third-base line (rather than dragged down the first-base line).

Correction

Angle the bat slightly toward first base.

Misstep

The batter opens his front side, pulling the bat away from the contact zone and causing the batter to miss the ball or to foul the ball to the right side.

Correction

Keep the front side closed.

Figure 5.7 **Drag Bunt**

a   b   c

PREPARE TO DRAG BUNT

1. Assume normal batting stance in left side of batter's box
2. Initiate running slap foot action

DRAG BUNT

1. Slide top hand up bat into bunting position; open hips
2. Hold bat out in front, slightly ahead of left foot
3. Angle bat slightly toward first base
4. Make contact ahead of home plate but slightly back in zone (off left heel)
5. Weight is on left foot
6. Give slightly on contact
7. Drag ball down first-base line

RUN

1. Make contact with ball with weight on left foot as you run toward pitcher
2. Take first step after contact with right foot, running toward first base
3. Get into foul territory as quickly as possible
4. Run through first base

Misstep

The batter brings the bat into the contact zone late, resulting in the ball going down the third-base line.

Correction

Adjust the timing so that the bat is in the contact zone just before the pitch enters the zone.

Misstep

The batter pulls her head on contact.

Correction

Keep your head still and your eyes on the ball on contact.

Drag Bunt Drill 1. *Drag Bunt Off a Batting Tee*

This drill provides the opportunity to work on drag bunt technique without having to worry about a moving pitch. Place the batting tee just off the front corner of home plate on the first-base side. Work on dragging the ball down the first-base line, and take five steps toward first base after contacting the ball. Repeat 10 times. Complete two sets of 10 repetitions.

Success Check

- Assume a normal batting stance in the left side of the batter's box.
- Take a short jab step with your right foot, and cross over with your left foot toward a cone representing the pitcher.

- Slide your top hand up the bat, and get into bunting position by opening your hips.
- Angle the bat slightly toward first base.
- Make contact ahead of home plate but slightly back in the zone, off the heel of your left foot.
- Make contact with the ball with your weight on your left foot as you run toward the pitcher.
- Drag the ball down the first-base line on the ground.
- Take your first step after contact with your right foot, running toward first base.
- Take five running steps toward first base with at least three steps in foul territory.

Score Your Success

Score yourself for two sets of 10 attempts. Earn 1 point for each successful drag bunt.

Your total score ___

To Increase Difficulty

Increase the speed of your running steps.

To Decrease Difficulty

- Repeat this drill.
- Walk slowly through the swing.
- Use a larger ball.
- Begin in the contact position, with your weight on your left foot and with the bat on the ball. Practice the dragging motion to place the ball down the first-base line on the ground.

Drag Bunt Drill 2. *Front-Toss Drag Bunt*

You and a partner set up as bunter and tosser. Place three cones parallel with and 5 feet (1.5 meters) away from the first-base line. The third cone should be approximately 15 feet (4.5 meters) from home plate. The cones represent the target area where you want the drag bunt to land. The bunt should not go beyond the third cone. The tosser has a bucket of 10 regulation balls and is positioned 10 feet (3.0

meters) from the bunter. Before tossing the ball, the tosser signals (e.g., raises an arm above the head) so that the bunter can time when to initiate the drag bunt. The bunter attempts to drag the ball on the ground into the target area and takes five running steps toward first base after making contact. Switch places after 10 attempts. Complete two sets of 10 repetitions.

Success Check

- Assume a normal batting stance in the left side of the batter's box.
- Take a short jab step with your right foot, and cross over with your left foot toward the tosser.
- Slide your top hand up the bat, and get into bunting position by opening your hips.
- Angle the bat slightly toward first base.
- Make contact ahead of home plate but slightly back in the zone, off the heel of your left foot.

- Give slightly on contact.
- Make contact with your weight on your left foot as you run toward the tosser.
- Drag the ball down the first-base line on the ground into the target area.
- Take your first step after contact with your right foot, running toward first base.
- Take five running steps toward first base with at least three steps in foul territory.

Score Your Success

Score yourself for two sets of 10 attempts.

Your total score ___

To Increase Difficulty

- Increase the speed of your running steps.
- Decrease the size of the target area by moving the cones to a position 3 to 4 feet (.9 to 1.2 meters) from the first-base line.

To Decrease Difficulty

- Repeat the previous drill.
- Repeat this drill.
- Use a larger ball.
- Increase the size of the target area.
- Begin in the contact position, with your weight on your left foot.

Drag Bunt Drill 3. *Drag Bunt a Pitched Ball*

This drill provides the opportunity to perform the drag bunt off a pitch. Set up in groups of three—pitcher, catcher, and batter. The catcher must wear full catching gear. (The catcher can be eliminated. Instead use a catch net with a target behind the batter. Work in pairs or make the third person the on-deck batter.) The batter takes a position in the batter's box. The catcher is behind the plate. The pitcher has a bucket of 10 balls and takes a position 15 to 20 feet (4.5 to 6.1 meters) from the batter; the pitcher should be in line with the pitching rubber behind a protective pitching screen. (If a screen is not available, the pitcher should be closer and should use Wiffle balls.) Create a target zone by placing three cones parallel with and 5 feet (1.5 meters) away from the first-base line. The third cone should be approximately 15 feet from home plate.

Before pitching the ball, the pitcher signals the batter so that the batter can time when to take the initial jab step before the delivery of the pitch. The

pitcher attempts to deliver a flat, moderate-speed pitch into the strike zone for the batter. (If available, a pitching machine could be used.) The batter moves into contact position and attempts to drag the ball into the target zone down the first-base line. The batter takes five steps toward first base. The bunt should not go beyond the third cone. After 10 balls are pitched, collect the balls, return them to the bucket, and rotate positions—bunter to catcher, catcher to pitcher, and pitcher to bunter. Complete two sets of 10 repetitions.

Success Check

- Assume a normal batting stance in the left side of the batter's box.
- Take a short jab step with your right foot, and cross over with your left foot toward the pitcher.
- Slide your top hand up the bat, and get into bunting position by opening your hips.
- Angle the bat slightly toward first base.

- Make contact ahead of home plate but slightly back in the zone, off the heel of your left foot.
- Give slightly on contact.
- Make contact with the ball with your weight on your left foot as you run toward the pitcher.
- Drag the ball down the first-base line on the ground into the target area.

- Take your first step after contact with your right foot, running toward first base.
- Take five running steps toward first base with at least three steps in foul territory.

Score Your Success

Score yourself for two sets of 10 attempts.

Your total score ___

To Increase Difficulty

- Increase the speed of your running steps.
- Increase the speed of the pitch.
- Decrease the size of the target area by moving the cones to a position 3 to 4 feet (.9 to 1.2 meters) from the first-base line.

To Decrease Difficulty

- Repeat previous drag bunting drills.
- Repeat this drill.
- Decrease the speed of the pitch.
- Use a larger ball.
- Make the target area larger.
- Begin in contact position, with your weight on your left foot.

SUCCESS SUMMARY

In fastpitch softball, the short game is an effective means of moving runners over and getting on base. Because some of the skills included in the short game depend on the player's speed, all players are not expected to use all these skills in a game. However, learning the skills included in the short game will help you to see the ball and increase your bat control skills.

All players should be able to perform the sacrifice bunt and either the push or slash bunt off the sacrifice bunt. The sacrifice bunt is designed to move runners over and does not depend on the batter's foot speed. A batter who does not have good foot speed might choose to perform a slash or push bunt from a sacrifice bunting position,

not to get on base, but rather to give the runners a better chance of moving over. Getting on base is a bonus, as long as you successfully move the runners over! If you have good foot speed, work on mastering several of the short-game skills. These skills will give you more options as a hitter and therefore make you more difficult to defend.

In the next step, you will work on the baserunning skills that are very important in the short game. Good baserunners make the short game even more effective. Before moving on to step 6, you should look at how you did on the drills in this step. Enter your score for each drill, and add up your scores to rate your total success.

Sacrifice or Surprise Bunt Drills (score yourself for each type of bunt)

1. Mimetic Bunts
   Sacrifice bunt ___ out of 10
   Surprise bunt ___ out of 10
2. Front-Toss Bunt
   Sacrifice bunt ___ out of 10
   Surprise bunt ___ out of 10
3. Bunt the Pitched Ball
   Sacrifice bunt ___ out of 10
   Surprise bunt ___ out of 10
4. Placing the Bunt
   Sacrifice bunt ___ out of 10
   Surprise bunt ___ out of 10

Push Bunt Drills

1. Front-Toss Push Bunt ___ out of 20
2. Push Bunt the Pitched Ball ___ out of 20

Slash Bunt Drills

1. Front-Toss Slash Bunt ___ out of 20
2. Slash Bunt the Pitched Ball ___ out of 20

Running Slap Drills

1. Fence Swing ___ out of 20
2. Catching a Ball From a Front Toss ___ out of 20
3. Slapping Off a Tee ___ out of 20
4. Slapping a Pitched Ball ___ out of 20

Drag Bunt Drills

1. Drag Bunt Off a Batting Tee ___ out of 20
2. Front-Toss Drag Bunt ___ out of 20
3. Drag Bunting a Pitched Ball ___ out of 20

Total ___ *out of 300*

Your total score provides an indication of whether or not you have developed the skills necessary to be effective in the short game. If you scored 225 total points or more—and a minimum of 68 points in the sacrifice bunt plus the push or slash bunt drills—congratulations! You have mastered the skills included in the short game. If your total score was 180 to 224 points, you would benefit from additional practice in selected drills. If you scored less than 180 points, you should continue to practice the short-game drills to improve your skills and increase your total score.

However, if you scored less than 225 total points but scored at least 68 points in the sacrifice bunt plus the push or slash bunt drills, you have the minimum short-game skills you need to be effective in a game. If you have good foot speed, you should strive to improve other short-game skills by getting additional practice to increase your total score. To consider yourself skilled in the sacrifice bunt and push or slash bunt drills, work to earn at least 68 points in those drills.

Baserunning

Now that you have learned several offensive and defensive skills, let's move on to another important offensive skill—baserunning. A good baserunner has many opportunities to contribute to the success of a team. Major league baseball Hall of Fame players Lou Brock and Maury Wills were valued for their baserunning skills more than their hitting skills. Current major leaguers Carl Crawford of the Tampa Bay Devil Rays and Coco Crisp of the Boston Red Sox are major scoring threats when they get on base, because a single followed by a sure stolen base puts a runner in scoring position almost immediately!

The success of the 2000 U.S. Olympic softball team in its quest for the gold medal in Sydney, Australia, was largely because of the baserunning abilities of players such as Dot Richardson and Laura Berg. Laura had great speed, while Dot's success was because of her smart baserunning decisions. A new baserunning star, Natasha Watley, emerged at the 2004 Olympics in Athens, Greece. At those Games, Watley broke the Olympic record for stolen bases with five in nine games!

Once you hit the ball, you must run to first base. *Batter-runner* is the official rule book term to identify the batter who, one way or another, has finished a turn at bat and is moving from home plate to first base. By definition, the term *batter* refers only to the person at bat and does not describe the person running to first base. Technically, then, as the batter, let's say you hit a ground ball to the shortstop. As you run to first base, you become the batter-runner until you either reach first base safely or are put out there. When you reach first base safely, you become a *baserunner*.

Baserunning is the only way you can advance around the bases and score a run. Your degree of baserunning skill often makes the difference between your being safe or out on a play. Thus, correct baserunning technique is essential to your team's offensive success. Baserunning technique is the same whether you are playing in a fastpitch, modified-pitch, or slow-pitch game. However, the rules for baserunning are different for fastpitch and slow-pitch games.

Running is a fundamental skill. However, baserunning is a skill specific to softball and baseball that involves more than simple physical running skills; you must exercise good judgment in executing those skills. The physical skill is the development of maximum speed in short distances as you run around a 60-foot (18.3-meter) square. Traveling the shortest distance possible, despite the fact that making a 90-degree turn at each base is impossible, is the tactical baserunning skill. In both fastpitch and slow-pitch games, you may overrun first base and home plate, but you must stop on second and third base when advancing directly to those bases. When baserunning in fastpitch softball, you may leave the base the moment the pitcher releases the pitch. This allows you to be off the base when the ball is hit, thus shortening your distance to the next base at the moment of the hit. In slow-pitch softball, though, you may not leave a base until the ball is hit or crosses home plate; thus, you must run the full distance to the next base after the ball is hit.

You must also know when and how to run. Will you try to advance or will you return to the base you just rounded? Will you slide or stand up coming into a base? The answers to these and many other questions depend on your ability to use good judgment when baserunning. Once you get on base, sound baserunning techniques and good judgment make it possible for you to score runs—and win games!

OVERRUNNING FIRST BASE

When you hit a ground ball that is playable by an infielder, you must get out of the batter's box as quickly as possible and run at top speed *over* first base. Remember that first base and home plate are the two bases you may overrun. (When batting, you are out if you step on home plate as you contact the ball with the bat, not because you stepped on home plate, but because you were out of the batter's box when you hit the ball.)

After hitting the ball, take your first step out of the batter's box with your back foot (figure 6.1a). You begin with your back foot because your weight shifts onto your front foot as you complete your swing, thus freeing your back foot to take that first step. Your run to first base must take you into foul territory (outside the baseline) and into the alley that starts halfway between home and first. If you run from home plate to first base in fair territory and you are hit by a thrown ball, you are out.

Misstep

You start to run out of the batter's box using your front foot, thus increasing the distance and time it takes to reach first base.

Correction

At the completion of your swing, be sure your full weight is on your front foot, so your rear foot is free to move.

For a left-handed batter, the first step with the back foot should be very close to foul territory, because most of the left-handed batter's box is in foul territory on the first-base side. A left-handed batter would step into fair territory only if she were batting in the very front of the box, in which case the batter would need to get to the foul side of the baseline as soon as possible. A right-handed batter must make a conscious effort to start her movement to first base toward the foul line and not run directly at the base from the point at which she completes the follow-through of the swing.

Once on the foul side of the first-base foul line, you should run directly over the first-base bag, contacting it with your foot on the front corner that is on the foul line (figure 6.1b). Overrun the base at full speed, traveling in a straight line (follow the foul line). Start to slow down by bending your knees, taking short steps, and leaning back until you can easily come to a stop. Turn to your left, toward fair territory (figure 6.1c). If you have been called safe, return directly to the base. If, as you turn toward the field of play, you see that the ball has been misplayed, you must decide whether to continue toward second base. Once you make an attempt to go to second base, you are no longer allowed to return to first base freely and may be tagged out.

Figure 6.1 | Overrunning First Base

LEAVING THE BOX
1. First step is with back foot
2. Get to foul territory
3. Accelerate quickly
4. Get to top speed
5. Look to coach, *then* focus on base

a

CONTACTING THE BASE
1. Run on foul ground
2. Continue running at top speed
3. Don't break stride
4. Focus on base
5. Contact front corner of base

b

RETURNING TO THE BASE
1. Bend knees
2. Take short steps
3. Lean back and stop
4. Turn to left
5. Go directly back to base

c

Misstep

You run all the way to first in fair territory.

Correction

Don't! Get over into foul territory as soon as possible.

Misstep

You leap for the bag or take short or long strides just before reaching first base.

Correction

Maintain a consistent running stride, and contact the front outside (foul line) corner of the base with either foot.

Overrunning First Base Drill 1. *Leaving the Batter's Box*

With a bat, assume your regular batting stance in the batter's box. Swing at 10 imaginary pitches using the technique described in figure 4.2 (page 64) for hitting. Put special emphasis on completing your swing by wrapping your hands around your shoulder. In addition, make sure your weight is on your front foot, your front knee is bent, and your body is leaning toward first base. Drive out of the batter's box, taking the first step with your back foot. Release your top hand and hold the bat with your bottom hand as you start toward first base. Drop (do not throw) your bat on the ground in foul territory as you take your second or third running step. Take several full strides toward first base (until you get into foul territory and have taken two more strides down the line if you are a right-handed batter, or four more strides if you are a left-handed batter).

Success Check

- Take a full swing.
- Wrap your hands around your shoulder.
- Shift your weight onto your front foot.
- Take your first step out of the batter's box with your back foot.
- Get into foul territory within 10 feet (3.0 meters) of home plate.
- Drop your bat on the ground in foul territory.

Score Your Success

Earn 1 point for each attempt out of 10 in which you demonstrate all the success check criteria.

Your score ___

To Increase Difficulty

Run over first base using the technique illustrated in figure 6.1.

To Decrease Difficulty

Try a few attempts in slow motion and then repeat the drill at regular speed.

Overrunning First Base Drill 2.   *Over the Base*

Initiate this drill exactly as you did the previous drill. Swing at 10 imaginary pitches and drive out of the batter's box with your rear foot. Instead of stopping after several strides, though, continue to run to first base. Do not slow down before you get to the base. After crossing first base, turn to the left and return to the base. Do not turn out to the right after crossing first base or return directly to home plate—go back to first base! Execute the skill according to the techniques illustrated in figure 6.1.

If other runners are practicing with you, quickly leave first base after you have returned to the base correctly. Get well out of the baseline so that you will be out of the way of the next runner.

Success Check

- Run in foul territory within the alley markings.
- Continue running at top speed until over the base.
- Come to a controlled stop.
- Turn to the left and return directly to the base.

Score Your Success

Earn 1 point for each attempt out of 10 in which you demonstrate all the success check criteria.

Your score ___

To Increase Difficulty

- Use a regulation base.
- After crossing the base and turning to the left, make a move toward second base, hesitate, and then continue eight steps at full speed toward an imaginary second base.
- After crossing the base and turning to the left, make a move toward second base, change your mind, run back to first base (the outfield baseline corner), and stop on the base.
- Use a batting tee. Hit a ground ball and run to first base.

To Decrease Difficulty

- Use an indoor base so that the height of the base does not make you afraid of tripping over it.
- Decrease the distance so you can maintain full speed over the base.
- Go from home to first without using a bat in the swing.

Overrunning First Base Drill 3.   *Tee Ball and Run*

In a game, you will have to hit a real ball and run to first base. Simulate this situation by hitting the ball off a batting tee and running to first base.

Set up a batting tee at home plate. Hit a ground ball off the batting tee and run to first base. If you are working alone, have a bucket of 10 balls so that you can hit all 10 balls, running to first base with each hit, and then collect them all.

This drill works much better when you work with a partner. Hit the ground ball to your partner, and run over first base using the correct technique. Your partner fields the ball, leaves the glove in the field for you, and takes the ball to home plate to take the next hit off the tee. After running over the base and returning to the base, you go to the fielding position. Repeat the drill until you have each hit and run out 10 grounders. You may increase or decrease the difficulty of this drill using the same ideas as outlined in overrunning first base drill 2.

Success Check

• Run in foul territory within the alley markings.
• Continue running at top speed until over the base.
• Come to a controlled stop.
• Turn to the left and return directly to the base.

Score Your Success

Earn 1 point for each attempt out of 10 in which you demonstrate all the success check criteria.

Your score ___

Overrunning First Base Drill 4. *First Baseman Covering*

Now you need to practice overrunning first base with a first baseman at the base attempting to catch the thrown ball. This is when it is critical that you contact the front foul-line side of the base as you overrun it. You must be sure that you do not go across the center of the bag because you may collide with the person making the catch.

This drill has two parts (no-throw and throw) and requires four participants. Two players are at the hitting position, one is a fielder at the shortstop position, and the fourth is the first baseman. The ball is hit from the tee. Place a bucket of 10 balls beside the tee. The shortstop has an empty bucket in which to place the fielded ground balls.

No-throw: The first batter hits the ball to the shortstop and runs to first base. The first baseman stands in front of the second-base side of the bag. The shortstop fields the ball, but holds it. The first baseman places one foot on the bag and reaches toward the shortstop as if a throw were coming. The shortstop then watches to see whether the batter-runner contacts the front corner of the base (on the foul-line side), comes to a controlled stop, turns left, and returns directly to the base. The batter-runner then returns to home plate, running well out of the baseline in foul territory as the next batter hits. After five hits, the two fielders switch positions. After each batter has completed five hits and runs to first base, rotate roles. The two batters go to the two fielding positions, and the two fielders come in to bat. Repeat the drill until all players have completed five hits and runs to first base and have been at each of the two fielding positions for five hits.

Throw: Conduct this part of the drill exactly the same as the first part, except this time the fielder (shortstop) throws the ball overhand to the player at first base after fielding the ball. The bucket is moved to the infield side of the first baseman. Be sure it is out of the way of both the first baseman and the batter-runner. Batters must wear batting helmets. After catching the ball, the first baseman drops the ball into the bucket. If the throw is off target, the first baseman should just let it go rather than chasing after it. The batter-runner returns to home plate, making sure to stay out of the way of the second batter. The rotation is the same as in the first part of the drill.

Score only the second part of the drill. Count the number of times you get to first base safely, either by beating the throw or because the first baseman does not catch the ball.

Success Check

• Run in foul territory within the alley markings.

• Maintain full speed and a consistent stride while running over the base.

• Contact the front corner of the base on the foul-line side.

• Come to a controlled stop, turn to the left, and return directly to the base.

Score Your Success

For the second part of the drill, score yourself based on the number of times you are safe at first base.

Four or five times = 5 points

Two or three times = 3 points

One time = 1 point

Your score____

To Increase Difficulty

• Have the batter hit a ground ball that makes the infielder move two or three steps to the right or left in order to field the ball.

• Make a team game out of the second part of this drill. The two batters make up one team, and the shortstop and first baseman make up the other team. Keep score. The batting team scores 1 point for each hit and run to first base in which a batter-runner is safe. Each player on the batting team gets five times at bat, then the two batters rotate to the fielding and first-base positions. Keep track of the number of points you score as a team. You only score in this game when your team is at bat.

To Decrease Difficulty

• Use an indoor base.

• Decrease the distance to first base.

• Swing without using the ball and batting tee.

Overrunning First Base Drill 5. *Safe or Out*

This drill involves playing a game using the same setup as in the second part of the previous drill. The game is similar to the team game described in the second suggestion for increasing the difficulty of the previous drill. However, for this game, both teams will score points.

For safety, batters must wear helmets. The batter hits a ground ball off the tee in the shortstop's range, making the shortstop move no more than two or three steps to the side or forward to field the ball. Otherwise, the fielding team scores 1 point. If the batter-runner makes it to first base safely on a good grounder, the batting team gets 1 point. If the shortstop and first baseman combine to get the batter-runner out (the first baseman has the ball in the glove and contacts first base before the runner contacts the base), the fielding team gets 1 point.

After each player on the batting team completes the hit-and-run sequence 5 times, the batting team and fielding team change positions. Continue the game until each player has hit the ball 10 times (two complete rotations or a maximum of 20 points per team). Keep track of your team's points.

Because this drill is a game, there is no need to increase or decrease difficulty.

Success Check: Hitter

• Hit the ball so that it goes within the range of the shortstop.

• Reach first base safely.

Success Check: Shortstop

• Field the ball cleanly.

• Make a successful throw to the first baseman.

Success Check: First Baseman

• Catch the ball while contacting first base.

Score Your Success

Team score is 15 to 20 points = 5 points

Team score is 10 to 14 points = 3 points

Team score is 5 to 9 points = 2 points

Team score is 4 points or less = 1 point

Your score ___

ROUNDING A BASE

You round a base when you think you might be able to advance beyond it or when you know you are advancing beyond it because of an extra-base hit. The technique used for rounding a base is designed to let you take the most direct route around the bases while maintaining top speed.

When you are about 15 feet (4.5 meters) from the base, curve your path to it by swinging out to the right about three strides, then heading back in toward the base. The pattern you run looks like the outside edge of a spoon, thus the term *spooning* is sometimes used for rounding a base. As you cross the base, lean toward the infield and make contact with the inside corner of the base with your left foot (figure 6.2).

If advancing to the next base, continue in a direct line toward that base. If you decide you cannot safely advance to the next base, take only a few steps past the base you rounded, bend your knees, shift your weight back, and come to a controlled stop. Retreat to the base by walking backward to it, keeping your eyes focused on the person with the ball.

When rounding a base in a game, you cannot return freely to it; instead, you are susceptible to being tagged out. If the ball is thrown to the person covering the base you have rounded, get back to the base in a manner that best avoids being tagged; otherwise, you will be out.

Figure 6.2 Rounding the base.

Misstep

You end up out in the right-field grass when making the turn at first base.

Correction

You started your rounding turn too late (too close to the base). Start to turn 15 feet before the base.

Misstep

You slow down at the base so you can make the turn.

Correction

Be sure to swing out to the right 15 feet before the base and head to the base at full speed.

Rounding a Base Drill 1. *Swing Out*

To round a base, start running directly at the base. When 15 feet (4.5 meters) from the base, swing out to the right of the baseline and run in a semicircular path to the base. Run across the inside corner of the base, heading in the direction of the next base. Continue running for several strides past the base and come to a controlled stop.

If practicing on a regulation softball field, start halfway between home plate and first base (in the marked alley in foul territory on the first-base line). Run in the alley toward first base and start to swing out 15 feet from the base, rounding it and heading toward second base at full speed (figure 6.3). Come to a controlled stop 10 to 15 feet (3.0 to 4.5 meters) past the base. Walk or jog to a position 30 feet (9.1 meters) from second base and repeat the drill. Continue in this fashion around all the bases, including home. Pay attention to the size of the semicircular path you need to take to be able to cross the base while heading in the general direction of the next base. Make sure you use the technique shown in figure 6.2 (page 114).

If practicing with just a single base set on the ground or floor, turn around when you have run 20 feet (6.1 meters) past the base and repeat the drill going to the same base (figure 6.4). Swing out to the right of the base each time, and cross the base from right to left. After four repetitions, you will be back to your original starting position.

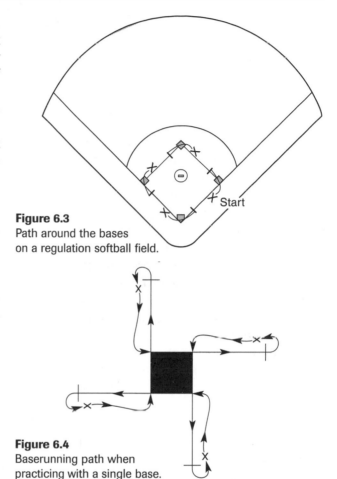

Figure 6.3
Path around the bases on a regulation softball field.

Figure 6.4
Baserunning path when practicing with a single base.

Success Check

- Swing out to the right when within 15 feet of the base.

- Lean to the left and head directly toward the base.
- Contact the inside front corner of the base with your left foot.
- Come to a controlled stop.

Score Your Success

Score yourself based on the number of attempts in which you demonstrated all the success check criteria.

  4 attempts = 5 points

  2 or 3 attempts = 3 points

  1 attempt = 1 point

  Your score ___

To Increase Difficulty

- Decrease the allowable arc size.
- Increase the speed of the approach and the rounding of the base.

- Reduce the length of the jog between bases so that ultimately you are running the length of the entire baseline.

To Decrease Difficulty

- Decrease the speed of the approach to the base.
- Decrease the distance that you run in the approach to the base.
- Begin with a relatively large arc and gradually reduce the size of the arc while maintaining medium speed.
- Jog through the entire rounding-the-base pattern.

115

Rounding a Base Drill 2. *Single, Double, Triple, Homer*

You need a partner who will time you with a stop-watch for this drill. Start at home plate.

Using a bat, swing at an imaginary pitch and, using the technique described in figure 6.2 (page 114), run out a single and round first base. Retreat to first base using the correct technique. Return to home plate.

Next, swing and run out a double, rounding first base and stopping at second base as you would in a game. Slide into the base, or run full speed to within 10 feet (3.0 meters) of the base, bending your knees, shifting your weight back, and taking smaller steps to come to a stop on the base without overrunning it. Return to home plate. Continue the drill with a triple, rounding first and second base and stopping at third. Return to home plate.

Finish the drill sequence by running out an inside-the-park home run. When you hit the ball over the fence for a home run, you may simply jog around the bases, waving to the crowd! On an inside-the-park home run, though, the ball remains in play, and you must arrive at home plate

before the defense gets the ball there to tag you out. Therefore, you must use good baserunning technique to beat the throw to the plate. Round all three bases, running at full speed all the way from home to home. Remember, you can overrun home plate, so don't slow down to stop on the plate. Run full speed over home plate.

Fatigue can be a factor for a single player running out each hit and returning to home plate to immediately run the next time. If possible, use two or three runners instead of a single runner, thereby giving each person a little chance to rest before her next attempt.

Success Check

* Take your first step out of the batter's box with your back foot.
* When running out a sure single or advancing to the next base, spoon out before crossing the base.
* Stop on the base for a double and a triple.

Score Your Success

Score yourself based on the times in table 6.1.

To Increase Difficulty

Hit a soft-tossed ball for each part of the drill.

To Decrease Difficulty

Practice with reduced distances between the bases. Then repeat the original drill, trying to improve your previous score.

Table 6.1 Scoring for the Single, Double, Triple, Homer Drill

Distance run	Time range (sec.)	Points	Your score
Home to first (single)	Less than 3.5	5	
	3.5 to 3.9	3	
	4.0 to 4.5	2	
	More than 4.5	1	
Home to second (double)	Less than 9.0	5	
	9.0 to 9.9	3	
	10.0 to 11.0	2	
	More than 11.0	1	
Home to third (triple)	Less than 13.0	5	
	13.0 to 13.9	3	
	14.0 to 15.0	2	
	More than 15.0	1	
Home to home (home run)	Less than 18.0	5	
	18.0 to 18.9	3	
	19.0 to 20.0	2	
	More than 20.0	1	
	Total score		

Rounding a Base Drill 3. *React to Base Coach*

In a game situation, the batter-runner is assisted by the first-base coach in deciding whether to overrun or round first base. A baserunner going from first to second base looks to the third-base coach for direction. At first base, the coach usually tells the batter-runner to round the base and look for the ball when the ball goes through the infield. The batter-runner must look at the coach before getting within 15 feet (4.5 meters) of the base in order to receive the base coach's instruction in time to round the base if necessary.

This drill is designed to help you develop your ability to react to the coach and to the call she is making. You need a partner for this drill: You are the batter-runner, and your partner is the coach. Swing at an imaginary pitch and run to first base. The base coach tells you either to overrun or to round the base, randomly calling "round and look

for the ball" or "run through." React to the base coach by following the call.

Run to first base five times. Count the number of times you react correctly to the coach's call. Switch roles. As in the previous drill, having additional participants (two or three batter-runners) can help facilitate this drill by giving each runner a chance to rest.

Little can be done to increase or decrease the difficulty of this drill. Simply proceed to the next drill. If you are having difficulty with this drill, continue to practice it.

Success Check

- Accelerate quickly.
- Look at the base coach, then focus on the base.
- Execute the called-for play at the base.

Score Your Success

Score yourself based on the number of times (out of five attempts) that you demonstrate all the success check criteria.

Five times = 5 points

Four times = 3 points

Three times = 2 points

Two times = 1 point

Your score ___

Rounding a Base Drill 4. *Double to the Outfield*

For this drill, you need four people. Two players wearing batting helmets position themselves at home plate with a batting tee and a bucket of 10 balls. One person is a left fielder, and the other person is a second baseman. Place an empty bucket to the outfield side of second base.

The first batter hits a line drive off the tee to the left fielder. The batter runs, rounds first base, and decides whether to run to second base. The outfielder fields the ball and throws it to the second baseman covering that base, who drops the ball into the empty bucket after the play is complete.

At the completion of the play, the first batter-runner returns to home plate, making sure to get out of the way of the second batter's hit and run to first. (Going home via the pitching area after the second player hits the ball is probably best.) As the batter-runner, try to make the correct decision:

either go back to first or get to second base before the ball is caught by the second baseman. Less experienced players do not need to make the tag at second on this drill. However, players with more experience who know the proper tagging technique may practice making the tag at second. All players must have practiced their sliding skill and must be proficient at it before sliding into second in this drill. Count the number of times you make the correct decision: either remaining at first base or continuing and being safe at second. Be honest! If the outfielder misses the ball and you remain at first base, you made the wrong decision!

After each batter has taken five hits, rotate roles. One hitter goes to the outfield, and the other goes to second base (bringing along the empty bucket). The outfielder and second baseman go to home plate, taking the bucket of 10 balls to hit. To maximize practice opportunities, the two players in the field should change places after five hits to gain experience as both an outfielder and infielder. The goal for this drill is primarily making appropriate decisions; therefore, there is no need to increase or decrease the difficulty of the drill.

Success Check

- Round the base using the correct technique.
- Reach the base before the ball does if you decide to go to second base.
- Remain at first base if the ball would arrive at second before you.

Score Your Success

Score yourself based on the number of times (out of five attempts) you successfully demonstrate all the success check criteria.

Five times = 5 points

Four times = 3 points

Three times = 2 points

Two times = 1 point

Your score ___

Rounding a Base Drill 5. *Overrun or Round Game*

Now we make the practice very similar to a game situation. For this drill, six players are needed. Two players are hitters, one is the first base coach, a fourth player is the shortstop, the fifth player is the left fielder (behind shortstop), and the sixth player is the second baseman. Set a bucket with five balls at home plate and an empty bucket near second base.

The batters alternate hitting the ball off the batting tee, attempting to get the ball by the shortstop and into deep left field. On hitting the ball, the batter runs to first base and reacts to the call of the base coach. If the ball goes by the shortstop, the base coach calls, "Round the base and look for the ball!" If the ball is fielded by the shortstop (no throw to first), the base coach calls, "Run through the base!" The batter-runner does as the coach signals. If the call is to round the base, the baserunner must then decide whether to return to first base or to try to advance to second base. When advancing to second, the baserunner has the option of practicing his sliding skills. As in the previous drill, if sliding is to be used, players must have practiced this skill before using it in the drill. Batters must wear helmets.

The fielders attempt to field the ball as it comes to them. If the outfielder fields the ball, she throws it to the second baseman covering second. More experienced players make the tag play on any runner attempting to advance to second. Second basemen drop the ball in the bucket at the completion of the play; the shortstop returns fielded balls to home. After 5 hits by each batter, rotate posi-

tions: one batter to shortstop (the second batter remains at bat and hits another round), shortstop to outfield, outfield to second base, second base to base coach, and base coach to batter. Continue the drill until each player has hit the ball 10 times. The first hitter to rotate out to shortstop needs to rotate into the hitting position one more time in order to complete 10 hits.

The goal of this game is to get as many doubles as you can. Count the number of times you make it safely to second base. See whether you can get more doubles than any of the other players in your group. When you are the outfielder or shortstop, you should take advantage of the opportunity to practice fielding. Watch the ball as it leaves the bat and quickly move into position to field the ball in front of your body. Field the ball cleanly and make an accurate throw to the second baseman. The base coach must watch the hit ball and the fielder making the play. Based on the result of that play, the base coach makes the appropriate call for the batter-runner. The primary goal of this drill is making appropriate decisions; therefore, there is no need to increase or decrease the difficulty of the drill.

Success Check: Batter-Runner

- Respond appropriately to the coach's call.
- After contacting the base, look for the ball and focus on the play.
- Make the appropriate decision on whether to advance to second or return to first.

LEADING OFF BASE

Advancing into scoring position (second or third base) is very important in any type of softball game. Once you have gotten on base and are stopped, you want to increase your chances of attaining the next base.

Moving a short distance off the base you are on is called *taking a lead*. This is not allowed in slow pitch, but in fastpitch, taking a lead is a baserunning technique that helps increase your chances of getting to the next base safely on a hit ball.

In fastpitch, the runner cannot leave the base until the ball leaves the pitcher's hand. For the runner on first base, the right-handed pitcher's hand is hidden from view by the pitcher's body. However, a study of pitching deliveries would reveal that for most pitchers the step with the left foot (for a right-handed pitcher), which is readily visible from first base, is timed with the release of the ball. When taking a lead, you should time your leaving the base with the pitcher's striding foot hitting the ground.

In fastpitch softball, you should take a lead off the base on every pitch, even if you are not intending to steal. (The offensive tactics of stealing will be dealt with in step 9.) If you've taken a lead on the pitch in a nonstealing situation and the batter hits the ball, you are several steps closer to the next base. The following techniques for leaving the base can be used for either taking a lead or stealing. The choice is usually a matter of personal preference or, in the case of stealing, the one that gives you the quickest start.

Although the method of leaving the base and the runner's foot placement on the base vary, most runners use one of the following two techniques. In the *rocker* start, the runner stands over the base with the preferred driving foot (the foot that pushes off) on the front edge of the base (figure 6.5). As the pitcher is in the windup phase of the delivery, the runner begins to shift her weight from back to front over the driving foot. The first step toward the next base is taken with the back foot, and that step is timed with the release of the ball by the pitcher. This technique is sometimes called a *rolling start* and has the advantage of putting the runner in motion before the release of the ball. The timing on this method is extremely important; your front foot cannot leave the base before the actual release of the ball by the pitcher. Remember, if you do leave before the release of the ball, you are out. The coach may want to let the umpires know which players use the rocker method so that the forward movement of the runner while still in contact with the base is not viewed as leaving the base too soon.

Another technique is for the runner to assume a track start position in front of the base, facing the base that the runner is advancing to (figure 6.6). The back foot is on the base; that foot takes the initial step. Experiment with each foot as

Figure 6.5 Rocker start position.

the foot on the base to see which one feels most comfortable and gives you the best jump off the base.

Another situation affects the manner in which you leave a base or take a lead on the pitch. A rule in softball applies when a baserunner is on base with less than two outs and a fly ball is hit. The baserunner must be in contact with the base when the fly ball is caught, or she can be put out by a throw to the base. You may leave the base when a fly ball is hit, but you must return to the base if the ball is caught. If you go too far from the base on a fly ball, the fielder who catches the ball will throw it to the base you left; if the fielder covering the base gets the ball and tags you while you are off the base—or steps on the base before you get back to it—you are out.

When you take a lead on a pitch and the ball is hit in the air, you must decide how far from the base you can venture. If you are on first base and a fly ball is hit to right field, go no more than two or three steps off base (8 to 10 feet [2.4 to 3.0 meters]). The right fielder has only a short throw to put you out at the base if the ball is caught. On the other hand, if a fly ball is hit to left field when you are on first base, you can go nearly half the distance to second base. If the ball is dropped, you will be that much closer to second base; if the ball is caught, you should be able to beat the throw back to first base.

When you are on second or third base, the same principles apply. If a fly ball is hit to an

Figure 6.6 Track start position.

outfield position close to the base you are on, do not venture too far toward the next base. On the other hand, if the fly ball is hit to an outfield position far away from the base you are on, you can leave the base and venture farther toward the next base.

You must decide how far you can progress toward the next base on a fly ball and still be able to get back to your original base before the throw if the ball is caught. If the fly ball is not caught or if any ground ball is hit, your job is to run at maximum speed to the next base and either stop or round it and go to the next base. This is the judgment and decision making of baserunning—one of the most challenging and fun parts of softball.

SLIDING

Previously, you learned that you may overrun first base and home plate but must stop on second and third base when advancing to those bases. You have just learned about different techniques to use when advancing to a base. When you must stop at a base, sliding into it is the fastest way to get there because you do not have to slow your run in order to come to a stop at the base. Sliding into a base is also an effective way to avoid a tag when the play is not a force-out (when the baseman has to tag you with the ball rather than just catching the ball and touching the base). You are not allowed to remain on your feet and crash into a defensive player who has the ball or is about to

catch the ball to make a play on you at that base, such as at home plate; therefore, you must slide whenever that situation arises.

Sliding involves lowering your body to the ground while in full running stride so that you go into a base feetfirst. Because serious injury can occur to the head, neck, shoulders, arms, and hands, headfirst sliding into a fielder or base is not recommended. Even some major league baseball players have been hurt using the headfirst sliding technique. When you are approximately 10 feet (3.0 meters) from the base and still running at full speed, throw your shoulders back and lift your legs, turning slightly to the side on which you want to slide. Keep your hands up and contact the ground with your body fully extended as explained in the various situations that follow.

Techniques for sliding vary, but some general principles apply to sliding in most situations. On a close tag play, slide away from the tag and present a very small target for the tag. On a throw from the center fielder to second base, slide to the infield side of the base on your left side, and hook the corner of the base closest to the pitcher with your right foot (figure 6.7a). If the throw is coming from the infield (e.g., from the catcher), slide to the outfield side of the base on your right side, and hook the base with your left foot (figure 6.7b).

The straight-in, or down-and-up, slide is used when you can see that the throw will not arrive in time to put you out; however, you still need to maintain full speed into the base to assure reaching it safely. Correct execution of this sliding technique also brings you to a standing position so that if the throw is off target and goes past the base, you are ready to advance to the next base. To end up facing in the direction of the next base, you should slide on your left side. As you lower your body into the slide, contact the ground with the outside part of your lower left leg (just below the knee) and the outside of your upper left leg and left buttock. The front of your knee should not contact the ground, nor should your hands. When your body is on the ground, bend your left leg so that the front of your entire lower leg or shin comes up against the base. Keep your right leg straight and lift it slightly so that your foot clears the base (figure 6.8a). Your forward momentum will be slowed as your left leg contacts the base. Your forward momentum will then be transferred to vertical lift, causing your body to come up over the base and allowing you to stand with your right foot on the far side of the base (figure 6.8b). You are now in a position to advance to the next base if the opportunity presents itself.

Although a fundamental skill, especially in fast-pitch softball, sliding technique must be taught to players before expecting them to execute the skill in practice drills or in a game. Usually, younger players find learning the skill easier than older players. The fear factor tends to be less in a young player. In addition, the distance the younger player has to fall to get to the ground is far less than for a young adult.

Figure 6.7 Hook slide (a) to the infield side of the base when the throw is coming from the outfield and (b) to the outfield side of the base when the throw is coming from the infield.

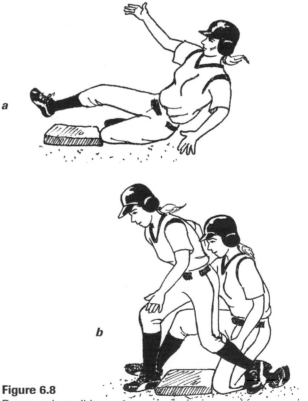

Figure 6.8
Down-and-up slide.

Sliding mistakes usually occur during the take-off or the landing. In the takeoff, there should be a smooth transition from an upright forward-lean running position to a backward-lean, body-extended, flat position. A common mistake is jumping into the takeoff rather than lowering into it. When you jump into the takeoff, you elevate your body, which makes for a greater distance to fall to the ground. Therefore, you not only have a much harder landing, but you are also slower getting to the base. Another common mistake is starting your slide too close to the base; a late takeoff will cause you to slide into the base forcefully, thus risking injury.

Sliding on the wrong side of the body, especially for the down-and-up slide, is a typical landing problem. When sliding into a base with the option of going on to the next base, you should land on the left side so that when you pop up you are facing the direction of the next base. If you slide into second base on your right side, you will come up facing cnter field rather than third base!

Before trying any of the baserunning drills in this step that include a sliding option, you should practice your sliding techniques using the following suggestions.

Misstep

You jump into the slide.

Correction

Don't! Lower your body and fully extend.

Misstep

You land on your hands.

Correction

Throw your hands and arms up as you start to slide.

Sand Walk-Through

In a large sand area, such as a long jump pit (or the beach!), sit down in the sand in the position shown in figure 6.8a. Be sure you are turned slightly onto your left side so you are resting on your left buttock and the outside of your bent left leg. Lean back and put both hands up in the air over and behind your head. Try to get the feel of where your legs, hips, seat, and arms are when you are in this sliding position.

Next, while walking through the sand, gradually bend your knees, lower your hips, throw your right leg forward (don't jump), bend your left leg, and fall back onto the sand in the same position. Be sure your hands are up over your head as you land; don't reach down to catch yourself with your hands. Try this a few more times, each time increasing your walking speed. Remember, do not jump into the landing slide position and do not catch yourself with your hands.

When you feel comfortable assuming the landing position in the sand, move on to one of the following techniques for practicing sliding.

Sliding Practice on Wet Grass

This is a great option for a nice hot summer day! Using plenty of water, wet down a thick grassy area that is free from any hazards such as glass and rocks. Wear an old pair of sweatpants or other long pants that you don't mind getting wet and grass stained, and take off your shoes so that you can run in socks (do not run barefooted). Do not wear cleats! Cleats can very easily get caught in the grass as you slide, causing injury to an ankle or knee. Place a loose base (with no spikes attached), a carpet square, or a similar flat object in the middle of the wet grass area to represent a base. Take a starting position 30 to 35 feet (9.1 to 10.6 meters) away from the base and run toward it. When you are 10 to 12 feet (3.0 to 3.6 meters) away from the base, while still running at top speed, lean back, lower your body, bend your left leg, throw your right leg out and forward (keeping your right foot off the ground), and land in the same position you assumed in the sand. Make sure you throw both hands up over your head and tuck your chin to your chest so you don't hit the back of your head on the ground. You should end up sliding into the base. If you didn't make it to the base, you probably weren't running fast enough when you started your slide or you started your slide too early. If you took the base with you in your slide, you may have started your slide too late or too close to the base. Be sure to start your slide at least 10 feet from the base and let your slide take you to the base.

If no water is available, put a large piece of plastic or cardboard on the grass and slide on that. Another option is to wait for a warm, rainy day!

Snow Sliding

If you live in an area that gets snow, a great way to practice sliding is on grass that is covered with just a few inches of snow. If the snow is too deep, it is too difficult to run. Set up your practice area and use the same technique as you did for sliding on wet grass.

TAGGING UP

Another important baserunning tactic is tagging up. *Tagging up* is a softball and baseball term that refers to the fact that in certain game situations, after you make contact with a base and leave that base, you must return to that base before taking any further action. Runners must tag up after a foul ball is hit. In baseball, the runner can take a lead before the next pitch after tagging up. In softball, the runner must tag up and remain on the base until the next pitch.

Advancing to a base after a caught fly ball is another example of a situation in which you must tag up at the base you were on at the time of the hit. This opportunity usually occurs when the ball is hit deep into the outfield. For example, a baserunner on second base would immediately return to second base on a deep fly ball that can be caught by the right fielder. Once the right fielder touches the ball, the baserunner may break contact with second base and advance to third base. In this situation, you must make sure you don't leave second base before the fielder touches the ball. The play on you is a tag play, so you must beat the throw to the base and avoid being tagged out. Remember, although you can overrun home plate, you cannot overrun third base. The same tagging-up strategy applies when you are a runner on third base and a fly ball is hit to any deep outfield position. In such case, you would not only be advancing a base, you would be scoring a run.

The following tagging-up drills can be set up and facilitated in a variety of ways and can be modified for less experienced players. For example, the fly ball for these drills can be delivered by hitting off a live pitch, a soft toss, a batting tee, or a pitching machine; the fly ball can also be delivered by a fungo hitter or by a player throwing the ball. The method used depends on the skill of the players involved. Remember that the practice task for these drills is tagging up and advancing to the next base on a caught fly ball. For this practice to occur, a catchable fly ball must be delivered to an outfielder. Therefore, the coach or teacher must select the best method of delivering that ball in order for the players to practice tagging up and advancing a base. Two or three runners taking turns executing the baserunning task make these drills run more quickly. Runners rotate into the waiting line of runners until the specified number of attempts for each runner are completed. If all players participating in the drill are to play fielding positions as well as run, set up a rotation for that to occur.

Tagging-Up Drill 1. *Second to Third*

In a game situation, if you are a runner on second base with less than two outs, and a deep fly ball is hit to the right fielder, you should tag up and advance to third base after the ball is caught. By advancing to third, you have the opportunity to tag up and score if another fly ball is hit to any outfield position with less than two outs, or you can score easily on a base hit.

You need a minimum of four people, and preferably six, for this drill. The first baserunner takes a position on second base. Two other runners stand well away from the base (to the left-field side and out of the way of the play). All runners must wear helmets. The on-deck runner can act as an observer for the runner and can verify her score based on the number of success check criteria the runner successfully demonstrates. The fourth player is the right fielder, and the fifth player is the third baseman. The sixth player delivers a fly ball by throwing the ball; hitting it off a soft toss, batting tee, live pitch, or pitching machine; or hitting a fungo hit. (For the soft-toss or live-pitch methods, additional players are needed.)

The right fielder takes a deep outfield position about halfway between a normal, straightaway position and the right-field foul line. From this position, the right fielder should be able to throw to third base without hitting the runner. The third baseman takes a normal fielding position for either fastpitch or slow pitch (figure 6.9).

The hitter (or thrower) delivers a fly ball to the right fielder. The fly ball must get all the way to the right fielder in her deep outfield position. The runner at second base takes her preferred starting position for leaving the base. As the fly ball goes toward the right fielder, the runner follows the ball by looking back over her left shoulder as it approaches the fielder. The runner decides whether to tag up and run based on the position the right fielder will be in when she catches the ball. If the hit causes the fielder to come in to short right field, the runner should not run, and the hitter should repeat the hit. If the hit is deep, as soon as the fielder touches the ball, the runner takes off from second base and runs to third. Remember, the runner is out if she leaves the base before the fielder touches the ball, and she may not overrun third base; she must stop on the base. If you have

worked on your sliding skills, this would be a good opportunity to practice your straight-in (down-and-up) slide or your hook slide to the outfield side of third base. The third baseman watches the ball go to the right fielder and moves to a position straddling third base so that she is in position to receive the throw from the right fielder and make a tag play on the runner. The right fielder catches the fly ball and throws the ball to third base to make a play on the runner.

Repeat the drill until all runners have run five times. If other players in the drill want to practice tagging up, the fielders should rotate in to the running position while runners rotate out to the other positions. The goal of this drill is primarily making correct decisions; therefore, there is no need to increase or decrease the difficulty of the drill.

Success Check

- Watch the ball from the hit or throw to the right fielder's glove.
- Maintain contact with second base until the right fielder touches the ball.
- Time your leave of second base with the ball contacting the outfielder's glove, and run at full speed all the way to third base.
- Do not overrun third base; stop on it.
- If sliding, use a down-and-up slide or a hook slide to the left-field side of third base.

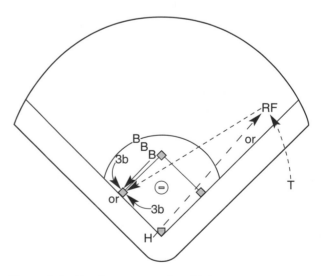

Figure 6.9 Tagging up second to third.

Score Your Success

Score yourself based on the number of times (out of five attempts) you successfully demonstrate all four (or five if sliding) success check criteria.

Five times = 5 points

Four times = 3 points

Three times = 2 points

Two times or less = 1 point

Your score ___

Tagging-Up Drill 2. *Third to Home*

The setup for this drill is the same as the previous drill, except the runner tags up at third base, the hit (or throw) could be to any deep outfield position, and a catcher is needed instead of a third baseman because the throw will come to home plate. Extra runners should stand in foul territory by third base. Again, all runners must wear helmets. The on-deck runner acts as observer. The catcher must be in full catching gear.

You should make this drill a little more gamelike than the previous one. The runner takes a short lead as if on a pitch (in fastpitch) or when the ball is hit (in slow pitch). As the fly ball is delivered to the outfielder, the runner must return to third, tag up, and wait for the fielder to touch the ball before taking off for home. In this drill, the runner must slide into home plate. It is against the rules for a runner to stand up and run into the catcher as she attempts to catch the ball and make a play. Rotate roles after all runners have had five tagging-up attempts. Again, the focus of this drill is decision making; therefore, there is no need to increase or decrease the difficulty.

Success Check

- Take a short lead just before the hit.
- On the hit, return to the base and tag up.
- Watch the fly ball go to the fielder.
- As the fielder touches the ball, take off for home.
- Slide into home, trying to avoid the tag. No headfirst slides!
- Be safe at home.

Score Your Success

Score yourself based on the number of times (out of five attempts) you successfully demonstrate all the success check criteria.

Five times = 5 points

Four times = 3 points

Three times = 2 points

Two times or less = 1 point

Your score ___

SUCCESS SUMMARY

Scoring runs is the ultimate goal of a softball team that is on offense (at bat). Your ability to run the bases efficiently and effectively contributes to your team's ability to score runs. Getting into scoring position in softball means getting to second base or, even more important, getting to third base. In slow-pitch softball, as in baseball, a single will usually score a runner from second base. However, in fastpitch softball, because the outfield distances are shorter than in baseball and the outfielders do not play as deep as in slow-pitch softball, scoring from second base on a single is more difficult. Baserunning is fun! Sliding into a base and avoiding the tag by the fielder is one of the most exciting aspects of the game for players—and also for the spectators.

This is the last step devoted to individual skill development. Although we provided a few gamelike drills in the skill development steps, the next few steps are designed to teach you about the game and various offensive and defensive strategies used in official game play. In the next step, we will be discussing the responsibilities that different defensive players have in the various situations occurring in a game. In these remaining steps, you will have an opportunity to continue to practice all of the individual fundamental skills that you have learned. Now, however, your focus will be on using these skills in combination in gamelike settings. Before moving on to step 7, take the time to look at how you did on the drills in this step. Enter your score for each of the drills. Add your scores to rate your total success in baserunning.

Overrunning First Base Drills

1. Leaving the Batter's Box   ___ out of 10
2. Over the Base   ___ out of 10
3. Tee Ball and Run   ___ out of 10
4. First Baseman Covering   ___ out of 5
5. Safe or Out   ___ out of 5

Rounding a Base Drills

1. Swing Out   ___ out of 5
2. Single, Double, Triple, Homer   ___ out of 20
3. React to Base Coach   ___ out of 5
4. Double to the Outfield   ___ out of 5
5. Overrun or Round Game   ___ out of 5

Tagging-Up Drills

1. Second to Third   ___ out of 5
2. Third to Home   ___ out of 5

Total   ___ *out of 90*

Your total score will give you an indication of whether or not you have developed the baserunning skills necessary to be successful in the next steps. If you scored 68 points or more, congratulations! You have mastered the skills of baserunning, and you are ready to move on to the next steps. If your total score was between 54 and 67 points, you are ready to move on to the next steps, although you might benefit from additional practice in selected drills. If you scored fewer than 54 points, you should continue to practice the baserunning drills in order to improve your skills and increase your total score.

Defensive Responsibilities and Tactics

Defensive players have different responsibilities depending on the positions they play and the game situation. When you play a position, you must read a developing situation and react by carrying out the duties of your particular position, including covering and backing up bases, knowing which position has priority in making the play to catch a fly ball, and executing both force and tag plays at the bases. You should know the duties of all the positions, not just the one you are playing, so that you can interact effectively with your teammates no matter where the ball is hit or thrown. All team members must work together smoothly. You cannot demonstrate good teamwork if you and your teammates are confused about responsibilities.

In addition to the varying responsibilities for defensive players at different positions, there are certain characteristics that players should have for playing specific positions. For example, a pitcher should have a strong throwing arm, good shoulder flexibility, and the ability to remain calm under pressure.

A fastpitch catcher must have a strong overhand snap throw to be able to throw out runners attempting to steal. As the only player on the team facing the full field of play, the catcher is in the best position to be the team leader on the field.

A tall, left-handed first baseman is an advantage for the rest of the infielders because she has greater range fielding balls hit to her right (her glove is on that side) and she is a big target for the infielders' throws to first base.

Second basemen are usually smaller; they must be quick, have good range both right and left, and possess a strong throwing arm in order to make the double play from second to first.

The shortstop is usually the strongest infielder. She must have a very strong throw and great range, especially going in the hole to her right.

Good teams are usually strong up the middle, with very skilled players at the catcher, pitcher, shortstop, and center fielder positions. The third baseman in fastpitch plays the hot corner. Because her starting position is so close to home plate, any ball hit down the line to third arrives very quickly. A third baseman must have very quick reflexes and a strong throwing arm.

All outfielders must have strong overhand throws because all outfielders must throw to home plate. Some people think that right field is where the weakest outfielder should play. On the contrary, the right fielder has to make the long throw to third base, whereas the left fielder does not usually throw to first base! In addition, a ball hit to right field by a right-handed hitter slices away from the right fielder toward the foul line, making it more difficult to field. In fastpitch, many balls are hit to right field because of the pitching.

Good position play requires an understanding of some basic concepts that are applied to the particular game and play situations as they arise. The two major categories of defensive duties are called *covering* and *backing up*. Table 7.3 later in this step includes all covering and backing-up responsibilities for each position. Only the basic concepts and some examples are described in the sections that follow.

When covering a base, you will usually make a tag play or a force play on a runner coming to your base. The techniques you use when executing these plays are explained later in this step. In addition, several drills for practicing force and tag plays are included in this step. Specific drills for practicing the skills of covering and backing up are not covered in this step; however, you will be able to apply these concepts while participating in many of the drills in later steps.

COVERING RESPONSIBILITIES

Each of the positions (9 in fastpitch and 10 in slow pitch) has a specific name, number, and coverage area. Figure 7.1*a* shows the regular-depth starting positions and the area coverage for each position in fastpitch softball. Figure 7.1*b* shows the regular-depth starting positions and the area coverage for each position in slow pitch.

Slow-pitch teams use the 10th player (usually an outfielder) in basically two different alignments. Currently, the more common approach is to have four outfielders spread out across the outfield approximately equidistant from home plate. We will focus on this alignment in all future references to the slow-pitch game. The other, less commonly used, alignment is to use the 10th player as a short fielder. This player positions herself in the short outfield in front of the other

three outfielders and in back of the infielders in an area determined by the strength of the offensive player at bat. We have illustrated the short fielder alignment in figure 7.1*b* for information purposes only.

In addition to differences in outfield alignment within slow pitch and between slow pitch and fastpitch, note the difference between slow-pitch and fastpitch starting positions for the first and third basemen (figure 7.1, *a-b*). Because the fastpitch game allows the batter to bunt the ball, the first and third basemen usually assume a starting position closer to home plate (in fair territory in front of their respective base). In the diagrams, the sections outlined by dashed lines identify the primary area of coverage for each starting position. The shaded areas that overlap

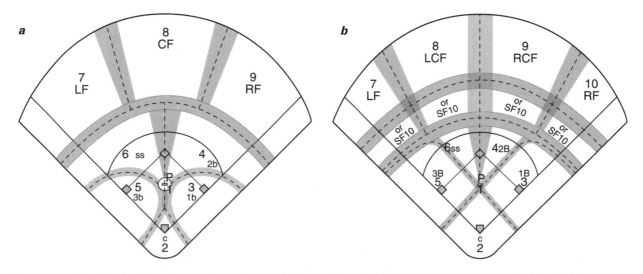

Figure 7.1   Regular-depth starting positions shown by the numbers and area coverage: *(a)* fastpitch; *(b)* slow pitch.

the dashed lines identify the interaction areas in which covering responsibility is shared by adjoining positions. The diagrams show flexible approximations of these coverage areas, which may vary depending on the relative range and other skills of teammates.

The term *covering* also describes the responsibility of an infielder at a base (figure 7.2). For instance, on a ground ball hit to the shortstop, the first baseman covers first base to take the shortstop's throw and to put the batter-runner out. The assigned coverage in area 6 (figure 7.1, *a-b*), by the way, enabled the shortstop to field the ground ball without interference from another defensive player.

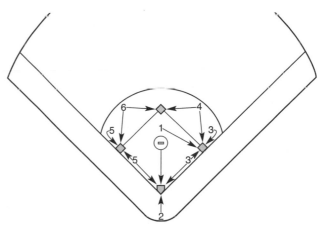

Figure 7.2 Base-covering responsibilities. The first- and third-baseman positions closest to home plate indicate fast-pitch starting positions.

PRIORITY SYSTEM FOR FLY BALLS

Any ball coming into a primary coverage area is mainly the responsibility of the defender playing the corresponding position (figure 7.1, *a-b*). A team's initial defense is based on the concept that each player has jurisdiction in her primary coverage area. Take, for example, a high pop fly hit to area 6. The third baseman, shortstop, second baseman, and pitcher all have time to move into position to field the ball. If they all did at once, however, there would be chaos. If everyone understands that area 6 is the shortstop's responsibility, though, this assigned jurisdiction allows the play to be made with minimal confusion.

Verbal signs or signals are extremely helpful for team defense. You should always call for the ball on a fly ball, and even sometimes for ground balls playable by more than one fielder. Your call of "I have it!" or "Mine!" must be loud and clear enough for all players in the immediate area to hear. In fact, it is helpful to call for the ball even when it is clearly in your area of responsibility. To indicate that they understood your call, other players should then call "Take it!" or call out your name.

Determining who should play a fly ball between two areas of responsibility is more of a problem, but it becomes less difficult when a priority system is established. In general, outfielders have priority over infielders. Because they are moving in on the ball, outfielders have an easier

time fielding and throwing than infielders, who are running back to the ball. When runners are on base and the ball is hit between two or more outfield positions, the fielder who would be in the best throwing position after the catch has

Table 7.1 Fly Ball Jurisdiction, Slow Pitch

Position number	Symbol	Player position	Has fielding priority over
1	P	Pitcher	No one
2	C	Catcher	Pitcher
3	1B	First baseman	Pitcher
4	2B	Second baseman	First baseman, pitcher
5	3B	Third baseman	Pitcher
6	SS	Shortstop	Third baseman, second baseman, first baseman, pitcher
7	LF	Left fielder	All infielders
8	LCF	Left center fielder	All infielders, left fielder
9	RCF	Right center fielder	All infielders, right fielder
10	RF	Right fielder	All infielders

priority. When a follow-up throw is needed, the outfielder with the strongest throwing arm has priority.

In the infield, the third baseman should cut off any ground ball he can reach while going to the left. Because it is easier to run laterally than backward, the shortstop should field any pop-up behind the third baseman. The second baseman should field any pop-up behind the first baseman.

Tables 7.1 and 7.2 show the player position number, symbol, and the priority system for calling most fly balls.

Table 7.2 Fly Ball Jurisdiction, Fastpitch

Position number	Symbol	Player position	Has fielding priority over
1	P	Pitcher	No one
2	C	Catcher	Pitcher
3	1B	First baseman	Catcher, pitcher
4	2B	Second baseman	First baseman, pitcher
5	3B	Third baseman	First baseman, catcher, pitcher
6	SS	Shortstop	Third baseman, second baseman, first baseman, pitcher
7	LF	Left fielder	All infielders
8	CF	Center fielder	All infielders, all other outfielders
9	RF	Right fielder	All infielders

BACKING-UP RESPONSIBILITIES

Backing up describes support or aid given to a covering player by another defensive player. The backing-up player does not make the initial play on a runner or on a hit ball. For example, the left center fielder (slow pitch) or the left fielder (fastpitch) backs up the shortstop fielding the ground ball. The catcher backs up the first baseman on an infield grounder fielded and thrown to first; the catcher's stopping a misplayed ball that has gone beyond the first baseman could prevent the runner from advancing to another base.

Backing up a play requires that you

- know all the possible backing-up responsibilities for the specific position you are playing,
- immediately recognize situations for which you have backing-up responsibilities when they arise, and
- move into the correct backing-up position.

Thus, backing up is two-thirds cognitive and one-third physical! The descriptions of backing-up responsibilities for each position in this step—and the game opportunity experience you will get in later steps—will help you learn this aspect of position play. Good anticipation will help you recognize situations as they unfold.

Figure 7.3 shows the backing-up responsibilities and approximate positions each fielder

would likely take. A backing-up position is actually determined by the ball's path. The backing-up player must get in a direct line with the source of the ball (the throwing fielder or the hitter) and its receiver (the fielder covering a base or the fielder making a play on the hit ball; see figure 7.4). The backing-up player must assume a position approximately 15 to 20 feet (4.5 to 6.1 meters) behind the primary receiver.

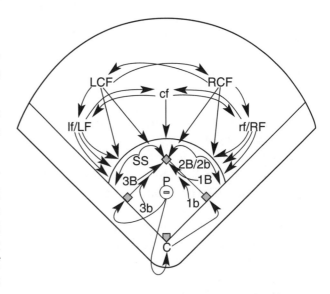

Figure 7.3 Backing-up responsibilities. The first- and third-baseman positions closest to home plate indicate fastpitch starting and backing-up positions.

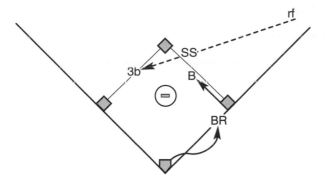

Figure 7.4 Backing up on the overthrow line.

Remember, your role as the backing-up player is to catch a misplayed ball to prevent additional advance by any baserunner. You are not trying to make the initial covering play. If you back up a play by standing too close to the covering fielder, a misplayed ball will go past you because you will not have time to react and catch the ball.

Once you catch the ball as the backing-up player, listen for verbal assistance from your teammates regarding what to do with the ball. Also look to see what the runners, especially the lead runner, are doing. Sometimes a runner seeing an overthrow or other error will automatically dash for the next base. That is when backing up a play really pays off because your team then gets a second chance on the same play to get the player out.

CHARTING RESPONSIBILITIES

Every player has individual responsibilities on every play. Defensive position play depends on the offensive situation and the duties of the player's position. To be a successful defensive softball player, you must think about your responsibilities before each pitch.

You can also become a better offensive player by knowing the concepts of defensive position play. If you thoroughly understand defensive positioning and likely responses, you can make offensive moves that attack the inherent weaknesses of any defensive setup.

Use table 7.3 to help yourself remember what to do when playing each position. Ask a trained observer to use the chart as a checklist to evaluate your position play during game situation drills, modified games, or official games.

DEFENSIVE SHIFTS

Special situations may alter the starting positions and the size of the coverage areas. For example, when playing against a strong right-handed pull hitter (whose swing pulls or hits the ball to the left-field side), most of the infielders, especially the third baseman and shortstop, and all the outfielders would shift around toward the left-field foul line, as shown in figure 7.5 (compare to figure 7.1, *a-b*). The areas covered by the left fielder and third baseman become smaller. In fastpitch, the center fielder's area remains about the same size but moves to the left; this increases the right fielder's area of coverage. In slow pitch, the left center fielder and right center fielder would shift toward the left-field area, leaving the right fielder with a larger area to cover. The second baseman's closer position to second base increases the coverage area for the first baseman.

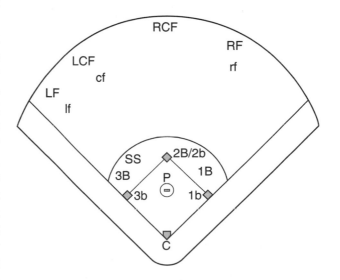

Figure 7.5 Shift for playing a strong right-handed pull hitter.

Table 7.3 Covering and Backing-Up Responsibilities

Position	Number	Covering responsibilities	Back-up responsibilities
Pitcher (P)	1	• Area 1 • First base on hit to 1B • Cutoff on throws to home from LF, LCF, RCF, or RF (SP only)	• Home plate on outfield throws • Second base on outfield throws • Third base on outfield throws
Catcher (C)	2	• Area 2 • Home plate	• First base on infield throws
First baseman (1B)	3	• Area 3 • First base • Cutoff on throws to home from CF, RF, or LF (FP only)	• Second base on LF throws
Second baseman (2B)	4	• Area 4 • First base when 1B is out of position • Second base on double plays and force plays from 3B or SS • Second base on LF, CF, or LCF throws	• Balls hit to 1B • Second base on throws to SS from P or C
Third baseman (3B)	5	• Area 5 • Third base	• Second base on RF throws
Shortstop (SS)	6	• Area 6 • Second base on double plays and force plays from P, C, 1B, or 2B • Second base on RCF or RF throws	• Second base on throws to 2B from P or C • Balls hit to 3B • Balls hit to P
Left fielder (LF)	7	• Area 7	• Balls hit to CF or LCF • Balls hit to 3B or SS • Second base on 1B, 2B, or RF throws • Third base on C, 1B, 2B, or RF throws
Left center fielder (LCF)	8	• Area 8 (SP)	• Balls hit to LF or RCF • Balls hit to SS • Second base on 1B or 2B throws
Center fielder (CF)	8	• Area 8 (FP)	• Balls hit to LF or RF • Balls hit to SS or 2B • Second base on P, C, or 1B throws
Right center fielder (RCF)	9	• Area 9 (SP)	• Balls hit to RF or LCF • Balls hit to 2B • Second base on 3B, P, or C throws
Right fielder (RF)	9 (FP) 10 (SP)	• Area 9 (FP) • Area 10 (SP)	• Balls hit to CF or RCF • Balls hit to 1B or 2B • First base on P or C throws • Second base on 3B, SS, or LF throws

Another special situation comes with the bases loaded (baserunners on first, second, and third base) and less than two outs. The infielders move in a little closer to home plate (compare figure 7.6 to figure 7.1) before the ball is pitched. This is called the *infield-in* position. If a ground ball is hit to an infielder, the force play at home plate on the lead runner or the home-to-first double play (for more experienced players) has a greater likelihood of success. The shortened distance the ball has to travel to the fielder and the resulting shortened distance of the throw to home plate make a successful play more possible than if the fielders had stayed back at their regular depth.

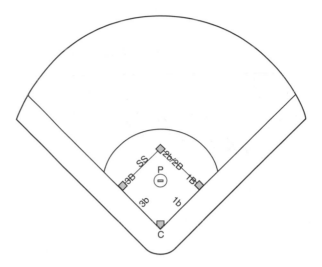

Figure 7.6 Infield-in positioning. The first- and third-baseman positions closest to home plate indicate fastpitch starting positions.

FORCE PLAYS AND TAG PLAYS

An offensive player can be put out by the defense in a number of different ways. Many of these plays fall into two categories: force plays and tag plays. A force play occurs whenever a baserunner must go to the next base because of the batter becoming a baserunner. The batter must always go to first base after hitting the ball. Only one baserunner may be on a base at one time; therefore, with a runner on first base, when the batter hits a grounder in the infield, the play at second base on the runner from first base is a force play, and the play on the batter-runner at first base is a force play.

The runner is put out in a force-play situation when the defense gets the ball to the base ahead of the runner. The ball itself need not actually come into contact with the base for a force-out, but the defensive player must have control of the ball and make contact with the base with some part of the body before the baserunner arrives (figure 7.7).

The simple force play is the fundamental defensive concept in softball. In beginning-level game play, the basic defensive strategy is to get one out at a time. When there are less than two outs and runners on base in a force-play situation, the fundamental defensive strategy is to *get the lead runner out* (the runner closest to home plate). With two outs, the play for the third out to end the inning is normally made at first base because that is always a force-out situation—and, unless the batter is left-handed, the batter has the greatest distance to go to get to the base.

The tag play is another fundamental defensive concept. A tag-play situation occurs any time a runner is not in contact with a base and is not

Figure 7.7
Making a force-out.

133

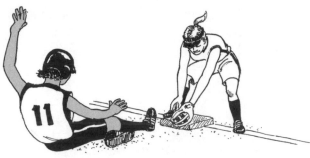

Figure 7.8 Executing a tag play.

allowed to move to any base freely. For example, a runner overrunning second base is not free to return to the base; conversely, a runner is free to return to the base after a foul ground ball. To put a baserunner out with a tag play, the defensive player must tag, or touch, the offensive player with the ball or with the glove holding the ball when the runner is off base (figure 7.8).

Infielders are the defensive players who normally execute force plays and tag plays because the plays occur on the infield (at or between the bases). These plays are the basic skills for getting baserunners out, thus preventing them from advancing and scoring runs. You must know the tag-play and force-play concepts and must be able to execute the skills in order to be a successful defensive player and help your team stop the offensive play of your opponents. This is especially important if you would like to concentrate on playing an infield position.

Making the Force Play

The force play can be executed at all three bases and home plate. The basic techniques and fundamental principles are the same regardless of the base.

Figure 7.10
Third-base coverage on a force play with a throw from the left fielder.

The throw for the force play should be about chest high. The defensive player covering the base moves to the side of the base nearest the source of the throw. This will shorten the throw's length and, thus, the time it takes for the throw to arrive in the fielder's glove. The quicker the throw arrives, the more likely it is that the fielder will get the baserunner out.

For example, on a force play at third base with a throw coming from the catcher, the player covering the base moves to the home plate side of third base to receive the throw, as shown in figure 7.9. On the other hand, if the throw were coming to third base from the left fielder, the covering player would stand on the outfield side of third base to receive the throw (figure 7.10).

Once the throw is on the way and the covering player knows exactly where the ball will arrive,

Figure 7.9 Third-base coverage on a force play with a throw from the catcher.

she places one foot on the base and stretches out her glove hand and the other foot to meet the throw. If the throw is slightly off target to the side, the covering player steps to meet the ball with the foot on the ball side and contacts the base with the other foot. For example, if the throw is off target to your left, step to the left with your left foot and contact the base with your right foot. If the play is going to be close, stretch as far as you can and catch the ball in your glove hand only. If the play is not going to be close, stretch a comfortable distance and catch the ball with both hands. Remember, you want to shorten the distance and time of the throw so the ball will get to you (and the base) before the runner does.

Making the Tag Play at a Base

Remember that the tag play is required when a baserunner is not forced to go to a base, such as in the following situations:

1. With no runner on first base, a runner on second base tries to go to third base on a ground ball hit to the second baseman.

2. A runner attempts to score from second base on a base hit.

3. A runner tagging up on a fly ball tries to advance a base.

4. A runner overruns second or third base.

5. In fastpitch softball, a baserunner attempts to steal a base.

The throw for the tag play should arrive just below the knees of the covering player. The runner will probably be sliding into the base, so the throw should be low and close to the runner. This minimizes the time it takes for the covering player to move the glove and ball into position to tag the baserunner.

There is more than one acceptable technique for covering the base on the tag play. The method recommended here places you in a position at the base where you can tag the runner but where your chances of committing obstruction and getting knocked down are limited. As your skill increases, if you choose to become more aggressive in your play, you may want to actually block the base (once you have the ball in your possession) from the runner with your body as you make the tag

play. For now, though, let's give the runner an open path to the base.

Your exact position at the base depends on the path the runner is taking to the base—for instance, coming into third base from second base as opposed to coming back to third from the direction of home plate. The other factor that affects your exact position is the source and direction of the throw. Is the ball coming to you from the outfield or the infield? In general, you should straddle the base or stand just to the side of the base facing the direction of the incoming runner. Do not, under any circumstance, place your leg between the base and the incoming runner! Leave the path to the base open to the runner.

Position yourself so that you can catch the ball and bring the gloved ball down to the edge of the base where the runner will arrive. As the runner slides in, let the runner tag herself out by sliding into the ball held in your glove. Then sweep your glove out of the way of the runner. Even if the runner does not slide, the runner's foot must get to the base—so tag the foot (figure 7.11). Don't reach out to tag the runner on the chest only to find out that the feet slid into the base before you tagged the chest.

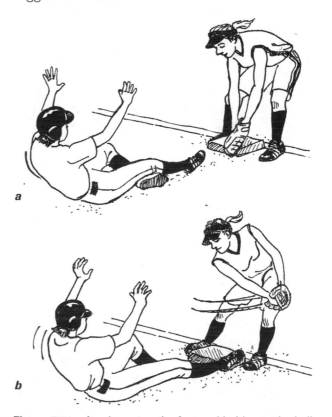

Figure 7.11 At a base, tag the foot and hold onto the ball.

Making the Tag Play Between Bases

Tagging out a player who is running between the bases is a fairly easy play. The baserunner is standing up, so you will have little trouble reaching her to make the tag. Hold the ball securely in both hands (the ball in your glove) to reduce the chance of dropping the ball. Tag the baserunner with the back of the fingers of your glove (figure 7.12). Immediately pull both hands away so the contact with the runner does not knock the ball out of your glove. Hold onto the ball!

Figure 7.12 A tag play between bases.

DEFENSIVE SKILL COMBINATIONS

In a game situation, there are two ways a ball can be hit off a pitch: into the air (either a line drive or a fly ball) and on the ground. However, in most cases, the defense must not only field the ball but also make the follow-up play required by the specific game situation. Basic defensive play calls for a player to use a combination of skills in order to achieve the desired result. Fielding the ground ball, line drive, or fly ball and making an overhand or sidearm throw or underhand toss to another player to make an out is a combination of actions that occurs frequently in a regulation game. Fly balls hit to the outfield can either advance runners into scoring position or enable them to score (sacrifice flies). Catching the fly ball or fielding a base hit and then throwing the ball quickly and accurately to the proper player or base makes it much more difficult for the offensive team to move runners.

Typical game situations that require a combination of defensive skills include the following:

- Fielding ground balls, line drives, or pop-ups that have been hit at varying speeds and that come to your glove side, throwing side, or directly at you while playing one of the five infield positions (pitcher included). You must then make throws of varying distances and in a variety of directions in order to make a tag play or force play at any of the bases or home plate.

- Fielding ground balls, line drives, and fly balls and making overhand throws from the various outfield positions to make a play on a runner at an infield base or home plate.

The following force-play and tag-play drills will give you the opportunity to practice using skills in combinations that typically occur in a game situation. You will work on fielding ground balls and fly balls and throwing the various distances that infielders and outfielders have to throw, in addition to moving in different directions to get in front of ground balls and under fly balls in order to make specific plays. Use these drills and work with a teammate to make a force play or tag play that requires each of you to make a specific contribution to the successful completion of the play. In addition, you will have the opportunity to practice with a teammate who is either trying to make the same catch as you or is backing you up as you make the catch. These basic defensive tactics and combinations of skills are used in all levels of softball, and you must master these in order to continue your development as a complete and effective defensive player.

Force-Play and Tag-Play Drill 1. *Mimetic Practice*

Proper footwork is required as you move from an infielder's starting position to the cover positions for force plays and tag plays. Although primarily designed for less experienced players as instructional practice, this drill could be used by experienced infielders as a quick review of correct technique for specific defensive positions. Practice this drill on a regulation softball field if possible. Placing an extra base in the area of second base would make it possible for both a shortstop and second baseman to practice at the same time. The drill is performed most effectively with partners working at each infield position. One partner executes the footwork for the force play and the tag play for each of the possible plays at that base. The other partner acts as observer and keeps score for the active partner. The observing partner stands about 10 feet (3.0 meters) from the base and moves to show the direction of the incoming throw for each play.

If practicing alone, place a loose base (home plate, if called for) on the ground or floor. Foul lines can assist you in orienting your fielding position in relation to the base. If no lines are available, place a cone about 15 feet (4.5 meters) from the base and use that cone to represent the direction to home plate. Draw an imaginary foul line from the cone to your base. Remember that the base lies in fair territory so the line (real or imaginary) goes on the left side of first base or the right side of third base (when facing home plate from your infield position).

When in the first baseman's role, position yourself slightly behind for slow pitch or slightly in front for fastpitch and about 8 feet (2.4 meters) to the right (infield side) of the base. When in the third baseman's role, position yourself slightly behind for slow pitch or slightly in front for fastpitch and about 8 feet to the left (infield side) of the base. When in the shortstop's or second baseman's role, position yourself in regular fielding position. When in the catcher's role, position yourself about 2 feet (.6 meters) behind the plate.

Without a ball, practice the footwork for force plays and tag plays at each base. Table 7.4 lists the covering positions, the general direction, and the possible thrower with whom you will practice the force and tag plays.

Table 7.4 Force-Play and Tag-Play Practice Situations

Covering player	General direction and possible thrower
1B (figure 7.13)	RF, 2B, SS, 3B, P, C
2B (figure 7.14)	LF, LCF, 3B, SS
SS (figure 7.15)	RF, RCF, CF, 1B, 2B, C, P
3B (figure 7.16)	LF, LCF, CF, RCF, RF, SS, 2B, 1B, P, C
C (figure 7.17)	LF, LCF, CF, RCF, RF, 3B, SS, 2B, 1B, P

Take your regular fielding position before each repetition in the drill, then move into cover position at the base to receive an imaginary throw. First move into position to make a force play. Mimic the stretch and the ball reception. Then practice the footwork needed on throws that are slightly off target to the left and to the right. Remember, on throws to your left, step with your left foot toward the throw and contact the base with your right foot; on throws to your right, step right and contact left.

Finally, do a series of repetitions in which you move to the base to make tag plays on imaginary throws from all positions listed in table 7.4. Mimic actual tagging movements in each situation. Do two repetitions of the footwork practice for a force play, two repetitions for off-target throws right and left, and two repetitions for tag plays at each position. When possible, use a different throw direction from the chart for each repetition. Players who are working with partners in an instructional setting and practicing each position should switch partner roles after completing repetitions; these players should rotate positions after both partners have completed their turns at each position. More experienced players will likely practice at their own positions only.

Success Check

- Start in regular fielding position.
- Move to the ball side of the base.
- Step with your ball-side foot and contact the base with your other foot.

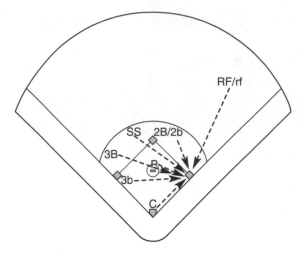

Figure 7.13 Throws to first baseman covering first base.

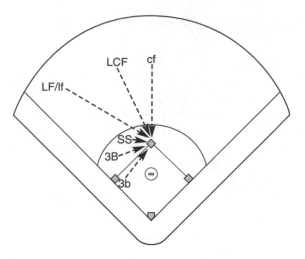

Figure 7.14 Throws to second baseman covering second base.

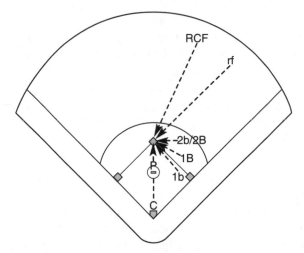

Figure 7.15 Throws to shortstop covering second base.

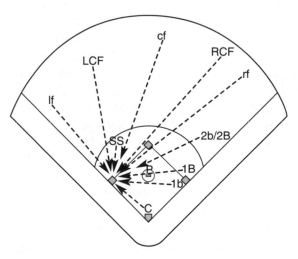

Figure 7.16 Throws to third baseman covering third base.

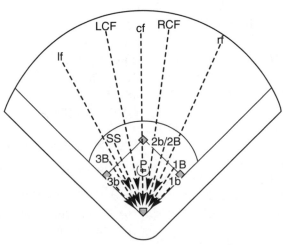

Figure 7.17 Throws to catcher covering home plate.

Score Your Success

For each infield position, score yourself based on the number of repetitions (out of eight—two force plays, two off-target throws right, two off-target throws left, and two tag plays) in which you successfully demonstrate all the success check criteria.

Seven or eight = 5 points

Five or six = 3 points

Three or four = 2 points

One or two = 1 point

Your total score ____

To Increase Difficulty

Have a feeder softly toss a ball to you as you cover the base.

To Decrease Difficulty

Practice either the force play or the tag play but not both.

Force-Play and Tag-Play Drill 2. *Game Simulation*

Fungo hitting is used in this drill. Before starting the drill, all players should review fungo hitting as covered in step 2 (page 24). Two pairs of partners set up on a regulation softball field. One pair includes a fungo hitter and a catcher at home plate; the other pair is a fielder to whom the ball will be hit and a fielder covering a base and making force and tag plays. Other players acting as observers can help with the scoring for the fielding players. The catcher and the hitter can observe for one another.

The covering fielder makes two force plays and two tag plays at each of the infield positions listed in table 7.4 for the previous drill. The fielder returns the ball to the catcher after each play at a base. The fielder fielding the hit ball moves to a different position (including outfield) for each of the repetitions for the covering fielder. Switch roles within pairs after the four repetitions (two force plays and two tag plays) at each infield position have been completed.

The fungo hitter hits the ball to the fielding play-er. Depending on the ability of the fielding player, the hitter can vary the distance the fielder has to move to field the ball and can vary the force of the hit. Exchange roles between pairs (fungo hitter and catcher go to the fielding positions, and vice versa) after both fielding partners have completed their repetitions.

Success Check

- Start in regular fielding position facing the hitter.
- Move to the ball side of the base to receive the throw.
- For on-target throws, catch the ball with two hands.
- For off-target throws, step with your ball-side foot and contact the base with your other foot.
- For very off-target throws, catch the ball with your glove hand only.

Score Your Success

For each infield position, score yourself based on the number of repetitions (out of four) in which you successfully demonstrate the relevant success check criteria.

Four = 5 points

Three = 3 points

Two = 2 points

One = 1 point

Your total score ____

To Increase Difficulty

Add baserunners. When using baserunners, some added factors come into play. The covering fielder must be sure to get to the ball side of the base and set his glove as a target that can be hit by the throwing fielder without the ball crossing the runner's path. Since the baserunner is bearing down on the covering fielder, this fielder has to be a very cool player to react calmly and correctly. For this drill variation, baserunners must always wear helmets.

To Decrease Difficulty

Have a fielder toss the ball from a short distance as you cover the base.

Force-Play and Tag-Play Drill 3. *Direct Grounders*

Set up in groups of three—hitter, catcher, and fielder. The hitter and the catcher assume positions at home plate; the hitter is in the batter's box, and the catcher is in the catching position. The fielder stands at one of the infield positions and assumes the infielder's ready position.

The hitter fungo hits a ground ball directly to the fielder. The fielder fields the ball and, using an overhand throw, throws the ball to the catcher. The catcher moves from the catching position into the position to cover home to receive the throw for a force or tag play. The catcher then tosses the ball to the hitter and returns to the catching position. As the ball is hit, the fielder tracks the ball and moves into position directly in front of the ball to execute the fielding skill. The catcher covering home plate gives the fielder a target with the glove: chest high for a force play or below the knees for a tag play.

If a ground ball gets by an infielder in a game, an outfielder would have to field the grounder and throw it to the appropriate person. To practice this situation, do this drill with the fielder in one of the outfield positions, thus extending the distance of the fielder's overhand throw. The drill is set up and executed as usual, but the fielder stands 130 to 160 feet (39.6 to 48.8 meters) from the hitter and catcher (the approximate distance from a regular outfield position to home plate). The distance can be adjusted to the fielder's throwing ability. The fielder assumes the outfielder's ready position—knees slightly bent, hands about waist high, weight on the balls of the feet, and eyes focusing on the hitter. As the ball is hit, the fielder tracks the ball and moves into position directly in front of the ball. If possible, the fielder moves in the direction of the catcher if she must field the ball on the move. As she brings the ball to the throwing position, the fielder takes a crow-hop step (step with the glove-side foot

toward the target, hop on the throwing-side foot while bringing the ball to the throwing position) and makes a strong overhand throw to the catcher, stepping toward the target with the glove-side foot as she throws. If the fielder cannot throw the ball all the way to the catcher in the air without an arc, she executes a one-bounce throw. The fielder aims her throw to hit the ground 10 to 15 feet (3.0 to 4.5 meters) in front of the catcher. The throw to that landing point should travel in a straight line.

After 10 repetitions, rotate roles. A successful force-play or tag-play attempt requires that the ball is fielded and thrown so that the catcher can catch the ball without moving more than one step from the cover position. The major focus of this drill is fielding and throwing to initiate the force play or tag play and catching to complete the play. The hitter is a facilitator in the drill, but the hitter's role is very important. The hitter must make the ball contact the ground at least 30 feet (9.1 meters) in front of the fielder and must hit the ball directly at the fielder. The scoring in this drill is for fielding and catching only.

Success Check: Fielder

- Move into position directly in front of the ball.
- Field and throw in one continuous motion.
- Make an accurate throw to the catcher.
- As an outfielder, use the crow-hop step when throwing to the catcher.

Success Check: Catcher

- From the catching position behind home plate, move quickly into position to cover home plate.
- Give a chest-high glove target for a force play and a below-the-knees target for a tag play.
- Catch the ball with two hands.

Score Your Success

Score yourself based on the number of successful fielding, throwing, and catching attempts (out of 10) you make in the fielding and catching positions.

    8 to 10 = 5 points

    6 or 7 = 3 points

    4 or 5 = 2 points

    2 or 3 = 1 point

Your total score ___

To Increase Difficulty

- Have the batter hit the ball with greater force.
- Have the batter hit the ball so that the fielder has to move to field it (see the next drill).
- Have the batter randomly vary the speed and direction of the ball hit to the fielder.

To Decrease Difficulty

- Have the batter hit the ball with less force.
- Reduce the distance of the throw.

- Use a softer ball, such as a Rag Ball or Incredi-Ball.

Force-Play and Tag-Play Drill 4. *Moving to the Ball*

Use the same three-player setup as in the previous drill. The fungo hitter begins by hitting 10 grounders, directing 5 to the fielder's glove side and then 5 to her throwing side. The fielder fields the ball and uses an overhand throw to return the ball to the catcher.

Next, the fungo hitter hits 5 slow grounders, forcing the fielder to come in on the grounder to make the play to the catcher. Finally, the fungo hitter hits 10 moderate-speed grounders, randomly hitting to the glove side, the throwing side, and directly at the fielder. Rotate roles after the full sequence of grounders to each fielder.

Although the fungo hitter is not scored in this drill, the hitter's role is very important. The hitter must hit grounders accurately for each of the field-

er's tasks. The hitter must also direct the grounder without telegraphing its direction.

Success Check: Fielder

- Start to move to your fielding position as soon as the ball comes off the bat.
- Whenever possible, field the ball in front of your body with both hands.

Success Check: Catcher

- When appropriate, catch the ball with two hands and use soft hands.
- Use correct technique when receiving the throw for a force play and for a tag play.

Score Your Success

For the fielding and catching positions, score yourself based on the number of successful attempts (out of 25) for the skill you are using.

20 to 25 = 5 points
14 to 19 = 3 points
8 to 13 = 2 points
2 to 7 = 1 point
Your total score ___

To Increase Difficulty

- Have the hitter randomly vary the speed and the direction of each hit. The fielder will not know in advance the direction or

the speed of the grounder. This will give you practice reading the ball's direction and speed as it leaves the fungo hitter's bat. This variation represents a gamelike situation for the more experienced player.
- Extend the fielder's range to the maximum without hitting the ball past her.
- Have the catcher randomly vary the target from chest to knee height as for force or tag plays.

To Decrease Difficulty

- Reduce the speed of the grounder.
- Reduce the range expected of the fielder.

Force-Play and Tag-Play Drill 5. *Triangle Drill*

Two pairs of partners take part: one pair, the hitter and catcher, positioned at home plate; and the other pair, fielders, positioned at the first- and third-base starting positions for either slow pitch or fastpitch.

The hitter hits ground balls to the two fielders, alternating between them. The person fielding the ball uses the overhand throw and makes the throw to the other fielder, who moves to cover her base—for a force play at first or either a force or tag play at third. After making the appropriate play at the base, the second fielder throws the ball to the catcher covering home for a force or tag play. The catcher then tosses the ball to the hitter.

After five grounders to each fielder, the hitter and catcher exchange roles, and the two fielders exchange positions. After the next set of five grounders to each fielder, both fielders exchange roles with hitter and catcher. Keep repeating the sequence. The major focus in this drill is on the combination skills of fielding, throwing, and catching the ball for a force or tag play. As the fielder, you must successfully field the ball and make an accurate throw on the same play in order to score points for an error-free play. The hitter is a facilitator in the drill and should try to hit the grounder so that it first contacts the ground within 10 feet (3.0 meters) of home plate. The hitter should try to match the difficulty of the hit with the experience level of the fielder. The scoring in this drill is for the fielders and the catcher only.

Success Check: First Base

- Field the ball with two hands.
- If right-handed, field the ball, pivot so your glove side is toward third base, and step toward third using an overhand throw.
- Use correct technique for making the force play at the base.

Success Check: Third Base

- Field the ball with two hands.
- On the throw, step in the direction of first base and use an overhand throw.
- Use correct technique for making the force play or tag play.

Success Check: Catcher

- Catch the ball with two hands.
- Use correct technique for making the force play or tag play at the plate.

Score Your Success

Score yourself based on the number of error-free plays (out of five attempts) for each task at each position.

Five = 5 points
Four = 4 points
Three = 3 points
Two = 2 points
One = 1 point
Your total score ___

To Increase Difficulty

- Have the hitter vary the force of the hit.
- Have the hitter vary the direction of the ground ball (glove side, throwing side, short).
- Have the hitter *randomly* vary the direction of the grounders (glove side, throwing side, short).
- Have the hitter randomly vary both the direction and the force of the hit.

To Decrease Difficulty

- Have the fielder play a rolled ball (instead of a hit ball).
- Use a softer ball.
- Decrease the distance of the throw from the fielder to the base.
- Lengthen the distance from the hitter to the fielder.

Force-Play and Tag-Play Drill 6. *Get One Out*

This drill is called "Get One Out" because in a real softball game, once you field a ground ball, you throw it to get a baserunner out. Outs are made one at a time in a game (even on a double play!), and they are only made if you can field the ball cleanly and make the throw to the base accurately and on

time. For this drill, set up with two sets of partners as in the previous drill. The fielders, however, are positioned at first base and shortstop. The hitter and the catcher are at home.

The hitter grounds the ball to the fielder at the shortstop position, who, in one motion, fields the ball and makes an overhand throw to the fielder at first base. The fielder at first base moves to the base in position to make the force play. Finally, the ball is thrown to the catcher, who tosses it to the hitter for the next hit. If desired, the catcher could take a position at the plate to make a tag play on the throw from the first baseman.

While taking the fielder's playing ability into consideration, the hitter should vary the placement of the grounders—to the glove side, to the throwing side, and directly at the fielder. The hitter should also vary the speed of the grounders, hitting both hard and softly (so the fielder must come in on the ball to make the play). All players should work on overhand throws only.

After 10 hits, the fielders exchange positions, and the hitter and catcher exchange roles. After the next set of 10, the fielders exchange roles with the hitter and catcher. Keep repeating the sequence. Vary the drill by having the fielding player at third base or second base instead of at shortstop.

Experienced fastpitch players can use fastpitch positioning and plays; the first baseman fields the ball, and the second baseman covers first base for the force-out.

Success Check: Fielder

- Quickly move to a position in front of the ball before fielding it.
- Field and throw the ball in one continuous motion.
- As the first baseman, use correct technique when making the force play at the base. Make an accurate throw to the catcher.

Success Check: Catcher

- Move quickly into position to cover home plate from the catching position.
- Catch the ball with two hands and mimic a tag play.

Score Your Success

Score yourself based on the number of error-free plays out of 10 attempts at each position.

8 to 10 = 5 points

6 or 7 = 3 points

4 or 5 = 2 points

2 or 3 = 1 point

Your total score ___

To Increase Difficulty

- Have the batter hit the ball so that the fielder does not know the direction it will go or the

speed at which it will travel (see the next drill).
- Have the fielder charge the ball as it is hit.
- Have the catcher give different targets for the throw.

To Decrease Difficulty

- Have the batter hit the ball with less force.
- Reduce the distance of the throw.
- Use a softer ball, such as a Rag Ball or IncrediBall.

Force-Play and Tag-Play Drill 7. *Rapid Fire*

Because of safety considerations, this drill is for more experienced players only. It should be done on a regulation infield with bases in position and foul lines marked.

Set up in two groups of three. One trio consists of a hitter standing outside the third-base foul line about 10 feet (3.0 meters) from third base down the line toward home, a third baseman, and a second baseman. The other group has a hitter standing outside the first-base foul line about 10

feet from first base down the line toward home, a shortstop, and a first baseman (figure 7.18). The hitter on the third-base side hits ground balls to the second baseman, who fields the ball and makes an overhand throw to the third baseman. The third baseman catches the ball, simulates a force or tag play at the base, and then tosses the ball to the hitter for the next hit.

The hitter on the first-base side hits ground balls to the shortstop, who fields the ball and makes an overhand throw to the first baseman. The first baseman catches the ball for a force play at the base and then tosses the ball to the hitter for a repeat play. The ground balls are hit simultaneously and therefore are crossing in the infield area. The hitters must hit the balls directly at the fielders. The fielders must stay behind the baseline to field the ball. Fielders should not charge a poorly hit ball because the other group is hitting at the same time. Work on good fielding and the quick release of throws. Having two balls in play increases the challenge of this drill.

After 10 repetitions, the players rotate within the group of three. After each player has had a turn at each of the three positions, the groups switch locations. This drill is designed to work on each player's quick response and reaction time; therefore, there is no need to try to increase or decrease the difficulty of the drill. Adjustments can be made by the hitter to accommodate varying levels of ability of the fielders.

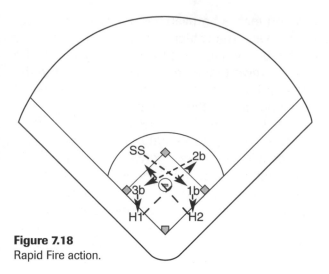

Figure 7.18
Rapid Fire action.

Success Check: Fielders

- Field the ground ball behind the baseline between first and second or second and third.
- Do not charge in on the ground ball.

- Field and throw in one motion with a quick release. Quickly return to ready fielding position.
- At the base, use proper footwork to make the force or tag play, especially to catch an off-target throw and still contact the base.

Success Check: Hitter

- Hit the ball hard.
- Hit the grounder directly at the fielder.

Score Your Success

Score yourself based on the number of error-free plays (out of 10 attempts) for each task at each position.

    8 to 10 = 5 points

6 or 7 = 3 points
4 or 5 = 2 points
2 or 3 = 1 point
Your total score ___

Force-Play and Tag-Play Drill 8. *In the Air*

Two pairs of partners are needed. One pair consists of a hitter and a catcher, positioned at home. The other pair is made up of fielders, one positioned in center field and the other at second base.

A fly ball is hit to the fielder in center field. This fielder catches the ball and, using the crow hop, makes a throw in the air (no bounces) to the partner at second base. The fielder at second catches the ball as if making a force play on a runner who left the base too soon on the fly ball; this fielder then pivots and throws the ball to the catcher. The

catcher moves up to cover the plate and simulates a tag play as she catches the ball. These throws are relatively short and should not be bounced; they should still be thrown overhand.

After 10 sequences, change roles within partners. After the next set of 10, the fielders exchange roles with the hitter and catcher.

Success Check: Outfielder

- Get behind the ball and make the catch while moving toward the second baseman.

- Use a crow hop and make a chest-high throw to the second baseman for the force play.

Success Check: Second Baseman

- Give a chest-high target with your glove.
- Pivot to your glove side and make a knee-high throw to the catcher for the tag play at home.

Success Check: Hitter

- Hit high fly balls.
- Hit fly balls directly at the fielder.

Success Check: Catcher

- Call "home" as the ball is thrown to the second baseman.
- Move to the front of the plate to receive the ball and simulate a tag play.

Score Your Success

Score yourself based on the number of error-free plays (out of 10 attempts) for each task at each position.

8 to 10 = 5 points

6 or 7 = 3 points

4 or 5 = 2 points

2 or 3 = 1 point

Your total score ___

To Increase Difficulty

- Lengthen the distance between the outfielder and the second baseman.
- Have the hitter vary the distance of the fly balls. The outfielder has to move to the ball and throw different distances to second base.

- Have the hitter vary the direction of the fly balls. The outfielder has to move to get into position to make the throw and must throw to second base from various locations.
- Have the hitter randomly vary the direction and distance of the fly balls. The outfielder has to react to the ball off the bat, then adjust the throw to second base according to direction and distance.

To Decrease Difficulty

- Use any type of softer ball.
- Adjust the positioning of the outfielder so that it is easy for the outfielder to make a throw on the fly to the second baseman.

RELAYS

You have now had the opportunity to work on some combination skills and game concepts used in game situations. An additional defensive skill is called the *relay*. One of the defensive responsibilities for the shortstop and the second baseman is to act as a relay person when an outfielder cannot make a throw all the way to the intended base or home plate. The relay is not a difficult defensive concept and can be used effectively by players at all levels.

Previous drills and steps have required you to make strong, accurate overhand throws and good catches. Less experienced players may not have had enough time to develop as strong a throw as they might like or need in certain game situations.

By using a relay, players have the help of a teammate to get the ball to the intended destination. Experienced players should have had enough practice time to develop sufficient throwing and catching skills so that they will have success executing the relay.

The relay, as its name implies, uses more than one player to get the ball to its intended destination. It is used when the throwing distance is too great for one player to execute a fast, accurate throw.

The relay is typically executed by the shortstop or the second baseman. When a hit ball goes past the outfielders in left and center fields, or when these fielders retrieve a hit ball and the throwing distance to the desired base is beyond their capabilities, the shortstop goes out to receive the throw and relay it to its ultimate destination. Similarly, when a ball is hit to right field in this manner, the second baseman is the relay person. When the 10th player in slow pitch is the 4th outfielder and all the outfielders are equidistant from home plate, the shortstop and second baseman must assume the relay responsibility as they would in fastpitch.

The player executing the relay moves to a position in the short outfield on a direct line from the outfielder to the intended destination of the ball. As the relay player, you should face the outfielder and raise your arms to make yourself a big target. The throw from the outfielder should arrive chest high to your glove side. Catch the ball, pivot by turning to the glove side, and throw the ball to the intended destination (figure 7.19).

Figure 7.19   Relaying the Ball

a   b   b

PREPARATION

1. Face outfielder who has ball
2. Identify yourself as relay person by calling "relay, relay"
3. Raise arms to increase your size as target
4. Focus on ball
5. Extend hands to prepare to catch
6. Begin pivot by stepping toward target with glove-side foot
7. Catch ball

CATCH AND THROW

1. Complete pivot
2. Use crow-hop step
3. Weight is on throwing-side foot
4. Glove side is toward target
5. Step toward target with glove-side foot
6. Throw ball using two- or three-finger grip

RELAY COMPLETION

1. Weight is on glove-side foot
2. Throwing-side shoulder is forward
3. Throwing hand is pointed at target

Relay Drill 1.   *Relay Pivot*

Three players are needed for this drill. Before actually starting the drill, have a veteran player, coach, or instructor observe you mimetically going through the three phases of the relay as illustrated in figure 7.19. This observer would be able to assist you in

developing the proper footwork and pivot that are necessary when you perform the relay skill in this drill.

Set up the drill with the three of you standing 30 feet (9.1 meters) apart from one another in a straight line. One of the end players starts with a ball. The middle player (the relay person) and the other end player face the player with the ball. To start the drill, the player with the ball throws to the relay person so that the ball arrives chest high. The relay person catches the ball, pivots to the glove side, and throws the ball to the other end person. Repeat the drill with a throw from the end person back to the relay person. The focus is on the relay person's pivoting action and throw. Rotate positions after the relay person has had 10 attempts. Continue until all three players have completed the drill. The success check and scoring in this drill are for the relay person only; however, the players in the end positions must make accurate throws so that the relay person can focus on catching the ball and making the correct pivot and throw.

Success Check

- Raise your hands up, ready to catch the ball.
- Focus on the ball.
- Pivot to the glove side.
- Make an accurate throw to the end person.

Score Your Success

Score yourself based on the number of times (out of 10 attempts) you successfully demonstrate all the success check criteria.

    8 to 10 = 5 points

    6 or 7 = 3 points

    4 or 5 = 2 points

    2 or 3 = 1 point

    Your score ___

To Increase Difficulty

- Increase the distance between players.
- Begin the pivot as you catch the ball.

To Decrease Difficulty

- Decrease the distance between players.
- Use a rebound net to receive the throw, pivot, and throw the ball at a wall.

Relay Drill 2. *Three-Person Relay*

Set up this drill like the previous one, except now stand 100 feet (30.5 meters) apart from each other. (Distance can be adjusted to the players' ability level.) One end person acts as an outfielder and the other as the catcher; the middle player is again the relay person. The relay person and the outfielder face the catcher.

The catcher throws a ball past the outfielder. (Using a fence or wall behind the outfielder to stop the ball facilitates this drill.) The outfielder turns, runs to retrieve the ball, pivots to the glove side, and throws to the relay person, who has turned to face the outfielder. At this point, the relay person has her back to the catcher and cannot see the straight-line relationship needed for an efficient relay play, that being the shortest distance between the outfielder and the catcher. Therefore, the catcher lines up the relay person by giving verbal directions of "right" or "left" so that the relay person is in a straight line between the outfielder (where the outfielder retrieves the ball) and the catcher. The relay person moves into position on the catcher's directions, catches the ball, pivots to the glove side, and throws to the catcher to complete the sequence.

After 10 sequences, rotate positions. One point is scored when the outfielder fields the ball and makes an on-target throw to the relay person and the relay person catches the outfielder's throw and makes an on-target throw to the catcher. The outfielder and the relay person are a team in this drill, so each scores 1 point when an error-free sequence is completed. Although the catcher's role is very important, players score points only when in the outfield and relay positions. Accumulate points for consecutive error-free sequences. Because your goal is consistency in performance, you must begin scoring again at 1 after any error in execution by either the outfielder or relay person in a sequence. At the end of three rotations, you should be back to your original starting positions, and each person will have had the opportunity to score a maximum of 20 points. Add the points you got for consecutive error-free sequences when in the outfield and relay positions to establish your total score. You will be working with different partners in each 10-sequence set in this drill. The success check and scoring in this drill are for the relay person and the outfielder only; however, the catcher must move the relay person into position by giving loud verbal directions.

Success Check: Outfielder

- As the ball is rolling away or stopped, use a two-hand scoop pickup, with the glove in front of the ball.
- Pivot to the glove side.

- Focus on the relay person as the target.
- Make a strong overhand on-target throw.

Success Check: Relay Person

- Raise your hands and arms up; make a large target.
- Focus on the ball; begin to pivot as you catch the ball.
- Pivot to the glove side, use a crow-hop step, and make an on-target throw.

Score Your Success

Score yourself based on the total number of cumulative sequence points you attained when in the outfield and relay positions.

15 to 20 = 5 points

12 to 14 = 3 points

9 to 11 = 2 points

6 to 8 = 1 point

Your score ___

To Increase Difficulty

- Have the catcher throw the ball past the outfielder to the right and left so that the relay person must move some distance to get into position.
- Have the catcher throw the ball past the outfielder at random speeds and in random directions.

- Add a baserunner to the play. The baserunner (who must wear a batting helmet) starts jogging toward home plate as the outfielder throws the ball to the relay person.

To Decrease Difficulty

- Have the catcher throw the ball less forcefully past the outfielder.
- Shorten the relay person's throw to home plate.
- Have the catcher throw the ball at a consistent speed and with consistent accuracy so that the outfielder won't need to move right or left (and the relay person will already be in proper lateral position).

SUCCESS SUMMARY

Successful team defense depends on your ability to read and react to specific game situations, to know the responsibilities for the position you are playing, and to know the responsibilities for all other positions as the situation develops. You need to know whether, and where, you have covering or backing-up responsibility on every play. You need to know whether the ensuing play is a tag play or force play in your covering situation. This is the foundation of knowledge for your comprehension of basic defensive tactics.

Skills such as fielding ground balls or fly balls and throwing are defensive skills performed by individuals. However, the important concept of team defense requires several individuals to effectively perform individual defensive skills in combinations, and in specific sequences, in order to reach a desired end. The various plans for achieving a desired end for the defense in softball are called *defensive tactics* or *strategies*. For you to be a contributing member of your team's defense and appropriately react to a particular situation as a defensive player, you must know your positional responsibilities, and you must be able to adjust your on-the-spot decision making to a continuously changing situation (such as runners moving around the bases or getting caught off base).

In the next step, we will introduce you to more advanced defensive tactics and techniques, such as those used for cutoffs, rundowns, and various double-play situations. You will have the opportunity to further develop your individual defensive skills. However, the focus of the drills will be on the defensive techniques and tactics called for in each given situation. You will be applying the individual skills and knowledge you have learned to achieve a team result. Before moving on to step 8, take time to review how you did on the drills in this step. Enter your scores for the drills that you participated in. Add up your scores to rate your total success in mastering the basic defensive tactics of the game of softball.

Force-Play and Tag-Play Drills

1.	Mimetic Practice	___ out of 25
2.	Game Simulation	___ out of 25
3.	Direct Grounders	___ out of 15
4.	Moving to the Ball	___ out of 15
5.	Triangle Drill	___ out of 25
6.	Get One Out	___ out of 20
7.	Rapid Fire	___ out of 25
8.	In the Air	___ out of 20

Relay Drills

1.	Relay Pivot	___ out of 5
2.	Three-Person Relay	___ out of 5

Total   ___ **out of 180**

Your total score will give you an indication of whether or not you have mastered the basic defensive tactics, concepts, and skills you need to be successful in the next step. If you participated in all of the drills in this step and you scored a total of 135 points or more, congratulations! You have mastered the concepts and skills of basic defensive play, and you're ready to move on to the next step. If your total score was between 108 and 134, you are ready to move on, but you would benefit from additional practice on those drills in which you had difficulty. If you scored less than 108 points, you should continue to practice the drills for the various defensive tactics presented in this step in order to improve your skills and understanding.

If you did not take part in all the drills, add up your scores for the drills you participated in, then add up the total possible number of points for those drills. If your score was 75 percent of the total possible points, you are ready to move on. If your score was 60 to 74 percent of the total possible points, you have done well but could benefit from additional practice on those drills in which you had difficulty. If your score was less than 60 percent of the total possible points, you need additional practice in order to master the skills and concepts needed to move on to step 8.

Cutoffs, Double Plays, and Rundowns

Your development as a softball player depends on your ability to select and execute the appropriate skill combinations in the variety of offensive and defensive situations that occur during a game. Seldom in a team sport like softball is one skill carried out in isolation. Unlike the diver or the gymnast who does a dive or a vault, the softball player must be able to field a ground ball or fly ball and make a follow-up throw. On offense, the softball player must follow a hit with baserunning. In addition, your ability to perform one skill influences your ability to perform the follow-up skill.

Your focus in this step is on executing the fundamental defensive skills of fielding and throwing in more advanced defensive game situations, such as double plays, cutoffs, and rundowns. You know how to execute four of the basic defensive skills used in the game of softball: catching, throwing the ball overhand, fielding ground balls, and fielding fly balls. You also know the offensive skill of hitting a pitched ball and the practice skills of hitting off a tee, hitting the soft toss, and fungo hitting. All of these skills will be used in the various practice drills in this step. In step 9 and 10, you will have the opportunity to practice these and other defensive plays in controlled and real-game situations.

CUTOFFS

Cutting off the ball—that is, interrupting the flight of a throw—is used when a throw intended to put a baserunner out will arrive too late, but a fielder cutting off the ball and throwing to another base will have the opportunity to put a different runner out.

As with the relay, the cutoff play is not a difficult defensive concept or skill, and it can be used by players of all abilities. In fastpitch, because the first baseman plays much closer to home, most teams use the first baseman as the cutoff player on all throws from the outfield to home, and the pitcher backs up the play at home (figure 8.1). In slow pitch, the pitcher is often the cutoff player on all throws to home; that leaves either the first baseman or the third baseman with the responsibility to back up home (figure 8.2). On throws to third base from all outfielders, the shortstop is the cutoff person in both slow-pitch and fastpitch softball (figure 8.3).

As the cutoff person, you should assume a position about 35 feet (10.6 meters) from the

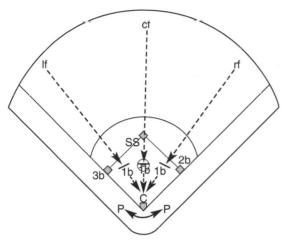

Figure 8.1 First baseman is the cutoff player on throws from the outfield to home. Pitcher backs up the play at home. Fastpitch only.

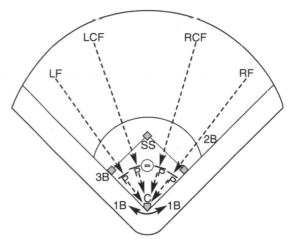

Figure 8.2 Pitcher is the cutoff player on throws to home. Either the first or third baseman backs up home. Slow pitch only.

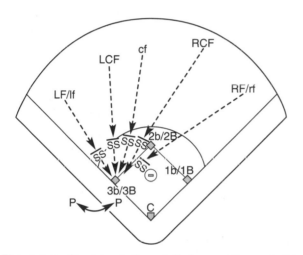

Figure 8.3 Shortstop is the cutoff player on throws to third base from any outfielder. Pitcher backs up third base. Both slow-pitch and fastpitch softball.

original target base, facing the thrower. Stand with the glove side of your body aligned with the ball's line of flight so that you do not block the covering player's view of the ball. Because the play on the baserunner will be a tag play, the throw from the fielder should arrive at the covering player about knee high. The throw should pass the cutoff person at about head or shoulder height.

Cutoff plays require strong communication between the covering fielder at the base and the cutoff person. The covering player directs the cutoff play. If there is still a play to be made on the incoming baserunner and the throw is on target, the covering player says nothing, and the cutoff person allows the throw to go through to the base. On the other hand, if the incoming runner is already safe or the throw is off target, the covering player calls "cut" and further indicates to the cutoff person by a verbal signal where (if at all) to play the ball. "Cut second" or "cut two" indicates that the cutoff person should cut off the incoming throw and then throw to second base, making a play on the batter-runner trying to advance. On an off-target throw to home, "cut home" or "cut four" tells the cutoff person to cut off the throw and relay the ball to home plate because there is still a play on the incoming runner. "Cut" with no further direction tells the cutoff person to cut off the throw and simply hold it.

As with the relay person, any pivot toward home by the cutoff player is done to the glove side. Pivoting to your glove side puts your body in direct throwing position with only a quarter-turn change of direction.

Cutoff Drill 1. *Cut Second*

Four players are needed for this drill. The outfield area on a regulation softball field will provide enough room for several groups of four to practice this cutoff drill. The next drill will be more gamelike when done on a regulation field.

Position three of the four players in a straight line. One end player is an outfielder, the other is the catcher, and the middle player is the cutoff. Overall distance is based on the participating players' abilities. The throw from the outfielder needs

151

to be able to reach the catcher with no more than one bounce. The cutoff person should be on the straight line between the catcher and the outfielder at a distance from the catcher that is about a third of the overall distance. The fourth player, the covering infielder, is in a position about halfway between the catcher and outfielder but off the line on the left side. For this drill, the covering infielder will be the second baseman.

The second baseman acts as the feeder for the start of the drill; she throws a ground ball to the outfielder. She then turns to face the catcher and cutoff person. The catcher and the cutoff person face the outfielder. The outfielder fields the ball and, using a crow-hop step, throws the ball to the catcher. If the outfielder cannot throw the ball to the catcher all the way in the air, she can make it a one-bounce throw. The ball should pass the cutoff person about head or shoulder height so she has the opportunity to catch it. Before the ball gets to the cutoff person, the catcher calls "cut second" or "cut two." The cutoff person cuts the ball and throws it to the second baseman. To be sure the outfielder has the idea of making the throw all the way to the catcher and not just to the cutoff person, it might be

helpful to let the first throw go all the way through to the catcher. If this is the case, the catcher does not say anything. After five repetitions, rotate positions—catcher to cutoff person, cutoff person to second baseman, second baseman to outfielder, and outfielder to catcher. After four rotations, you should be back at your original positions.

Success Check

- As the second baseman, throw the ground ball accurately to the outfielder.
- As the outfielder, throw the ball on a line to the catcher so that it reaches the catcher with one bounce maximum.
- As the cutoff person, catch the outfielder's throw on the command from the catcher.
- As the cutoff person, make an accurate throw to the second baseman.
- As the catcher, give commands to the cutoff person in a timely manner.
- As the catcher, catch the ball and simulate a tag play on throws allowed through.

Score Your Success

For each position, score yourself based on the number of attempts (out of five) in which you demonstrate all the applicable success check criteria for that position.

All five attempts = 5 points

Four attempts = 3 points

Three attempts = 2 points

One or two attempts = 1 point

Your total score ___

To Increase Difficulty

Have the catcher randomly call "cut second" or give no call to let the ball come through.

To Decrease Difficulty

Shorten the distances and redo the drill to improve your skill.

Cutoff Drill 2. *Cut Two, Cut Three, Cut Four*

On a regulation field, position an outfielder, a cutoff person, a base-covering player, and a catcher (and a fungo hitter, if desired) to practice cutoff plays for each of the following simulated gamelike situations (no actual runners or batter-runners):

1. Runner on second, ball hit to the left fielder: cut two, cut three, cut home, no call (let the ball go through to home).

2. Repeat the drill with the hit going to the center fielder.

3. Repeat the drill with the hit going to the right fielder.

For each gamelike situation, players take the appropriate positions. As an example, on the play from left field for the "cut two" variation, the outfielder takes the position of the left fielder, the covering player is the second baseman, the cutoff person is either the pitcher (slow pitch) or first baseman (fastpitch), and the catcher is at home plate. The catcher throws a ground ball to the left fielder (or use a fungo hitter). The left fielder fields the ball and makes the throw toward home plate. The appropriate cutoff person moves into position from her regular starting position. The second baseman moves into the cover position at second base. The catcher calls directions to the cutoff person to line her up on a straight line between the outfielder and home plate. As the ball approaches the cutoff person, the catcher calls "cut second," then the cutoff person cuts the ball and makes the throw to the second baseman covering second. After five repetitions, players rotate positions and the drill is repeated, or the drill could be repeated for the "cut three" variation with the covering player changing her covering responsibility to third base.

Success Check

- As the outfielder, field the ball cleanly and use a crow hop to initiate the throw. Make a throw that is on target, would reach the catcher, and would pass the cutoff person chest high.
- As the covering player, arrive in the appropriate cover position before the cut call. Catch the cutoff person's throw and make a simulated tag play.
- As the cutoff person, move quickly into position, arriving before the ball. Catch the ball and make an accurate throw to the covering player.
- As the catcher, line up the cutoff person and make a timely call of "cut." Catch the ball on "cut home" plays and make a simulated tag play.

Score Your Success

For each position, score yourself based on the number of attempts (out of five) in which you demonstrate all the applicable success check criteria for that position.

All five attempts = 5 points

Four attempts = 3 points

Three attempts = 2 points

One or two attempts = 1 point

Your total score ___

To Increase Difficulty

- Add a relay person to the drill.
- Cause the outfielder to move laterally to field the ball.
- Add baserunners. Baserunners must wear batting helmets.

To Decrease Difficulty

Make a short-distance toss to the cutoff person, who is already in the appropriate cutoff position. The cutoff person then makes a throw to the covering person, who is already in position at the base.

DOUBLE PLAYS

If you want to gain more experience and play at a higher level, you must increase your knowledge and physical ability to execute advanced defensive tactics successfully. For both slow pitch and fastpitch, more experienced players must be able to execute the double play if they intend to play in the infield. In addition to new footwork, two new throwing skills—the sidearm throw and the underhand toss—are introduced in this section because they are used by some infielders when executing the double play.

For less experienced players, the basic defensive strategy is to get one out at a time. When there are fewer than two outs with runners in a force situation, the play is on the lead runner. Now you are going to focus on the double play, an advanced defensive tactic that calls on the defense to get two outs from continuous action.

The most common double-play opportunity occurs when there is a runner on first base and less than two outs. The batter hits a ground ball to an infielder, who throws to second base to put out the lead runner, immediately followed by that covering player's throw to first base to put out the batter-runner. Infield double plays are also made from third to first when runners are on first and second and from home to first when the bases are loaded.

In addition to infield double plays, double plays occur anytime two players are put out during continuous action. Here are some examples:

- A fly-out or line drive out is followed by a baserunner being put out after failing to tag up.

- A fly-out is followed by a baserunner being thrown out attempting to advance after tagging up.

- In fastpitch, the batter strikes out, and a baserunner is thrown out trying to steal a base.

However, in this section, your focus is on infield double plays with runners on first base, first and second base, or the bases loaded, and a ground ball hit to the infield. The skills that you will work on for this double play are the sidearm throw, the underhand toss, the shortstop's drag step and inside pivot techniques, and the second baseman's crossover and rocker pivot techniques.

The double play is important because the defense can get two players out on one pitch. Not only is the baserunner already on base put out as a lead runner, but the batter-runner is also put out as part of the continuous play.

In game play, the successful execution of a double play can deal a psychological blow to the offensive team and, at the same time, motivate the team that has successfully executed it. Thus, the momentum in a game often changes hands as a result of a successful double play.

Double plays on ground balls are typically initiated by a throw from an infielder to second base, third base, or home plate. The infielder playing the base to which the initial throw was made then throws the ball to first base. The first out is made on the lead runner, who is forced; the second out is made on the batter-runner at first base, also a force-out. In fastpitch softball, where runners can lead off the base on the pitch, the only hope of getting the second out is to make that play on the batter-runner. Even in slow pitch, the batter will be at least a step behind the other baserunners be-

cause of completing the swing and shifting gears to get out of the batter's box. The right-handed batter, in particular, has a greater distance to run than any other runner because she is on the side of home plate farther away from first base. The recommendation for both fastpitch and slow-pitch play is to always get the second out of the double play at first base.

You have already had experience executing portions of the double play—namely, throwing overhand, catching, and executing footwork for a force play. The sidearm throw is a skill used by the shortstop when executing a medium-range feed (throw) to the second or third baseman for the first out of the double play, and by the second baseman when making the feed to the shortstop covering second base for the front end (first out) of the double play. When a short throw or toss is required for these same plays, you should use the underhand toss. Use the overhand throw, which you can execute well by this point, when a long throw is needed for either of the outs in the double play. You will first have the opportunity to develop your sidearm throwing and underhand tossing skills before we start using them in the double-play drills.

Tossing Underhand

When the shortstop fields the ground ball about 8 to 10 feet (2.4 to 3.0 meters) away from second base, the quickest way to get the ball to the second baseman covering second is to toss the ball underhand so that it arrives chest high to the fielder. In this instance, the sidearm throw would be too strong a throw and too difficult for the second baseman to handle. Likewise, the second baseman fielding a ground ball close to second base would use the underhand toss to the shortstop who has moved in to cover the base.

No specific drills are included for the underhand toss. Practice this skill by working in groups of three. Set up in a triangle formation about 10 feet apart from each other. Player one starts the practice by rolling the ball to player two. Player two fields the ball, turns, and tosses the ball underhand to player three. Player three rolls the ball to player one, and the sequence is repeated. Continue around the triangle in this manner. All three players will have the opportunity to roll the ball, field the ball, and underhand toss the ball.

You can add a more gamelike quality to the practice by putting a loose base down on the ground. Players two and three position as shortstop and second baseman about 10 feet from the base. Player one stands on line with the base, equidistant from the other two players. Player one rolls the ball to the shortstop, who fields the ball and tosses it underhand to the second baseman covering the base. Next, player one rolls the ball to the second baseman, who fields the ball and tosses underhand to the shortstop covering the base. Continue to alternate rolling the ball to the two players. Rotate positions so that all three players have an opportunity to practice fielding the ball and using the underhand toss to feed the covering player. Remember to aim your toss to arrive about chest high.

Throwing Sidearm

The sidearm throw should be used sparingly by less experienced players because it is difficult to throw it as accurately and with the same force as the overhand throw. At an elite level of softball, the sidearm throw is sometimes used by shortstops and third basemen when a quick-release throw is needed to make a play on a batter-runner at first base. However, there are instances when a less forceful throw is needed. Most players can use the sidearm throw for short-distance throws, such as the second baseman's throw to first base

after fielding a ground ball and the close feeds at any base for a single force play or the first out of a double play.

The trajectory of the sidearm throw is horizontal or slightly low to high. Most throws should arrive to the fielder about chest high. A short-distance overhand throw tends to go high to low, thus arriving at the fielder's feet and making for a very difficult catch. The short-distance sidearm throw stays horizontal or rises slightly to the fielder, arriving at the desired chest height. Although the sidearm throw is less accurate than the overhand, the shorter distance in which the throw is used reduces the likelihood of error. The sidearm throw also gets to the intended base more quickly because the thrower releases the ball from the crouched fielding position rather than taking the time to come to the erect overhand throwing posture.

As you field a ground ball, keep your back flat, knees bent, and torso parallel to the ground while bringing the ball to the throwing position. If you are a right-handed second baseman throwing to first or a right-handed shortstop throwing to second, your glove side is already pointed toward your target, so you don't need to pivot. Simply bring the ball across the front of your body, keeping your throwing arm parallel to the ground (figure 8.4). All other aspects of the throw are exactly the same as for the overhand throw.

| Figure 8.4 | **Throwing Sidearm, Glove-Side Target** |

READY TO THROW

1. Ball is in glove
2. Back is flat
3. Shift weight to throwing side
4. Start glove and hand to throwing shoulder; use two- or three-finger grip
5. Stay low; flex at waist
6. Bring ball to throwing position
7. Glove elbow is toward target

155

b

c

THROW

1. Step toward target
2. Shift weight to glove side
3. Hips are square to target
4. Throwing arm is parallel to ground
5. Snap wrist on release of ball

THROW COMPLETION

1. Weight is on glove-side foot
2. Knees are bent
3. Throwing arm moves horizontally toward target
4. Glove elbow is back

Misstep

The ball goes to the right or left of the target.

Correction

Snap your wrist directly at the target, not before or after.

Misstep

The trajectory of the ball is high or low.

Correction

Do not stand up to throw—stay low. Bend and keep your torso parallel to the ground.

When using the sidearm throw to your throwing-arm side—for example, the second baseman throwing to second or the shortstop throwing to third—pivot your feet after fielding the ball so your glove side is toward the throwing target (figure 8.5), and then proceed as described for throwing to the glove side. Use the following sidearm throwing drills to perfect this technique before going on to the double play.

Figure 8.5   Throwing Sidearm, Throwing-Side Target

a

b

c

READY TO THROW

1. Ball is in glove
2. Back is flat
3. Weight is on throwing-side foot; start pivot to throwing-side target
4. Start glove and hand to throwing shoulder; use two- or three-finger grip
5. Stay low; flex at waist
6. Bring ball to throwing position
7. Glove elbow is toward target

THROW

1. Step toward target
2. Shift weight to glove side
3. Hips are square to target
4. Throwing arm is parallel to ground
5. Snap wrist on release of ball

THROW COMPLETION

1. Weight is on glove-side foot
2. Knees are bent
3. Throwing arm moves horizontally toward target
4. Glove elbow is back

Misstep

You push the ball rather than throw it.

Correction

Lead with the elbow as you bring the ball across your body.

Misstep

When you throw to a target on your throwing side, the ball is off target.

Correction

Stay low, but pivot your body so your glove side is toward the target.

The next three drills can be done inside or outside, using a wall or fence, respectively, for the throwing target. Because the ball will not rebound off a fence and come back to you, when you're practicing outside, you should have a partner with a bucket of balls roll a ball to you from a short distance. If no partner is available, take 10 balls and place them 1 foot (30.4 centimeters) apart in a straight line in front of you, going away from you. Move up to field each ball and make the sidearm throw to the fence. Remember, these are not accuracy drills; your target is simply the wall or the fence. If your sidearm throwing skills are good and you want to work on accuracy, make small targets on the wall or fence and throw to hit those targets.

Sidearm Throwing Drill 1.   *Wall Practice to Glove Side*

This drill is best done in a gymnasium. Position yourself 30 feet (9.1 meters) from each wall in a corner of the gymnasium. Face one wall, with the other wall to your glove side. Throw the ball against the front wall so that a ground ball rebounds to you, then field the ball and make a sidearm throw to the wall on your glove side using the techniques described in figure 8.4. Turn to the wall on your glove side, field the rebounding ball, and move it directly into throwing position. Do not throw the ball; instead, resume your starting position and repeat the sequence.

The major purpose of this drill is for you to practice the sidearm throw. However, you can also take this opportunity to work on your ground ball fielding skills. Ask a more experienced player or instructor to watch you complete the drill and rate your success based on the success checks.

Success Check

- Field the ball with two hands.
- Stay low, flexed at the waist, with your back flat. Move your arm to a horizontal throwing position.
- Step toward the target.
- Keep your throwing arm parallel to the ground during the throw and follow-through.

Score Your Success

Earn 1 point for each attempt out of 10 in which you demonstrate all the success check criteria.

Your score ___

To Increase Difficulty

- Have a partner roll or bounce the ball to you with varying speed.
- Have a partner roll or bounce the ball to you so that you must move laterally.

- Use a target to increase accuracy.
- Have a partner fungo hit the ball from various directions with different speeds.

To Decrease Difficulty

- Start with the ball stationary on the floor.
- Use a softer ball for a slower rebound.
- Practice, practice, practice!

Sidearm Throwing Drill 2. *Wall Practice to Throwing Side*

Stand as in the previous drill, except that what was the side wall is now the front wall (or rebounding wall), and the side wall (or throwing-target wall) is now on your throwing-arm side. Face the new front wall and throw the ball to the wall so that the rebound is a ground ball. Field the ball, pivot to your throwing side so your glove side is toward the throwing-target wall, and deliver the ball to that wall using a sidearm throw. Field the rebound, return to your starting position, and repeat the sequence for a total of 10 trials.

Success Check

- Stay flexed at the waist and keep your back flat throughout the pivot and throw.
- Make sure your weight is on your throwing-side foot as you start to pivot.
- Complete the pivot so that your glove side is to the target.
- Step toward the target.
- Move your throwing arm horizontally toward the target throughout the throw and follow-through.

Score Your Success

Earn 1 point for each attempt out of 10 in which you demonstrate all the success check criteria.

Your score ___

To Increase Difficulty

- Use a target to increase accuracy.

- Have a partner roll the ball in the opposite direction of the throw so that the pivot to make the throw is more difficult.
- Have a partner fungo hit the ball from various directions with different speeds.

To Decrease Difficulty

- Start with the ball stationary on the floor.
- Use a softer ball for a slower rebound.
- Have a partner roll the ball more toward the throwing-target wall so you are already moving in the direction of the pivot.

Sidearm Throwing Drill 3. *Four Player*

Now you will practice fielding a ball and making a sidearm throw to a partner. One important consideration in this drill is that you make the short sidearm throw with the appropriate amount of force (not too much) so that it can be caught.

This drill requires four people. Whether inside or outside, set up this drill as if you are on a field. The primary fielder takes the position of shortstop. The fungo hitter stands at home plate with a bucket of 10 balls. The third player is the second baseman, and the fourth is the third baseman.

The hitter hits 10 ground balls to the shortstop at varying speeds and to varying directions (either glove side or throwing side). In one smooth motion, the shortstop fields each ball and throws sidearm to the base on the side of the body the ground ball came to. For example, if the ball is hit to the left of a right-handed player (glove side), he fields the ball and makes the sidearm throw to second base. If the ball is hit to his right (throwing side), he fields the ball, pivots, and makes the sidearm throw to third base. The shortstop fields 10 balls and throws sidearm to the proper base. Focus first on clean fielding, then on the throw. Be sure that your throw does not overpower the base player. The base player catches the ball and rolls it back to the hitting station.

Count the number of good fielding plays and sidearm throws. After 10 attempts, rotate positions and repeat the drill. Continue until each participant has completed 10 attempts at fielding and throwing sidearm to a base player. Were you more successful throwing to your glove-side base or your throwing-side base? Were your throws at a force that was catchable? Work on those areas that gave you problems so that you can perform sidearm throws consistently.

Base players need to remember to assume the force-play cover position on the ball-side corner of the base. The fungo hitter must hit the ball accurately so the fielder can make at least four throws to each base.

Success Check: Shortstop

- Get in front of the ball to field it with two hands.
- Stay low with your back flat throughout the fielding and throwing sequence.
- Make sure your arm travels horizontally throughout the throw and follow-through on all throws.
- Field the ball, pivot, and make the sidearm throw in one fluid motion when making the play to third base.

Score Your Success

Score yourself based on the number of successful fielding and sidearm throwing plays (out of 10 attempts as the shortstop) in which you demonstrate all of the success check criteria.

7 to 10 = 5 points

4 to 6 = 3 points

1 to 3 = 1 point

Your score ___

Because this is a game situation drill, there is no need to increase or decrease difficulty. Those adaptations occurred in previous drills. The double-play drills that follow the next instructional section will include several combination drills in which you will have an opportunity to further practice the sidearm throw.

Turning Double Plays

As described in the introduction to this step, the double play is an advanced defensive tactic that results in the defense getting two outs from continuous action. When executing the double play from home to first or from third to first, you need to make only slight additions to the footwork technique you have already practiced for force-outs at home and third. To make a strong throw for the second out of those double plays, you need to take a step toward first base as you throw the ball. Thus, for the first out of the double play from home or third, do not stretch out as far as you would to catch the ball on a regular force-out. You need to be in balance and be able to take a step toward first base on your throw for the second out. If you stretch out with one leg while reaching to catch the ball for the first out of the double play, you will use valuable time getting your body back into position to be able to take a step toward first base. You will consequently be slower and less powerful in your throw to first base. On the other hand, the first baseman who is catching the throw for the second out of the double play must stretch as far as possible in order to shorten the length of that throw (and therefore the time it takes for the ball to arrive at first base). In softball, the play at first base on the double play is usually very close.

You have not had experience to date with the footwork involved in making the first out of the double play at second base. The footwork at second is much different from the footwork used at third or home. In your practice as both shortstop and as second baseman, you have learned how to make a force play at second base, but not a force play that must be followed by a throw to first base. The footwork for the double play at second base is called a *pivot*. Basically, the pivot positions you to make the force-out on the runner coming into second, lets you get out of the way of that runner, and puts you in a position to make a strong throw to first base for the second out.

In softball, unlike baseball, the first out of the double play at second base is almost always made with the runner close to the base. To be able to make a strong throw to first for the second out, you must have a clear path for the ball to travel, and you must not get knocked down by the runner before your throw. The runner has no option but to go to the base. You, therefore, must be the one to move away from the base in order to find the clear path needed for your throw. The following sections provide the techniques used by the shortstop and the second baseman when making the pivot on the double play at second base. In addition to the sidearm throw you have just worked on, you will practice different methods used to get the ball to the pivot player for the double play. All the double-play drills are presented at the end of the instructional sections for both the shortstop's and second baseman's techniques. The basic drill setup is the same whether the shortstop or the second baseman is making the play at second base. As you finish the instructional material for each of the techniques presented, go to the drill section and select drills that will give you practice opportunities for that particular technique. For example, after learning about the shortstop's drag step in the first instructional section, go to double-play drill 1, Mimetic Footwork, and practice that footwork technique. Then proceed to the portion of double-play drill 2, Simulated Hit, that deals with the shortstop's drag step (see the first variation for slow and fastpitch and the second variation for slow pitch).

Following each instructional section, select specific double-play drills to practice each of the techniques used by infielders when making the double play. Practice the drills from distances requiring you to use the underhand toss and the sidearm throw. You will then be able to experience the excitement of turning the double play in a real softball game. Experienced players who are playing either shortstop or second base should review the techniques for their positions and select some of the more gamelike drills, such as drill 3, Fungo Double Play. As a challenge, you might want to try the other infielder's techniques. For example, if you are a shortstop, try the second baseman's crossover and rocker techniques!

Note: Descriptions of techniques for executing the first out of the double play at second base as used by the shortstop (and later, the second baseman) are for a right-handed player. A left-handed player would have great difficulty getting into position to receive the throw at the base, and then getting out of the way of the runner while still leaving an unobstructed path for the throw to first base. For this and other reasons, left-handed players do not usually play shortstop or second base.

Shortstop's Drag Step

The *drag step* is the pivot used by the shortstop to make contact with second base while catching the ball for the force-out and positioning the body for the throw to first base for the second out. This technique gets the shortstop out of the baseline to avoid the runner and provides a clear path for the throw to first base. The drag step is used when the feed for the play at second is thrown by the second or first baseman from the outfield side of the baseline between first base and second base.

When a ground ball is hit to the first-base side of the infield in a double-play situation, the shortstop moves from her initial fielding position to just behind second base. She straddles the back corner of the base (the corner pointing to center field) with the inside of her right foot contacting the very corner of the base. Her shoulders are parallel with an imaginary line between first and third base. If there is not enough time to get to the base and stop in the straddle position over the back corner, the shortstop moves through that position without stopping. As she catches the ball to make the force-out, the shortstop steps toward the right outfield grass with her left foot (figure 8.6a), dragging the toes of her right foot across the back corner of the base (figure 8.6b). Still moving, she steps to close her right foot to her left (figure 8.6b), then steps left again and throws to first base for the second out (figure 8.6c). To accomplish these objectives without the runner's interference, the direction of your movement past the base must be toward the right outfield area, not down the baseline toward first base!

| Figure 8.6 | **Shortstop's Drag Step** |

APPROACHING THE BASE

1. Straddle back corner
2. Weight is on right foot
3. Face thrower
4. Focus on ball

FOOTING AND LEAVING THE BASE

1. Catch ball
2. Step past base with left foot
3. Drag right foot across back corner
4. Close right foot to left

FINISHING THE THROW

1. Step with left foot
2. Bring ball to throwing position
3. Throw to first base
4. Weight is on glove-side foot
5. Knees are bent
6. Throwing arm is horizontal
7. Glove arm is back

Now go to the double-play drill section and select drills appropriate for your experience level to practice the shortstop's drag step. When you feel comfortable making that play, come back to this next section to learn about the shortstop's inside pivot.

Shortstop's Inside Pivot

In step 7, you learned that the shortstop is responsible for covering second base on a double play when the ball is hit to the catcher or to the pitcher. The reason for this coverage is that the shortstop has easier skills to execute than the second baseman does when making the play at second base. The shortstop, when moving toward second base from the regular fielding position, is already going in the general direction of first base. Thus, the whole flow of the play is in the direction of the throw for the second out of the double play. The movement of the second baseman going to cover second base, on the other hand, is away from first base and therefore away from the direction of the throw for the second out.

Similar principles apply to covering a base for a double-play force-out as apply for any force play. As you know, when the feed for the force play is coming from the infield side of the baselines, the cover position is at the inside corner of the base. In a double-play situation, when the ball is hit up the middle and is fielded by either the pitcher or the catcher, the shortstop covers second on the inside corner and uses an inside pivot to make the force-out and complete the throw to first base for the double play. On the other hand, if the ball is clearly hit to the first- or third-base side and is played from the infield side of the baselines, the regular guidelines for base coverage apply (grounder to first-base side, shortstop covers second base; third-base side, second baseman covers).

When the ball is hit up the middle, the shortstop comes to the inside corner of second base, steps on the inside corner of the base with her left foot, and faces the player making the feed (figure 8.7a). As she makes the catch for the force-out, the shortstop bends her knees, taking the weight fully on her left foot, and springs away from the base off her left foot toward the pitching rubber, landing on her right foot well clear of the baserunner (figure 8.7b). The shortstop steps toward first base with her left foot and makes the throw for the second out of the double play (figure 8.7c).

| Figure 8.7 | Shortstop's Inside Pivot |

a

b

c

APPROACHING THE BASE

1. Step on inside corner with left foot
2. Hips are square to thrower
3. Focus on ball

FOOTING AND LEAVING THE BASE

1. Catch ball
2. Take full weight on left foot
3. Bend knees
4. Spring from base off left foot
5. Land on right foot
6. Step toward first with left foot
7. Bring ball to throwing position
8. Throw to first base

FINISHING THE THROW

1. Weight is forward
2. Knees are bent
3. Throwing arm is horizontal
4. Throwing shoulder is forward

Again, go to the double-play drill section and select drills to work on the shortstop's inside pivot. When you feel comfortable with this technique, come back here and learn how the second baseman makes the pivots at second base.

Second Baseman's Cross-over Pivot

For the second baseman, turning the double play at second base involves a true pivot or change of direction. The second baseman must clear the base after making the force-out, stop the momentum of the body going away from first base, and step back toward first on the throw. The second baseman uses the *crossover pivot* when the feed is coming from the infield side of the baseline between second and third, or when timing demands shortening the distance the feed has to travel (that is, on any throw from the third baseman or a long throw from the shortstop).

From her regular fielding position, the second baseman should move to cover second base so that she can cross the base in a direct line toward the person feeding her the ball. If time allows, she moves to a position just short of the base, facing the direction of the incoming throw (figure 8.8a). As the thrown ball approaches, the second baseman steps on the base with her left foot, moves over the base, and catches the ball on the far side of the base (third-base side) while still in contact with the base with her left foot for the force-out (figure 8.8b).

The second baseman immediately stops her forward momentum by landing on her right foot and bending her right knee. This step onto her right foot should carry her well clear of the base in order to get out of the runner's path. The second baseman shifts her weight to the left side. She steps left toward first and throws the ball to first base (figure 8.8c).

The major-league style of play in which the second baseman leaps straight up into the air over second base to avoid the incoming runner, spins in the air, and—while suspended in mid-air—makes the throw to first base is a technique above and beyond our expectations of you in this book!

Figure 8.8　　Second Baseman's Crossover Pivot

a | b | c

APPROACHING THE BASE

1. Weight is on right foot
2. Face thrower
3. Focus on ball

FOOTING AND LEAVING THE BASE

1. Step on base with left foot
2. Raise hands to ball height
3. Body moves forward over base
4. Catch ball
5. Step off base and block with right foot

FINISHING THE THROW

1. Step left to target
2. Shift weight to left foot and throw
3. Knees are bent
4. Hips are square to target
5. Throwing shoulder is forward

Go to the double-play drill section and select drills to work on the second baseman's crossover pivot. When you feel comfortable with this technique, come back here to learn the final pivot technique for the second baseman, the rocker.

Second Baseman's Rocker Pivot

The second baseman uses the *rocker pivot* when the shortstop's feed is initiated very close to second base. The second baseman moves to the base and places the toes of her right foot in contact with the outfield side of the base. With her weight on her left foot, the second baseman catches the ball (making the force-out), steps back onto her right foot, steps left toward first base, and throws the

ball. Stepping back with the right foot in this way, called the *deep drop* (figure 8.9), gets the second baseman out of the runner's path.

Another rocker technique involves standing with your weight on your right foot, kicking the base with your left foot for the force-out, and stepping left to throw. This move, the *short drop,* is quicker by one step, but it leaves you in the baseline. You should base your choice of footwork technique on the position of the runner at the time of the play at the base: Use the deep drop if the runner is close, and use the short drop if the runner is farther away. Figures 8.9 and 8.10 show how to execute both the deep- and short-drop rocker pivots.

Figure 8.9 Second Baseman's Rocker Pivot: Deep Drop

a *b* *c*

APPROACHING AND FOOTING THE BASE
1. Approach base; weight is on left foot
2. Raise hands to ball height
3. Focus on ball
4. Right foot contacts base
5. Catch ball

LEAVING THE BASE AND THROWING
1. Weight is on left foot
2. Step back behind left foot with right
3. Bring ball to throwing shoulder
4. Step left toward target
5. Right hip drives forward
6. Left elbow points toward target; throw to first base

FINISHING THE THROW
1. Weight is on glove-side foot
2. Hips are square to target
3. Throwing hand is low
4. Throwing shoulder is forward

Figure 8.10 | Second Baseman's Rocker Pivot: Short Drop

a

b

c

APPROACHING AND FOOTING THE BASE

1. Approach base; weight is on right foot
2. Raise hands to ball height
3. Focus on ball
4. Left foot contacts base
5. Catch ball

LEAVING THE BASE AND THROWING

1. Weight is on right foot
2. Step left toward target
3. Bring ball to throwing shoulder
4. Shift weight to left side
5. Right hip drives forward
6. Left elbow points toward target; throw to first base

FINISHING THE THROW

1. Weight is on glove-side foot
2. Hips are square to target
3. Throwing hand is low
4. Throwing shoulder is forward

Double-Play Drill 1. *Mimetic Footwork*

This drill is most appropriate for players who are just learning to execute double-play pivots at second base. With a partner, get in position at the regular shortstop and second-base fielding positions. Without using a ball, you will each practice the various footwork techniques executed by the shortstop and second baseman at second base during the second-to-first double play. When your partner is performing the footwork technique at the base, act as observer and give feedback to your partner on her demonstration of the success check criteria for the specific technique being practiced.

First, the shortstop moves to second base and executes the correct footwork for the drag step. The second baseman could mimic a feed throw to the shortstop; however, her major role is to watch

the shortstop's performance and give accurate feedback on her footwork technique. The shortstop returns to the shortstop position and repeats the drag step portion of the drill for a total of five repetitions.

Next, the second baseman executes the rocker pivots, both deep and short drops, while the shortstop acts as observer. The shortstop finishes her footwork practice using the inside pivot, and the second baseman completes her practice using the crossover pivot. Be sure to go back to your regular fielding position between each repetition.

If you are learning both the shortstop and second baseman positions, after each player practices the pivots in the initial fielding position, switch positions and practice the other pivots.

Success Check: Shortstop

Drag Step

- Raise your hands up, ready to receive the throw.
- Step toward right field, beyond the base, with your left foot.
- Face the thrower while dragging your right foot across the base.
- Close your right foot to your left, step to the left, and mimic the throw to first base.

Inside Pivot

- Raise your hands up, ready to receive the throw.
- Step on the inside corner with your left foot.
- Spring from the base off your left foot to get out of the baseline.
- Land on your right foot, step left toward first base, and mimic the throw.

Success Check: Second Baseman

Rocker Pivot, Deep Drop

- Raise your hands up, ready to receive the throw.

- With your weight on your left foot, contact the base with your right foot.
- Step back behind your left foot with your right foot.
- Step left and mimic the throw to first.

Rocker Pivot, Short Drop

- Raise your hands up, ready to receive the throw.
- Stand with your weight on your right foot behind the base.
- Reach forward with your left foot and contact the base.
- Shift your weight back over your right foot, step left, and mimic the throw to first.

Crossover Pivot

- Raise your hands up, ready to receive the throw.
- Come from behind the base, moving in the direction of third.
- Step on the base with your left foot, moving forward over the base.
- Block with your right foot, step left, and mimic the throw to first.

Score Your Success

For each type of double-play pivot, score yourself based on the number of times (out of five attempts) you demonstrate all of the success check criteria for the shortstop or second baseman.

Five = 5 points

Three or four = 3 points

One or two = 1 point

Your total score ___

To Increase Difficulty

Add the use of a ball so that you receive a short toss while executing the pivots (no throw after the catch).

To Decrease Difficulty

Walk through each of the sequences to improve your footwork skills.

Double-Play Drill 2. *Simulated Hit*

This drill is set up to provide practice of the second-to-first double play for players learning all infield positions. If the participants play only one position, select the variations appropriate for the players involved. The drill requires three pairs of partners: a feeder and a pivot player (shortstop and second baseman); the first-base cover player and a hitter; and a catcher and a pitcher or third baseman (this person plays either position, according to table 8.1). This drill and all drills that follow may be practiced for either slow pitch or fastpitch. See figure 7.1, page 128, for proper regular-depth fielding positions.

All fielders take regular-depth fielding positions (figure 8.11, variation A). The hitter stands with a bucket of five balls 20 feet (6.1 meters) from the feed player. The catcher should have an empty bucket.

The hitter rolls a ground ball to the feed player (1). The feed player, using either a sidearm throw or underhand toss, depending on the distance, throws to the pivot player covering second base (2). This player, after using correct footwork to tag the base, throws overhand to first base for the completion of the double play (3). The first baseman throws the ball to the catcher (4), who tosses the ball to the hitter.

Repeat the sequence five times for each of the variations in table 8.1. After completing all five variations (FP or SP), exchange positions within the pairs. After both partners have completed the double-play variations, the pairs rotate. The hitter and first baseman become the shortstop and the second baseman. The catcher and pitcher (or third baseman) become the hitter and first baseman. The shortstop and second baseman become the catcher and the pitcher (or third baseman).

More experienced players can add complexity to the drill by having a baserunner run from first to second base on each play. If you do, be sure the baserunner wears a batting helmet to protect against errant throws.

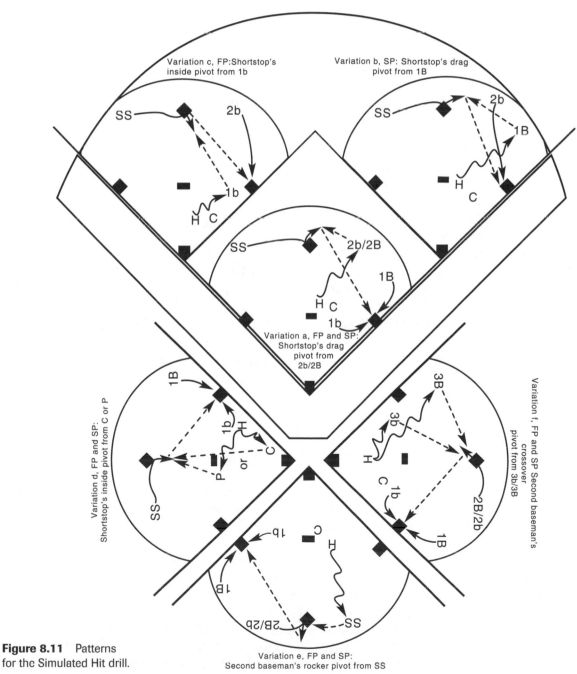

Figure 8.11 Patterns for the Simulated Hit drill.

167

Success Check

- Based on the feed source, use the appropriate pivot.
- Use correct footwork for the pivot.
- Successfully catch the feed throw or toss.
- Make an accurate throw to first base.

Table 8.1 Variations for the Simulated Hit Drill

Variation	Feeder	Pivot player	First-base coverage
A	Second baseman	Shortstop (drag step)	First baseman (FP and SP)
B	First baseman (SP)	Shortstop (drag step)	Second or first baseman (SP)
C	First baseman (FP)	Shortstop (inside pivot)	Second baseman (FP)
D	Catcher or pitcher	Shortstop (inside pivot)	First baseman (FP and SP)
E	Shortstop	Second baseman (rocker pivot)	First baseman (FP and SP)
F	Third baseman	Second baseman (crossover pivot)	First baseman (FP and SP)

Score Your Success

Although many participants are involved in this drill, because the focus of the drill is on the pivot play, scoring is applied only for the shortstop and second baseman (based on their successful execution of the pivot play at second base and accurate throw to first base to complete the double play). However, good fielding plays, catches, and accurate throws for all position players are necessary for the successful completion of the drill practice.

For each of the pivots at each position, score yourself based on the number of repetitions (out of five) in which you successfully demonstrate all success check criteria.

Five repetitions = 5 points

Four repetitions = 3 points

Three repetitions = 2 points

One or two repetitions = 1 point

Your total score (shortstop) ___

Your total score (second baseman) ___

To Increase Difficulty

- Vary the force of the "hit" ball.
- Vary the direction of the "hit" ball.

To Decrease Difficulty

- Practice only one variation per practice session.
- Have a partner call out the footwork cues as you do the pivot.

Double-Play Drill 3. *Fungo Double Play*

This drill is practiced like the previous drill, except a fungo hitter is at home, and a defensive player (feeder) is at each of the infield positions, including pitcher. (Although a fungo hitter is preferred, a batting tee could be used for the hitter to deliver the ball to the feed players.) The hitter fungo hits ground balls from home plate to the feed players. The feed player makes the throw to the pivot player at second base, who in turn completes the double play by throwing to the first-base cover player, who returns the ball to the catcher. To help speed up the drill, the catcher should hold a second ball and toss it to the hitter after the first ball is hit. In addition, a fourth pair of players serve as runners.

This drill is more gamelike than the previous one because you execute the double play from a hit ball. Furthermore, on the last three repetitions (out of the set of five) of each play variation (see the previous drill), baserunners are added. One runner goes from home to first on the ground ball, while the other runs from first to second. Baserunners must wear batting helmets. In this drill, both the feeders and the pivot players score points. The scoring system is designed for a practice in which players rotate to all positions and score points accordingly.

Because this drill is designed to practice game-like situations, there is no need to increase or decrease difficulty. Return to one of the previous drills for further practice on the basics of the double play if this drill is too difficult.

Success Check: Feeder

* Field the ball cleanly.

* Use the appropriate throwing technique based on throwing distance.
* Make an accurate throw to the pivot player.

Success Check: Pivot Player

* Complete the pivot using appropriate footwork.
* Successfully catch the feed player's throw.
* Avoid the baserunner on three repetitions.
* Make an accurate throw to first base.

Score Your Success

When you are the feeder, score yourself based on the number of times (out of five repetitions) that you successfully demonstrate all success check criteria for the feeder. When you are the pivot player, score yourself based on the number of times (out of five repetitions) that you successfully demonstrate all success check criteria for the pivot player.

Five = 5 points

Four = 3 points

Three = 2 points

One or two = 1 point

Your total score (feeder) ___

Your total score (shortstop) ___

Your total score (second baseman) ___

Double-Play Drill 4.   *Home-to-First Double Plays*

By now you should be proficient as both the pivot player and the feeder for all double-play combinations from second to first base. Table 8.2 shows the possible combinations for home-to-first double plays.

Table 8.2 Home-to-First Double Plays

Feeder	Pivot player	First-base coverage
Third baseman	Catcher	First baseman
Shortstop	Catcher	First baseman
Second baseman	Catcher	First baseman
Pitcher	Catcher	First baseman
First baseman (FP)	Catcher	Second baseman (FP)
First baseman (SP)	Catcher	First baseman (SP)

All previous drills can also be used to practice the double play when the first out occurs at home. The coverage at home is by the catcher, and the coverage at first is by the first baseman (or the second baseman when the first baseman is the feed player).

Set up with a catcher, a first baseman, a fungo hitter, and a fielder who moves around to play each of the various feed positions. The fielder plays second base and covers first when the ball is hit to the first baseman. Two runners should be positioned at third base (one on the base to run and the other in foul territory waiting to run). Two runners are also positioned at home to run to first base; these runners need to stand in foul territory to the side of home plate, out of the hitter's way. All runners must wear helmets.

The hitter hits two balls to the fielder at each different infield position to give the fielder good practice making feeds (overhand throws) of varying distances to the catcher. The hitter must hit balls that are within reasonable fielding range of the fielder. For safety, the hitter must step back out of the way of the runner and catcher after each hit. The catcher practices positioning to receive throws from the various infield positions to make the force-out at home while at the same time getting out of the way of the incoming runner and making the throw to first base. After each hit, the runner coming in from third base goes to the end of the runner's line at home, and the runner running to first goes to the end of the runner's line at third. After two double plays from each fielding position have been made, the four runners switch places with the fielders and hitter. The fielders and hitter rotate positions when coming back in to the fielding and hitting positions. Rotate positions a total of four times in order to play each position.

Runners are included in this drill to add a sense of gamelike play. However, because the ball is hit by a fungo hitter and the hitter is not actually running to first base, the success of the play is not based on the runners being out but rather the successful completion of the total play (hit ball is fielded cleanly; accurate throw is made to home; catcher catches the throw, uses appropriate footwork to contact the plate, and makes an accurate throw to first base; first-base cover player catches the throw from catcher and contacts the base).

Success Check: Feeder

- Set up in infield-in starting position.
- Charge a slowly hit ball.
- Field the ball cleanly.
- Make a strong, accurate throw to home.

Success Check: Catcher

- Start in regular catching position.
- When the ball is hit, move up to the front of the plate.
- Make a clean catch and use the appropriate footwork to contact the plate.
- Step and make a strong, accurate throw to first.

Score Your Success

Earn a team score based on your participation in the successful completion of the play. When in a fielding and hitting rotation, score yourself based on the number of successful double plays out of 10 attempts in each of your fielding and hitting rotations. You will be in a fielding rotation a total of four times for a total of 40 attempts.

8 to 10 successful double plays = 5 points

5 to 7 successful double plays = 3 points

4 or fewer successful double plays = 1 point

Your total score ___

To Increase Difficulty

To increase the challenge for your fielding and hitting team, have the hitter direct balls to the fielder at varying speeds and directions.

To Decrease Difficulty

If your fielding and hitting team found this drill too difficult, eliminate the use of runners.

Double-Play Drill 5. Third to First

The third-to-first double play is a very difficult play to make successfully unless the ball is hit to the shortstop side of the infield, hit directly back to the pitcher, or stops close to home plate directly in front of the catcher. Unless the runners are very slow, the distance the ball has to travel from the first or second baseman to third and back again to first makes the play very difficult. In addition, with a left-handed batter hitting, the play is even more difficult to complete. As in the other double plays, the second out of the double play should be made at first base. Remember, the right-handed batter has a longer distance to run than the runner on first base going to second.

This drill is most appropriate for a team practice of more experienced fastpitch players, although it could be used for slow pitch. In either case, participants play their normal positions. Set up this drill with two teams made up of a first baseman, a pitcher, a third baseman, a shortstop, and a catcher. The defensive team is in the field in their positions, and the other team is up to bat. The at-bat team places runners on first and second base. One player is at bat, and the others are on deck.

The drill is conducted as a real game. The game situation is runners on first and second and no outs or one out. The catcher must be in full catching gear, and the runners and batters must wear helmets. The pitcher facilitates this drill by pitching a ball that the hitter can place hit to the shortstop, third baseman, pitcher, or in front of home plate to the catcher so that the defensive team can work on the third-to-first double play. The fastpitch pitcher's focus is on throwing strikes and working on her change-up.

During the initial series of plays, the batter on the offensive team attempts to hit the pitched ball to the shortstop or pitcher, or drop the ball down for the catcher. In fastpitch softball, a ball hit to the third baseman requires the shortstop to cover third, which is a more difficult play and should be worked on later in the drill. After hitting the ball, the batter runs to first base. The runners take a lead on the pitch (fastpitch) and react to the hit ball. If the ball is popped up, the infield fly would be in effect, and the runners would hold their bases. If the ball is hit on the ground, they would run. After each play, the runner coming to third joins the offensive team's on-deck group as the other runner and batter-runner move up a base.

A team's turn at bat lasts until the hitters have successfully hit two ground balls to the shortstop, pitcher, and catcher for a total of six plays. The defensive team scores 1 point for each successful third-to-first double play. In this case, because the ball is hit off a pitch and the batter runs to first base, *successful* means both runners are put out. The offensive team scores 1 point for each play in which at least one runner is safe on the play. Teams switch roles after each series of six plays. The fastpitch play in which the ball is hit to the third baseman and the shortstop covers third can be added to make a total of eight plays for a team's turn at bat.

Because this is a game situation drill, there is no need to increase or decrease difficulty.

Success Check: Defensive Team

- The feed player cleanly fields the ball.
- The feed player makes an accurate throw to third.
- The third baseman moves to the inside corner of third base.
- The third baseman catches the feed throw while contacting the base.
- The third baseman steps toward first base and makes an accurate throw to first.
- The first baseman catches the ball while contacting first base.
- The runner is out at third, and the batter-runner is out at first.

Success Check: Offensive Team

- Fastpitch runners take a lead on the pitch.
- The hitter accurately hits the ground ball to the designated fielder.
- The runners read and react appropriately to the hit ball.
- The runner and batter-runner are safe at their respective bases.

Score Your Success

Score yourself based on the number of successful plays your team makes out of six (or eight) in a turn at bat or in the field.

Six (eight) = 5 points

Five (seven) = 4 points

Four (six) = 3 points

Three (four or five) = 2 points

Two (three) or less = 1 point

Your score (defensive team) ___

Your score (offensive team) ___

Your total one-inning score ___

Double-Play Drill 6. *Live-Pitch Double-Play Game*

The final drill in this section provides an opportunity to practice all double-play variations while hitting off live pitching. Accurate pitches are necessary for this drill to be successful, so more experienced players are needed. A pitching machine can be used if the pitching participants' accuracy is still in the developmental stage!

The drill is set up as in the previous one, except teams are made up of fielders for all infield positions (including pitcher, even if a pitching machine is used). One team starts in the field, and the other team is at bat. Conduct the drill as follows:

1. The game is played in innings. A half inning continues until all members of the team at bat have had a turn at bat, regardless of the number of outs.

2. The team at bat determines a batting order. In each half inning, the last player in the batting order starts as a runner on first base. Additional runners can be placed on base in order to practice third-to-first and home-to-first double plays (or see number 8).

3. The pitcher must throw a strike on the first or second pitch; otherwise, the batter is awarded first base.

4. The batter must hit a fair ground ball to the infield on the first strike pitch, or the batter is out.

5. After hitting the ball, the batter runs to first base.

6. The fielders attempt the appropriate double play.

7. If the defense just wants to work on the second-to-first double play, the runner going to second returns to her place in the batting order while play continues.

8. If the defense wants to work on the third-to-first double play or the home-to-first double play, the batter-runner stays on first, or other runners stay on to run for the next batter.

Score Your Success

Earn a team score for this drill. Your team score is based on combined points scored for defensive play and offensive play during an agreed upon number of innings. When on defense, your team scores 1 point for each runner you put out. Subtract 1 point for each error made in the field. When on offense, your team scores 1 point for every fair ground ball hit. Subtract 1 point for every ball hit that is not a fair ground ball.

Team wins the game = 10 points

Team takes second place = 5 points

RUNDOWNS

The final defensive situation you will deal with in this step is the *rundown* play. Rundowns occur when the defense catches a runner between bases (when the runner is not free to return to a base). Remember, baserunners may freely overrun first base and home plate, but not second or third base. If a baserunner rounds any base going toward the next base, the defense can make a play on the runner, attempting to get the runner in a rundown.

The defense wants to take advantage of any mistake made by a baserunner and get an out. The baserunner, however, does not want to be caught in a rundown unless a run can score on the play. A baserunner who gets caught in a rundown when there is no opportunity for a run to score has made a mental mistake—this runner was not concentrating and got caught between bases. Defensive players need to be alert to the fact that a runner caught in a rundown when

Figure 8.12 Rundown between second base and third base.

another runner is on third base may be trying to distract the defense to allow the run to score. The defense must be sure to keep an eye on the runner at third base.

Rundown Defense

Planned and practiced techniques are necessary to ensure that a runner caught off base will be tagged out. If no set play is used, the runner can more easily escape the situation and reach a base safely. Teams can select from among several options for set plays. The drills at the end of this section will give you the opportunity to practice those options.

Rundown defense is more effectively executed when the defensive players have back-up help in case the runner gets past one of the original chasers. The defensive players closest to the bases that the runner is caught between, the original chasers, are called *primary fielders* for the play.

Table 8.3 Fielder Responsibilities in Rundowns

Runner caught between	Primary fielders	Back-up fielders
First and second base	First baseman Second baseman	Pitcher Shortstop
Second and third base	Shortstop Third baseman	Second baseman Pitcher
Third base and home plate	Third baseman Catcher	Shortstop Pitcher

The players next closest to the two bases involved back up those original chasers and are called the *back-up fielders* for the play. A back-up fielder takes an initial position in front of the base she is responsible for. As the rundown play develops, the back-up fielder should stay at least 10 feet (3.0 meters) behind the primary fielder unless the play has moved close to the base (figure 8.12). Table 8.3 identifies the fielders and their responsibilities in rundown plays.

The primary fielders can execute the rundown alone unless one is passed by the baserunner. When passed, the primary fielder steps aside to allow the back-up fielder to move up to receive the throw. The original primary fielder rotates back behind the now-active back-up fielder and assumes the back-up role. The original back-up fielder has now moved up to assume the new primary role. Rotation in this manner continues each time a primary fielder is passed by the baserunner. Of course, this rotation should not be necessary if the runner is put out with no throws or one throw! All persons involved in the rundown must maintain positions in front of the bases. The back-up fielder, particularly, must not line up behind the base, because a runner passing a primary fielder could then get to a base safely before encountering the back-up fielder.

Several possible rotation methods can be used for executing the rundown play in addition to the one just described. However, certain principles apply to any rundown situation, regardless of the method used to get the runner out:

1. Try to get the runner out with the least possible number of throws. The ideal is no throw at all; one is good, two is all right, and more than two is too many.

2. The person with the ball (not necessarily one of the primary or back-up fielders) initiates the play by holding the ball and running directly at the runner until the runner commits to moving toward one base or the other. This person can actually make the tag if he is close enough before the baserunner gets to the base. If the tag is not made by the initiator, the ball is thrown to the fielder toward whom the runner is going.

3. Keep the runner away from the bases, but closer to the base last touched than to the one not yet reached.

4. Throw the ball back and forth beside the runner, not over the runner's head. Hold the ball at head height in your throwing hand, close to your throwing shoulder. Use a short snap throw (with a motion like throwing a dart) from this position to get the ball to the covering fielder.

5. When making the tag, grip the ball with your bare hand and hold the ball and hand securely in your glove. Tag the runner with the back of your glove.

Rundown Offense

The runner must watch the person with the ball. Once the initial throw is made, the runner must decide whether to run at full speed toward the base away from the throw or to stay in the rundown situation. If the throw is a long throw and the runner is fairly close to the person throwing the ball, the runner's chances of making it to the base are good. If a preceding runner has a chance to score while the defense has the runner in the rundown, the runner should stay in the rundown and try to avoid being tagged out until the run scores.

Because the following drills are in a progressive order of difficulty, there is no need to increase or decrease the difficulty of each drill. The succeeding drill will increase the difficulty for the participants, and repeating the previous drill will decrease the difficulty for the participants.

Rundown Drill 1. *Mimetic Rotation*

This drill requires four players positioned between two bases—two in primary roles and two in back-up roles. No runner is used. One primary fielder with a ball starts the drill by throwing the ball to the other primary fielder. After each throw, the assumption is made that the imaginary runner passes the thrower. Therefore, the thrower in the primary role rotates back, and the person in the back-up role moves up to receive the next throw. You score 1 point for every on-target throw, successful catch, and appropriate rotation movement you make in 30 seconds.

Success Check

- Give a glove target outside of your glove-side shoulder, not in front of your body.
- Throw the ball beside the imaginary runner and hit the glove target.
- As the primary fielder, rotate back to the back-up position after every throw.
- As the back-up fielder, always be in front of the base.

Score Your Success

Score yourself based on the number of points scored in 30 seconds.

20 or more = 5 points

15 to 19 = 3 points

10 to 14 = 2 points

9 or fewer = 1 point

Your score ___

Rundown Drill 2. *Rundown With Baserunner*

Use the same setup as in the previous drill, except add a runner and rotate only when the runner actually passes a primary fielder. The baserunner must wear a batting helmet. Rotate a fielder into the runner position after 30 seconds.

Success Check: Fielders

- Try not to exceed two throws in getting the runner out.

- Throw beside the runner.
- Rotate back to the back-up position when you are passed by the runner.

Success Check: Runner

- Watch the fielder with the ball.
- Reach base safely or stay in the rundown for 30 seconds without being tagged out.

Score Your Success

As the runner, score yourself based on the number of seconds you stay in the rundown.

30 seconds or more = 5 points

20 to 29 seconds = 3 points

10 to 19 seconds = 2 points

9 seconds or less = 1 point

Your score ___

For defense, score yourself based on the number of seconds it takes you to tag the runner out. Record your best defensive score from the four bouts.

9 seconds or less = 5 points

10 to 19 seconds = 3 points

20 to 29 seconds = 2 points

30 seconds or more = 1 point

Your best score ___

Rundown Drill 3. *Rundown With Initiator*

This drill requires three sets of partners. The first set acts as the primary fielders, and the second set acts as the back-up fielders. These four players stand in front of two bases. The third set acts as the runner and the initiator. The initiator, with the ball, stands 20 feet (6.1 meters) from the runner, who is positioned in the baseline midway between the bases. The runner must wear a helmet. The initiator starts the drill by running directly at the runner. The initiator tries to tag the runner, but once the runner commits to run to a base, the initiator throws the ball to the primary fielder at that base. From that point, the drill proceeds as in the previous drill. After three 20-second rundown bouts, rotate roles within each set of partners. After the next set of three 20-second bouts, sets of partners rotate roles: The base 1 pair becomes the runner and initiator; the runner and initiator become the base 2 fielders; the base 2 fielders move to base 1. Continue the drill until the rotation has gone full circle. The success checks and scoring are for the runner and the fielders. However, the initiator is a major participant in any rundown play and should hold the ball and run directly at the runner, trying to tag the runner out before making any throw.

Success Check

- As the primary fielder, rotate to the back-up position when passed by the runner.
- As the primary fielder, make throws beside the runner.
- As the back-up fielder, maintain a position in front of the base.
- As the back-up fielder, rotate to the primary position in a timely manner.
- As the runner, focus on the fielder with the ball.
- As the runner, reach base safely or stay in the rundown for 20 seconds.

175

Score Your Success

Score yourself based on the number of bouts (out of six as a primary fielder, six as a back-up fielder, and three as the runner) in which you successfully demonstrate all the success check criteria for the primary and back-up fielder or the runner.

Primary and back-up fielder

Six bouts = 5 points

Four or five bouts = 3 points

Three bouts or less = 1 point

Runner

Three bouts = 5 points

Two bouts = 3 points

One bout = 1 point

Your total score ____

Rundown Drill 4. *Rundown Competition*

Equipment needed for this drill includes two cones, gloves, helmets, and a softball. The game is played on a regulation softball diamond.

The group is divided into two equal teams (approximately 8 to 10 people on each side), making one group of fielders and one group of baserunners. The fielders divide up equally among the three bases and home plate. Rundowns occur between first and second and between third and home. Fielders at these bases assume primary and back-up positions. One fielder with the ball starts in the middle of the diamond around the pitching rubber. A cone is placed halfway between first and second base approximately 10 feet (3.0 meters) behind the baseline to the outfield side. Another cone is placed halfway between third base and home plate 10 feet behind the base path in foul territory. The running group divides up equally behind the two cones, waiting their turn to run. One runner starts in the baseline between first and second base, and one starts in the baseline between third base and home.

Play begins when the fielder with the ball runs in the direction of one of the baserunners, causing the runner to break toward the lead base or back toward the trail base. No runner may break toward either base until the fielder with the ball crosses the center of the field (pitching rubber). Once the rundown begins, fielders play out the situation until the runner is either tagged out or is safe at either base. As soon as the runner is tagged out or is safe at the base, the fielder in possession of the ball immediately turns and runs at the baserunner between the opposite set of bases, beginning another rundown. The original initiator takes the place of that fielder. This continues until time is out (usually two to three minutes). The defense earns 1 point for each runner who is tagged out. The objective of the drill is for the fielding group to tag out as many runners as possible in the allotted time. Fielders should play out every situation to completion, including overthrows. Once the allotted time is up, the two groups switch. Runners should stay in the rundown for as long as possible, forcing the fielders to make multiple throws—and possibly causing an error—while trying to arrive safely at either base. Scoring is for the fielding groups only. The fielding group earning the most points is the first-place finisher. Points are awarded to remaining teams for second through fourth place.

Success Check: Fielders

- Hold the ball up in the air and out of the glove so it is visible to the receiver. Keep the ball in a position to make a three-quarter throw at a pace that can be handled at a short distance.
- Run the baserunner back to the trail base whenever possible.
- Never fake a throw or pump the ball in a way that might "fake out" the receiver.
- As the receiver of the throw, initiate the toss of the ball by calling out "now" when you want the thrower to release the ball.

- As the receiver at the trail base, wait as long as possible to call out "now" so that the timing of the throw allows you to catch the ball and make the tag.
- As the receiver at the lead base, call out "now" when the baserunner is committed to moving up to the base you are covering, but early enough so that you can run the baserunner back to the trail base.
- Tag out the runner using as few throws as possible.
- Make the area where the runner is running smaller by moving toward the other fielder, thus shortening the distance (often referred to as "squeezing the pickle").
- As a back-up player at a base, give enough distance so that an errant throw does not get by you, but also be ready to step in once the player ahead of you has thrown the ball.
- Leave an open pathway for the ball to be thrown between yourself and the other fielder so that the throw does not hit the runner.

- When receiving the throw, move toward the thrown ball, making it more difficult for the runner to change direction.
- When running toward a baserunner in a rundown, run hard in order to give the baserunner less of a chance to change direction on a release.
- After releasing the ball on a throw, either peel away and return to the base you came from to become the next back-up or follow your throw and become the next back-up player at the base you threw to.

Success Check: Runner

- Stay in the rundown for as long as possible, forcing the fielders to make multiple throws—and possibly causing an error—while trying to arrive safely at either base.
- Get in the way of the path of the ball.
- Stay on your toes and stay low so that you can change direction quickly and easily.

Score Your Success

Each member of a fielding team receives points based on the team's placement at the end of the allotted time.

Winning team (most number of points) = 5 points

Second-place team = 3 points

Third-place team = 2 points

Fourth-place team = 1 point

Your score ___

To Increase Difficulty

- Give an additional point if the tag-out is made in less than three throws.
- Give an additional point if the tag-out is made at the trail base.

SUCCESS SUMMARY

From the first step in this book, we have stressed the concept that softball games are won on solid defensive play. During any softball game, certain situations tend to repeat themselves. With runners on base and less than two outs, there is usually a double-play possibility when the ball is hit on the ground in the infield. If your goal is to be an infielder in slow pitch or fastpitch, the ability to execute all variations of the double play is an absolute must.

A rundown play is used when the defense catches a runner off base. If you want to be an infielder, you must understand the concept of primary and back-up fielders in the rundown play, and you must be able to properly execute the techniques for both roles. With runners on base, a cutoff play is used on throws from the outfield intending to put a runner out at a base. If you want to be a shortstop, a fastpitch first baseman, or a slow-pitch pitcher, you must understand and be able to perform the role of cutoff person in a game. You have had the opportunity in this step to increase your knowledge of the defensive tactics used in these situations. You have also had a variety of practice opportunities to develop the skills used to apply the appropriate strategy to the various game situations.

In the next step, you will have the opportunity to not only increase your knowledge of the various offensive tactics used in fastpitch and slow-pitch softball games but also learn how the defense attempts to counter these offensive strategies. You will participate in gamelike practice settings that will require you to read the defense and make on-the-spot decisions about the best technique to use in specific offensive situations, such as advancing a runner. Double steals and delayed steals are just two examples of new offensive tactics that are in store for you in the next step. However, before moving on, let's see how well you have mastered the defensive tactics and techniques of the cutoff, double play, and rundown. Enter your score for each drill in the chart that follows. Add them up to rate your success as a defensive player.

Cutoff Drills

1. Cut Second ___ out of 20
2. Cut Two, Cut Three, Cut Four ___ out of 20

Sidearm Throwing Drills

1. Wall Practice to Glove Side ___ out of 10
2. Wall Practice to Throwing Side ___ out of 10
3. Four Player ___ out of 5

Double-Play Drills

1. Mimetic Footwork
 Shortstop ___ out of 10
 Second baseman ___ out of 15
2. Simulated Hit
 Shortstop ___ out of 20
 Second baseman ___ out of 15
3. Fungo Double Play
 Feeder ___ out of 30
 Shortstop ___ out of 25
 Second baseman ___ out of 15
4. Home-to-First Double Plays ___ out of 20
5. Third to First ___ out of 10
6. Live-Pitch Double-Play Game ___ out of 10

Rundown Drills

1. Mimetic Rotation ___ out of 5
2. Rundown With Baserunner
 Runner ___ out of 5
 Fielder ___ out of 5
3. Rundown With Initiator ___ out of 15
4. Rundown Competition ___ out of 5

Total ___ *out of 270*

Your total score will indicate whether or not you have sufficiently mastered the defensive tactics and techniques needed to move on to the next step. If you scored a total of 203 points or more, congratulations! You have mastered the tactics and techniques of cutoffs, basic double plays, and rundowns, and you are ready to move on to the next step. If your total score was 162 to 202, you can move on, but you might benefit from getting additional practice on those drills that were difficult for you. More experienced players who scored less than 6 on the last two double-play drills would benefit from additional practice on those drills before moving on.

STEP

9

Offensive Tactics and Defensive Responses

The offensive objective for a softball team is to score runs. Your team has to score more runs than the opposing team in seven innings to win a game. The defensive objective is to prevent the opposing team from scoring more runs than your team. This step provides you with knowledge and experience in offensive and defensive situational play to help you play the game of softball.

To score runs, batters have to get on base, advance around the bases, and ultimately cross home plate safely. The batter becomes a baserunner by reaching first base safely by a hit, a base on balls (walk), an error by the defense, being hit by a pitched ball (in fastpitch), or on a fielder's choice, a play in which the defense makes a play on a baserunner other than the batter-runner to get an out. To prevent runs from scoring, the defense must respond to what the offense does and make the plays in the field.

The number of outs, the location of the runners on base, the inning, the score of the game, the ball–strike count, the strengths and weaknesses of the batter, and the strengths and weaknesses of the pitcher or other defensive players are all factors that characterize offensive and defensive situations. These factors influence the decision of the coach or player regarding the potential choices presented by the situation, especially in fastpitch softball.

Offensively, for example, in the top of the seventh inning with the home team ahead 1-0, the pitcher walks the first batter, who is the ninth batter in the order. The next batter, the leadoff batter, lays down a bunt to the first-base side, which the right-handed first baseman fields and throws to second base for the force-out on the lead runner. The throw is slightly off target and draws the shortstop off the bag, leaving runners on first and second base with nobody out.

To this point in the game, the home team pitcher has allowed only a scratch infield hit and three fly balls to the outfield—one by the number three hitter (a left-handed hitter), two by the cleanup hitter—and has struck out 10 batters. The next batter, the number two hitter in the batting order, is a good contact hitter and also a good bunter. Based on the performance to date of the opposing pitcher, the location of the baserunners, the fact that there are no outs in the potential last time at bat, and the strengths of the next three batters, the coach makes the decision to try to advance the runners with a bunt. The coach instructs the batter to square around early to see where the defense moves to cover the bunting situation—and instructs her to then either call time (and step out of the box) or, if there is no opportunity to call time-out, don't bunt the first pitch. Does the third baseman stay back to cover third, in which case the pitcher will play the bunt on the third-base side? Or, does the third baseman come in and the shortstop move over to cover third base, leaving no cover at second base? Knowledge of how the defense intends to play the bunt situation will help the batter decide the best placement for the bunted ball.

The fact that the first baseman is right-handed means she must pivot after fielding the bunt on the first-base side, thereby slightly delaying the throw to third. The right-handed pitcher would have the same problem if she is covering the bunt on the third-base side. If these two players were left-handed, the throws would be released quicker and would add a different factor for consideration. Advancing the runners to third and second via a sacrifice bunt puts the tying runner on third base—in scoring position with only one out—for a potential sacrifice fly.

A *sacrifice fly* is a play in which, with fewer than two outs, the batter scores a runner with a fly ball or line drive. The batter is not charged with a time at bat when hitting a sacrifice fly. Because the third batter is left-handed and a good pull hitter, a fly ball to right field would not only score the runner from third but also allow the runner on second to advance to third. Obviously, a base hit by the third or fourth batter would score at least the tying run. In fastpitch, the sacrifice bunt is a good and often-used option to advance runners into scoring position. However, in slow pitch, bunting is not allowed, so hitting to right field behind the runners to advance them to second and third base might be the play of choice. In a coached game, the coach usually makes the decision on the play of choice. In a game where players are given the decision-making responsibility, the players involved need to go through the same thought process as described for the coach to arrive at the best tactic to use given the situation.

From a defensive perspective, the coach would have several options based on the original example: runner on first with no outs. Based on the performance of the pitcher to this point in the game, in fastpitch it is fairly predictable that the offensive team will attempt to bunt the lead runner over to second. Defensively, the coach can have the first and third basemen charge, forcing the batter to attempt to slash or push bunt, which are more difficult. If the batter lays down the bunt, the charging fielders will be in a better position to field it, and

they will have a much better chance at getting the runner at second (assuming the fielder makes a good throw!). Or, the coach may decide to go for the sure out at first, which then eliminates the possibility of bunting the runner to third with less than two outs, thus eliminating the use of the sacrifice fly to score the runner. If they decide to go to first, the defensive team may play the bunt differently, having the first baseman stay back and having the pitcher cover the bunt to the first-base side. However, regardless of the defensive play, it is always risky to put a runner into scoring position (second base) with less than two outs, especially with batters coming up who have had the only success off the pitcher so far in the game. A base hit will potentially score the runner or at least put her at third with less than two outs, where a sacrifice fly can again be used to bring in the run.

In slow pitch, the defensive options are less complex, but the coach still needs to make the decision about whether to go for the lead runner with no outs, or to get the sure out at first. In slow pitch, hitting behind the runner is an important strategy; therefore, the outfield may shift toward right field, forcing the batter to be more precise in the placement of the hit.

The complexity of the cognitive aspect of the game of softball for players and coaches is what makes the game so appealing to many people. They like the challenge of outthinking the opponent. You need to understand the game so that you can make effective decisions in response to the offensive and defensive situations that are presented to you. As your level of play increases, the options you have as a hitter or fielder increase—as a result, you and your team become more difficult to defend or to score on. The offensive and defensive strategies presented in this step include the basic to the more complex. The strategies you and your team choose to use will depend on the skill level and game knowledge that you and your teammates possess. Becoming a student of the game will help you become a better softball player and will help to make the game more exciting and challenging!

Before each pitch, you should mentally check off aspects of the offensive and defensive situations that are presented. At first glance, the lists in figures 9.1 and 9.2 look long. However, as you work with this mental exercise in a modified or regulation game, you will find the task easier than it looks. The batter or baserunner should know

Figure 9.1
Reading an Offensive Situation

1. What inning is it?
2. What is the score?
3. How many outs are there?
4. Are any runners on base? Which bases?
5. How fast are the runners on base?
6. What is the batter's major objective (get on base, advance the runner, sacrifice bunt [fastpitch], score the runner, sacrifice fly)?
7. What is the ball-and-strike count?
8. How is the outfield positioned (straightaway; shifted to left; shifted to right)?
9. Where are the largest gaps (left-field foul line, left center, right center, right-field foul line)?
10. Which outfielder has the strongest arm (left fielder, left center fielder [slow pitch], center fielder, right center fielder [slow pitch], right fielder)?
11. Which outfielder has the weakest arm (left fielder, left center fielder [slow pitch], center fielder, right center fielder [slow pitch], right fielder)?
12. How is the infield positioned (regular depth, infield-in, double-play depth)?
13. Is the third baseman shifted toward the shortstop, toward the foul line, deep, or shallow?
14. Is the shortstop shifted toward second base, toward third base, deep, or shallow?
15. Is the second baseman shifted toward second base, toward first base, deep, or shallow?
16. Is the first baseman shifted toward second base, toward the foul line, deep, or shallow?
17. Which infielder has the strongest arm (pitcher, catcher, first baseman, second baseman, third baseman, shortstop)?
18. Which infielder has the weakest arm (pitcher, catcher, first baseman, second baseman, third baseman, shortstop)?
19. In fastpitch, is the infield in a bunt defense? If so, which one (first and third in; first in, third back; first back, third in)?

Figure 9.2
Reading a Defensive Situation

1. What inning is it?
2. What is the score?
3. How many outs are there?
4. Are any runners on base? Which bases?
5. How fast are the runners on base?
6. Is the batter right- or left-handed?
7. What is the batter's running speed?
8. What type of batter is at the plate (strong pull hitter, line drive hitter, long-ball hitter, contact hitter)?
9. Can the batter hit to the opposite field? Can the batter hit with power to the opposite field?
10. Is the batter a good bunter (fastpitch)?
11. What is the ball-and-strike count?
12. How does the pitcher like to pitch to the batter (inside, outside, high, low)?

what inning it is, how many outs there are, where the runners are, what the batter's responsibility is, where the defense is positioned, and, as the at-bat continues, what the ball-and-strike count is. Before every pitch, defensive players should know the number of outs, the position of runners on base, and the ball-and-strike count on the batter. Get to know these lists so that reviewing them becomes a habit before and during your at-bat and when you are on defense.

Fastpitch is still a pitcher's game. Although the pitching distance in fastpitch has been moved back to 43 feet (13.1 meters) for collegiate women and is 46 feet (14.0 meters) for men's ASA, the increased distance has not seemed to have had the desired effect of making fastpitch more of a hitter's game at the elite level. Because of the normal depth positioning of the fastpitch outfielders, a single going directly to an outfielder will seldom score a runner from second base. A ball hit in the gap between outfielders or over the head of outfielders is normally needed to score a runner from second base. Therefore, it is advantageous in fastpitch softball to get runners to third base with less than two outs so that the runner can score on a single or a sacrifice fly ball. Because pitching still dominates the fastpitch game, the sacrifice bunt and the suicide squeeze are major offensive weapons used to advance runners and even to score runs. In addition, hitting behind the runner; drag, sacrifice, surprise, push, and slash bunting; the hit-and-run and run-and-hit; and steals are offensive strategies commonly used to advance runners into scoring position and score runs. Because of the many fastpitch offensive options, the defense must be able to respond to those options by using effective defensive strategies. The fastpitch offensive tactics of bunts, running slap hits, hit-and-runs, run-and-hits, and steals as well as the defensive responses to those tactics are described in this step.

SACRIFICE, SURPRISE, PUSH, AND SLASH BUNTS

In fastpitch softball, moving runners into scoring position with less than two outs increases the likelihood of the runners being able to score on a base hit, a sacrifice fly, or a defensive error. The sacrifice bunt (see step 5) is a relatively high-percentage play to advance runners into scoring position. It is typically used when there are no outs or one out, with a runner on first base, runners on first and second base, or, in certain instances, with a runner on second base. The surprise, push, and slash bunts are lower-percentage plays, but they can be equally productive and make it more difficult for the defense to know what the offensive tactic will be. Therefore, a team that has the ability to use a variety of offensive bunting tactics is less predictable, making the short game more productive.

The bunter is responsible for seeing what the defense is doing so she can place the bunt in the best spot to successfully move the runners. Does the defense charge hard? If so, she needs to place the bunt so that the fielder has to move to one side, preventing the fielder from having a good opportunity to get the lead runner. Or, if the batter is able, she may choose to use the push or slash bunt (see step 5) to put the ball by or over the fielders. Is the defense staying back? If so, hitting a soft bunt down the first- or third-base side is an option.

If one or more of your teammates have attempted a bunt before you are asked to bunt, you should have had an opportunity to see what the defense does on a bunt. If you are the first player asked to sacrifice bunt, you may want to square to bunt on the first pitch but take the pitch (do not offer to bunt at it) in order to see what the defense does. Remember, your job is to move the runner or runners to the next base. If you get on base while accomplishing your job, it is a bonus!

Bunting is not allowed in slow pitch because of the distance that the corner infielders play from home plate. If the first and third basemen in fastpitch played at the same depth as their counterparts in slow pitch, any bunt on the ground down either baseline would be a hit most of the time. Hitting in slow pitch is so strong that the first and third basemen would be in serious jeopardy from a hit ball if they had to play closer to

home plate to protect against the bunt. Therefore, bunting or intentionally hitting the ball weakly (full-swing bunt) in the infield is against the rules in slow-pitch softball.

In most sacrifice bunt situations in fastpitch softball, the resolve of the defense is to deny the sacrifice and get the lead runner out. When one run can mean victory, the defense needs to keep runners out of scoring position. Aggressive bunt defense is a necessity for a successful advanced-level fastpitch team and can be very important for less experienced teams.

The way that the defense will counter the strategy used in a sacrifice bunting situation depends on several factors. The first is the game situation—Is the potential run represented by the lead runner important? Second, the position of the runners on base dictates where the play on the lead runner will be. With a runner on first base only, the play on the lead runner will be to second base. The play will be to third when runners are on first and second. Therefore, in addition to covering first base, the defense needs to cover the base to which the lead runner is going. Although the intent is to get the lead runner, if that play is not likely to be successful, the batter-runner must be put out at first base. Third, the skills of the players involved in the bunt defense and the skills of the offensive players will help determine the defensive coverage scheme. Do the first and third basemen have good reaction times? Can they react quickly to a push or slash bunt after charging home plate? Is the pitcher quick enough off the pitching rubber to be able to field a bunt on the first- or third-base side if those fielders stay back to cover their respective bases? How fast are the lead runner and the batter-runner? What are the tendencies of the offensive team? Do they use a run-and-bunt, or do they use a safety sacrifice in which the runner, after taking a good lead on the pitch, must see the ball go down toward the ground before going to the next base? Can the batter be influenced not to bunt by a hard-charging defense at the corners? On the other hand, is the batter a good slash or push bunter? These are some of the questions that must be answered as a team prepares its bunt defensive scheme for an opponent.

The offensive team will ask many of the same questions to make decisions about whether to use the sacrifice bunt, where to place it, and if they should run-and-bunt or use a safety sacrifice. If the batter has the skill (which she should!), she must also decide whether or not to use the slash or push bunt to thwart a charging defense. When the sacrifice bunt is anticipated, the pitcher will try to keep the pitch up in the strike zone, trying to force the bunter to pop the ball in the air. The batter must be disciplined enough to only bunt strikes and to lay off pitches up in the zone.

Teams with mostly less experienced players may have limited offensive options. It is difficult for less experienced players to read the defense and make split-second decisions about whether to bunt, push, or slash and then make the necessary adjustments. More experienced players will be able to read the defense and make the best offensive decisions. The offensive options will be presented based on what the defense is doing, and the batter is responsible for making the necessary adjustments. For less experienced players, the coach may call the option to be used regardless of what the defense does. This allows the less experienced players to use the skills in a game situation without having to make decisions. It also makes the defense unsure of what offensive strategy will be used.

Having a sound offensive and defensive strategy for the bunt is an important part of fastpitch softball. For each of the following bunting situations, potential offensive tactics and defensive strategies are presented.

Runner on First Base

Offensive option 1. With a runner on first base, the batter squares to bunt and puts the bunt down. The baserunner takes a lead, sees the bunt down, and runs to second base. The baserunner should be prepared to slide straight into second base and pop up, ready to run to third. This option is most effective if the defense is not charging aggressively.

Offensive option 2. The batter squares to bunt and reads the defense. If the defense is aggressive and charging hard, the batter attempts to push or slash bunt past the defense. If the defense is not charging, the batter drops the bunt down (see offensive option 1).

Offensive option 3. The run-and-bunt option is more aggressive and more risky. In this option, the baserunner leaves on the pitch, and the batter has the responsibility to square early and get the bunt down. The runner peeks toward home without breaking stride and will only put on the brakes and attempt to get back to first if the ball is popped up. If the ball is not bunted, the baserunner continues to second as though he were stealing. If the ball is bunted, the play will most likely go to first, and the baserunner should anticipate going all the way to third. This can be a very effective play, particularly with a fast team.

The defense has three options for countering the situation when a runner is on first base, although the first option is used by the majority of teams and is considered to be the best option.

Defensive option 1. Before the pitch, the first and third basemen move to positions approximately halfway to home. The second baseman shifts slightly toward first base, and the shortstop shifts slightly toward second base, their respective covering responsibilities. As the batter squares around to bunt, the first and third basemen charge the plate and then stop in a low fielding position approximately 15 feet (4.5 meters) from the batter. To protect their faces, they should hold their gloves at about shoulder height. If the ball is bunted, they have the time to lower their gloves, but if the ball is slashed, their raised gloves will protect their faces. The second baseman and shortstop begin to move toward the bases they are to cover; however, they must watch and see the ball bunted before committing to the base. They must be ready to react to a push or slash bunt hit toward their vacated positions. The center fielder moves toward a back-up position at second base. The left fielder moves to back up a slash bunt or hit to the regular shortstop position, especially if she sees the shortstop moving to the base before the ball is bunted. If the ball is bunted, the left fielder runs from the position backing up shortstop to a position backing up third to protect against the runner going all the way to third when the play is made to first base. This is particularly important if the third baseman fields the bunt. Some teams will have the catcher or the pitcher cover third in this case, but the left fielder should always be there as a safety in case the player responsible for the coverage does not get there in time. The danger of having the left fielder as the primary coverage is that there will be no back-up for an overthrow on a play to third, resulting in at least one run scoring. If the third baseman does not field the bunt, she returns to cover third base, and the left fielder backs up the base on any play made there.

While this is happening, the right fielder is positioned off the line behind the second-base hole and not too deep. She must be prepared to field a ball slashed or hit through the hole if the second baseman moves toward first before the ball is bunted. Once the ball is bunted, the right fielder must move to a back-up position behind first base for any throw going to that base. The pitcher assumes a fielding position at the front edge of the 8-foot (2.4-meter) circle. She does not charge in toward home because she needs to protect against the push or slash bunt. The catcher prepares to field a ball that falls directly in front of the plate, and also—of greater importance—she directs the play by calling the base that the play should be made to. The catcher is the only defensive player who is facing the field of play and can see the relative positions of the runner, the batter-runner, and the other defensive players. The catcher should make the call just as the fielder is beginning to field the ball so that the fielder knows early enough where the play will be. This will enable the fielder to move smoothly from the fielding to the throwing position. The defensive players should anticipate making the throw to second base and make the adjustment if the catcher calls for the throw to go to first.

Defensive option 2. Although defensive option 1 is more desirable for the defense and provides the best combination of aggressive play and defensive protection, sometimes a team may decide to have the first baseman stay back and cover first and have the pitcher cover the bunt on the first-base side. If the first baseman is slow or immobile, a team might select this option. Everything else is the same as in option 1, except the second baseman stays in position and does not cover first. This allows her to cover second if the ball is hit or slashed to the shortstop. The danger of using this option is that the middle of the infield is open for the push or slash bunt. The pitcher must be anticipating the bunt and must begin to move toward the first-base side after releasing the pitch and seeing the batter square to bunt. It would be difficult for the pitcher to change directions and make the play on a ball hit up the middle. This

defense should not be used if the offense is known for their ability to push or slash bunt.

Defensive option 3. This defensive option may be used against a team that is very skilled in the push or slash bunt and is difficult to defend. This option will help ensure that the defense gets an out, but the out will usually be at first base. The first and third basemen play in front of their bases but do not begin to charge the bunt until it has been put on the ground. Because of the delay in fielding, the play will most likely have to go to first. The speed of the batter will determine how far in front of first or third the fielders will start. This defense can prevent the baserunner from getting the extra base, and it protects against the use of the push or slash bunt more effectively than defensive option 1.

Runners on First and Second Base

Offensive option 1. The batter squares to bunt and places the bunt down. The baserunners take a lead, see the bunt down, and run to the next base. The baserunners should be prepared to slide straight into the base. If the defense is keeping the third baseman back, the hitter should try to bunt the ball down the third-base line.

Offensive option 2. The hitter squares to bunt and reads the defense. If the defense is aggressive and charging hard, the hitter attempts to push or slash bunt past the defense. If the defense is not charging at third, the hitter drops the sacrifice bunt down the third-base line (see offensive option 1) or attempts to push or slash bunt between and past the pitcher and first baseman. If the pitcher is covering the bunt down the third-base line, the hitter attempts to push or slash bunt up the middle in the space vacated by the pitcher.

Offensive option 3. The run-and-bunt option is more aggressive and more risky, especially in this situation because of the potential for a triple play. However, an aggressive play such as this might surprise the defense and cause a throwing error because so much is happening. In this option, the baserunners leave on the pitch, and the batter has the responsibility to square early and get the bunt down. The runners peek toward home without breaking stride and only put on the brakes and attempt to get back to the base they left if the ball is popped up. If the ball is not bunted, the baserunners continue to the next base as though it was a double steal. This can be a very effective play, particularly with a fast team.

Defensively, the coverage is the same as for defensive option 1 with a runner on first base, with a few exceptions. In the first defensive option with runners on first and second, the shortstop covers third base and leaves second base uncovered. Chances are the play is either going to be made on the lead runner going to third base or the batter-runner going to first. The center fielder moves in to cover a possible throw to second if the runner from first makes an aggressive turn around second base. In the second defensive option, the third baseman stays back to cover third base, and the pitcher covers a bunt to the third-base side.

Runner on Second Base

Offensive option 1. The hitter squares to bunt and places the bunt down. The baserunner at second takes a lead, sees the bunt down, and runs to third. The baserunner should be prepared to slide to the outfield side of the base to force the fielder to reach around for the tag. Remember, this is a tag play, so it is more difficult for the defense to get the baserunner out. If the defense is keeping the third baseman back, and the pitcher is covering the third-base line, the hitter should try to bunt the ball down the third-base line.

Offensive option 2. This option is the same as offensive option 1, except the baserunner takes a lead, makes the defense look at him, and waits until the ball is released for the throw to first before going to third. Again, the baserunner should slide to the outfield side of the base.

Offensive option 3. The hitter squares to bunt and reads the defense. If the defense is aggres-sive and charging hard, the hitter attempts to push or slash bunt past the defense. If the defense is not charging at third, the hitter drops the sacrifice bunt down the third-base line or attempts to push or slash bunt between and past the pitcher and first baseman. If the pitcher is covering the bunt down the third-base line, the hitter attempts to push or slash bunt up the middle in the space vacated by the pitcher. The runner takes a lead and goes when the ball is down, sliding into the outfield side of third base. If the play goes to third, the batter-runner should look to go to second.

Offensive option 4. In the run-and-bunt option, the baserunner leaves on the pitch, and the bat-ter has the responsibility to square early and get the bunt down. The runner peeks toward home without breaking stride and only puts on the brakes and attempts to get back to second if the ball is popped up. If the ball is not bunted, the baserunner continues to third base as though it was a steal. This can be risky because there is the potential for a double play. If the ball is not bunted and the catcher has a strong arm, the baserunner could be thrown out at third, taking a runner in scoring position off the bases.

With a runner at second, the defensive op-tions are the same as for runners at first and second, with slight modifications. Because the runner at second does not have to run to third, the coverage of second by the center fielder is very important. However, fielders must remem-ber that the center fielder has no back-up, so any throws made to second must be accurate. If the runner is not going on the bunt, the defense should check the runner and make the throw to first, with the second baseman covering. The sec-ond baseman should be ready to make a return throw to third because the runner will most likely leave for third on the release of the throw.

Sacrifice, Surprise, Push, and Slash Bunt Drill 1.
React to the Defense, Alternating

The defense alternates charging aggressively and staying back on every other pitch. The bunter attempts to alternate placing the bunt down (de-fense stays back) and pushing or slashing the ball (defense charging). Use each offensive situation: runner on first; runners on first and second; runner on second. All nine players can be in position and practice their appropriate defensive responsibili-ties (coverage and back-up), or only the infielders, pitcher, and catcher can be involved.

Sacrifice, Surprise, Push, and Slash Bunt Drill 2.
React to the Defense, Random

This drill is similar to drill 1, except that the defensive strategy changes randomly and the batter does not know what the defense will do until the pitch is coming in. The bunter must respond to the defense and attempt to place the bunt down if the defense stays back or attempt to push or slash the ball if the defense charges. The defensive strategy option can be called by the teacher, coach, or a player.

Sacrifice, Surprise, Push, and Slash Bunt Drill 3.
Pressure Points

This practice activity is designed to put pressure on the batter by forcing her to bunt, push, or slash the first strike. For this activity, divide players into three groups—a hitting group, a fielding group, and a practice group—with at least six players per group. If you don't have enough players for three groups, eliminate the practice group. Each group needs a pitcher and a catcher. If you don't have enough pitchers and catchers, either rotate them in and out of the fielding group or use a coach as the pitcher. Place the fielders in the infield positions. Because the primary focus of this activity is on the bunter being successful, the fielders can either play out the bunt or simply field the bunt and give the ball to the pitcher.

Each person in the bunting group will have an opportunity to bunt two times before the groups rotate. Points are earned only by the bunting group. The bunting group gets 1 point for each successful bunt, push, or slash put down on the first strike. If the batter does not offer at the strike, fouls it off, or pops it up, the at-bat is over and the bunting group does not earn a point. Regardless of the success of the bunt, the batter should run out each attempt, being sure to get into foul territory as quickly as possible and run straight through first base.

The practice group works off to the side in groups of three (tosser, fielder, bunter). These players work on bunts only unless a protective screen is available. After the bunting group completes two rounds, they move to the field, the fielders move to practice, and the practice group moves to bunt.

SQUEEZE BUNT

A fastpitch team needs to take advantage of an offensive situation in which a runner is on third base and there are less than two outs. Advancing that runner means the team scores a run. Runs are hard to come by in fastpitch, so that runner on third needs to be brought home somehow. With a good contact hitter or long-ball hitter at bat, the base hit or sacrifice fly to score the run are viable strategy options. Another option used in fastpitch softball is a *squeeze bunt play.*

For the squeeze bunt, the element of surprise is advantageous, unlike the offensive situation when executing the sacrifice bunt. The defense at first and third will tend to charge the plate when the batter shows that she is going to bunt. Because the play will be made at home, the farther away from home plate those two fielders are when the bunt is put down, the better. The pitcher is the other fielder usually involved in making a play on the squeeze bunt. That player's distance from home plate is governed by the pitching distance and can only be altered after the pitch is delivered. To maintain the element of surprise on a squeeze bunt, the batter delays moving into the sacrifice bunting position in the batter's box. Rather than squaring when the pitcher's arm is at the top of the windup , the batter waits until the pitch is released. The batter must pivot quickly and get the bat into bunting position so that she can see the ball well. Just as with the sacrifice bunt, the batter's responsibility is to put the ball on the ground, making it difficult for the defense to make the play on the runner coming home. The likelihood of a successful squeeze bunt is increased when the batter gets a good look at the pitch coming in, just as it was with the sacrifice bunt. However, in executing the squeeze bunt, the batter does not have as much time to see the ball. In addition, the batter's role can be complicated by what the runner has been instructed to do. The defense should anticipate the squeeze bunt in this situation, especially if there is a fast runner at third and a batter who is not known as a fly ball hitter and hits for a low average.

For each of the offensive options for the squeeze bunt, the element of surprise is important. If the first pitch is not bunted when the squeeze play is called, the element of surprise is gone, and the batter will probably be asked to hit away on the next pitch.

Offensive option 1. In the suicide squeeze, the baserunner at third leaves on the pitch, and the batter must bunt the next pitch, or at least foul it off, to protect the baserunner coming home. The baserunner should attempt to slide to the back of home plate, making the tag play more difficult for the catcher. If the batter does not bunt the pitch, the baserunner should put on the brakes and attempt to get into a rundown, hoping for an errant throw that allows her to get back to third or maybe even score.

Offensive option 2. In the safety squeeze, the runner will take a big lead on the pitch and continue home only if the bunt is put down success-

fully and she thinks she can make it home. The hitter does not have to try to bunt a difficult pitch or one that is way out of the strike zone. This option is much less risky but can be very effective, especially with a fast runner at third.

Defensive option 1. If it is a close game and the runner is going home on the pitch (a suicide squeeze), this is really the only option. The third and first basemen should anticipate the possibility of the squeeze play and creep in toward home. As soon as the batter squares, the first and third basemen should charge hard toward home, and the pitcher should charge after the release of the pitch. The catcher should get in position to receive the flip toss from the fielder and attempt to make the tag play on the baserunner. The shortstop should cover third in case the baserunner chooses to get into a rundown. The defense must also keep the batter-runner from going to second during the play at home, so the center fielder must come in to cover second base.

Defensive option 2. If the offense decides to use a safety squeeze—in which the baserunner will take a big lead on the pitch and continue to home only if the bunt is put down successfully—the defense has a little more time to get the ball home. Again, in most instances, the play at home should be the first option (see defensive option 1).

Defensive option 3. If the defensive team has a comfortable lead, the objective should be to get a sure out. In this instance, the first and third basemen should charge the bunt, but they should make the throw to first, with the second baseman covering.

RUNNING SLAP

The running slap can be an effective weapon, especially for teams with good speed. The running slap adds an additional dimension to the offensive tactics available to a team and increases the defensive challenge.

Offensive option 1. The objective for a running slapper is to put the ball where the defense is not. Therefore, the first option is for the slapper to attempt to place the ball to the left side of the infield on the ground in a place that makes the fielders

move right or left. Because this is a skill designed to be used by runners who have good to excellent speed, the fielder's movement before fielding the ball should give the slapper the time to reach first base safely.

Offensive option 2. For more experienced slappers, the second option is to attempt to hit the ball over the heads of the infielders. This forces the defense to protect against two possibilities, making the slap more difficult to defend.

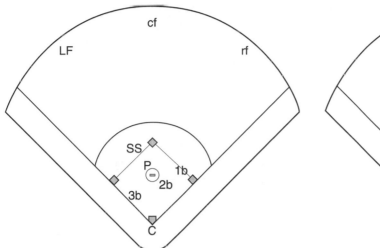

Figure 9.3 Running slap prevent defense.

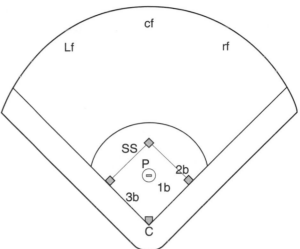

Figure 9.4 Variation of the running slap prevent defense.

Offensive option 3. This option is again for more experienced slappers who can switch hit or are natural left-handed batters who can perform the running slap. In this option, the batter alternates between taking a full swing from a regular batting stance and performing the running slap. If the defense is in a running slap prevent defense, the batter takes a full swing. When the defense retreats to normal depth, the batter becomes a running slapper. This offensive option is very difficult to defend, and an experienced slapper with this skill is usually very effective.

Defensive option 1. The most common defensive strategy for the running slap is a prevent defense (figure 9.3). In this defensive alignment, the first baseman plays back, even with or behind first base. The second baseman plays up, even with the pitching rubber about halfway between the first-base line and the pitching rubber. The third baseman plays in, just off the line. The shortstop plays even with the baseline, filling the space between the pitcher and the third baseman. The left and center fielders play at a short depth. The right fielder plays at regular depth, defending against the possibility of a full-swing hit. The goal of this strategy is to get the hitter out at first. When there is a runner on first, this strategy will force the defense to go for the out at first, allowing the baserunner to move to the next base.

Defensive option 2. This defense is also a prevent defense, with a slight variation from defensive option 1. All fielders play in the same position as in option 1, except the first and second basemen switch positions (figure 9.4). This allows the first baseman to play in, and the second baseman plays back. In this alignment, these fielders play at depths that they are more used to.

Defensive option 3. The third defensive option is for the infield to play in, similar to the positioning for a bases-loaded situation: second baseman and shortstop even with the baseline; third and first basemen halfway down the baseline. This enables the defense to adequately defend against the running slapper who can also take a full swing. It is a compromise defense, because it gives a little advantage to the very fast slapper (since the defense is playing further back than in options 1 and 2), but it does allow the defense to counter the possibility of the full-swing hit. This option also allows the defense to be able to get the lead runner when runners are on base.

STEALS

Teams that have the capacity to advance runners via stealing bases have a tremendous advantage, because they do not have to waste an out on a sacrifice bunt or other play that has the potential for producing an out. Stealing also has the potential for making an out. However, runners such as Coco Crisp in baseball and Natasha Watley of the U.S. Olympic softball team have a high base-stealing percentage, meaning they are safe in the majority of their steal attempts. The successful base stealer not only has the physical ability to run fast, but also has studied pitchers and their deliveries, as well as the timing of getting the jump start allowed by the rules.

In fastpitch, the runner cannot leave the base until the ball leaves the pitcher's hand. For the runner on first base, the right-handed pitcher's hand is hidden from view by the pitcher's body. However, a study of pitching deliveries would reveal that for most pitchers the step with the left foot (for a right-handed pitcher), which is readily visible from first base, is timed with the release of the ball. Most base stealers will time their jump off the base with the pitcher's striding foot hitting the ground.

Runner on First, Stealing Second

This is the most common situation for stealing. Usually, the coach will determine when a runner should steal, but in some situations, runners will make the decision. For a steal to be most effective, there should be a positive count (2 balls, 1 strike; 2 balls, 0 strikes; and so forth) on the batter, which makes it possible for the batter to take a pitch or swing and miss to protect the runner. The runner attempts to get a good jump on the pitcher. If the coach calls the steal and the batter knows not to hit the pitch, the stealer should run straight to second, using a hook slide. If the runner is stealing on her own, then after two or three steps she should peek in at home to make sure the ball was not hit into the air.

Defensive option 1. The most common strategy for defending against a runner stealing second is to have the shortstop cheat over toward second; however, the shortstop should hold his position until the pitch crosses the plate. The shortstop has to defend against the possibility of the batter hitting the ball into the hole created by the shortstop moving too soon to cover second base. As soon as the runner breaks toward second, the second baseman should yell "going" to alert the catcher and shortstop that the runner is stealing second. The shortstop moves to cover second, using the technique described in step 7. The second baseman moves into a back-up position behind second base.

Defensive option 2. This defensive strategy is more common in baseball but is occasionally seen in softball. The shortstop or second baseman covers the steal, depending on whether the batter is right- or left-handed. For a right-handed batter, the second baseman covers second. For a left-handed batter, the shortstop covers. This prevents creating a hole on the batter's strong side.

Runner on Second, Stealing Third

This offensive option can be very effective, especially with a team that has a good short game. When the defensive team has to defend against the bunt or running slap, this forces the shortstop and third baseman to play in, leaving third base vulnerable. Also, in a game situation with a right-handed batter up to bat, the batter is in the way of the catcher's throw to third. Therefore, after catching the pitch, the catcher must step in front of or behind the batter to make the throw. This delay in getting the throw away is often enough time for the steal of third to be successful. The runner at second or the coach should look for this defensive alignment and wait for a positive count on the batter. The stealer should attempt to slide to the outfield side of third, forcing the fielder to reach to make the tag.

Defensive option 1. Because this is a potential bunting situation, the third baseman typically plays in. Therefore, the shortstop cheats toward third, being sure that she can get there ahead of the runner.

Defensive option 2. The pitcher covers the third-base side in case of a bunt. The third baseman stays back to defend against the steal of third.

Runners on First and Second, Double Steal

This offensive tactic can cause havoc for even the most experienced defensive teams. It is almost impossible to get both runners out, and if the double steal is done at the most opportune time, the split second of defensive confusion can result in both runners safely stealing the bases. Again, the stealers should be running on a positive count and looking for advantageous defensive alignments (fielders playing in or at slap defense depths).

Runners on First and Third, Double Steal

The objective for this offensive tactic is to score a run. This double steal option can be attempted with less than two outs or with two outs. Offensive and defensive tactics vary depending on the number of outs.

Less Than Two Outs

With less than two outs, the objective is to score a run or at least move the runner on first into scoring position. The runner on first steals second, leaving on the release of the pitch and sliding to the outfield side of second base. The runner on third takes a small lead, trying to avoid having the catcher throw down to third. Before making the move to steal home, the runner on third should look for the following: The throw to second is high over the head of a cut player or goes straight into second base; the throw is in the dirt; or the throw is off line. The runner on third needs to make sure that the throw is not going straight to third and that the defense is not trying to trick the runner by throwing the ball to the pitcher or to another fielder. The batter should take the pitch and do nothing to distract the catcher from being able to make the throw.

With less than two outs, the defense is going to be aggressive and attempt to get an out and prevent the run from scoring. When the runner on first breaks for second, the catcher takes a quick look at third, making sure the runner is not too far off third, which would create a pickoff opportunity. The catcher then throws the ball to second. In the meantime, the second baseman cuts in halfway between the pitching rubber and second base, and the shortstop covers second for the steal. The second baseman has to make a split-second decision just before the ball passes by her position—Is the runner far enough off third to allow her to be thrown out or forced into a rundown? If the answer is yes, the second baseman cuts the throw and either throws the ball to third or home or runs at the runner, forcing a movement to home or third. A throw is then made to the appropriate base, resulting in a rundown.

If the second baseman decides that the runner at third is not too far off the base, she allows the throw to go into second base, attempting to get the runner stealing from first. If the runner on third breaks for home at that point, the shortstop should attempt to get the out at second and then make the throw home. If the shortstop thinks that she has a sure out at home, she can choose not to make a tag attempt and throw directly home. However, in this option, she must be sure to get at least one out.

In a less aggressive option, but one that does attempt to get an out and prevent a run from scoring, the catcher fakes a throw toward second and then throws quickly to third. In this option, the defense gives up the runner moving to second with the hopes of getting the runner at third out and preventing the run from scoring. This option can be used with two outs or less than two outs.

The least aggressive defense is often used when a team cannot afford to have a run score. This option can be used with two outs or less than two outs. In this option, the catcher pops up and makes it look as if the throw is going to second. Instead, the throw goes directly to the pitcher. The hope is that the runner at third will think the throw is going through and will take a large enough lead to get picked off. However, typically there is no pickoff throw, the runner at third stays at third, and the runner on first moves to second uncontested.

Two Outs

With two outs, the runner at first begins running to second on the release of the pitch, but she runs at a jogging speed. As soon as the catcher throws the ball to second base, the runner stops and attempts to get into a rundown. At the same time, the runner on third inches her way down the third-base line, looking for the right moment to break for home. The runner on third waits for the rundown to begin and looks for the following to make the attempt toward home:

- If the first baseman is a lefty, the runner on third should break for home on the release of the second baseman's throw to first. A left-handed first baseman will have to catch the ball and turn all the way around to make the throw home.

- If the first baseman is right-handed, then the runner at third should break for home on the release of the first baseman's throw to second. The second baseman will have to spin around and will have a longer throw to home.

If the defense chooses to ignore the runner at third and attempts to get the third out by tagging the runner in the rundown between first and second, the job of the runner in the rundown is to not get tagged out until the runner from third crosses home plate. In effect, the runner on first is sacrificed to score the run. If she is tagged before the run crosses the plate, it is the third out and no run scores. If the run scores first, it counts.

If the defense makes no play, the runner from first should jog into second, putting two runners in scoring position. The batter should take the pitch.

With two outs, the defensive goal is to get the third out before the run scores, or at the very least, prevent the runner at first from advancing. If the runner at first gets into a rundown, fielders should attempt to run the runner back to first base while keeping an eye on the runner at third. If the runner at third breaks toward home, the ball should immediately be thrown to the catcher covering home. If the fielders playing the rundown can minimize or eliminate throws, they have the best chance of preventing the run from scoring.

Delayed Steal

The delayed steal can be attempted with less than two outs or with two outs. The runner on first takes a lead on the pitch and begins to walk back to the base after the pitch crosses home plate (the batter takes the pitch). If the catcher does not wait until the runner returns to first before throwing the ball back to the pitcher, the runner waits for the release of the throw by the catcher to the pitcher. The runner turns and runs toward second as soon as the throw is released. (The runner must be off the base and moving toward second when the pitcher receives the throw. If the runner goes back to the base and then leaves after the pitcher has the ball, the runner is out.) The intent of this option is to confuse the defense. If the pitcher turns and throws the ball to second, the runner on third, with less than two outs, should break for home. If there are two outs, the runner from first should stop when the throw goes to second and get into a rundown. It then becomes a first-and-third situation with two outs.

To protect against the delayed steal, the catcher should always pay attention to the runner on first and make sure that he returns to the bag. The first baseman should cover the bag. However, if faced with a delayed steal tactic, the pitcher should immediately turn and throw the ball to second with the shortstop covering. The shortstop should be on the bag after every pitch to protect against the steal. The shortstop then runs the runner from first back to the bag while watching the runner on third.

Stealing Drill 1. *First to Second*

This drill requires six people: a runner at first base, two additional runners waiting off first base in foul territory, a pitcher, a catcher, and a shortstop or second baseman. On a regulation softball field, all players take their normal positions. All runners must wear helmets, and the catcher should be in full catching gear. To provide additional experience as a fielder covering second base for the throw from the catcher, alternate coverage coming from the shortstop position and the second baseman position.

Before starting this drill, all players should review the methods of leaving a base on a steal (figures 6.5 and 6.6, pages 119 and 120). More experienced players will probably already have a preferred method of leaving the base. However, this drill provides the opportunity in a nongame situation to practice different methods. Runners should slide into second base during the drill, so participants should also review the hook slide and down-and-up slide (figures 6.7 and 6.8, page121).

The drill begins with the pitcher delivering a pitch to the catcher. As the ball leaves the pitcher's hand, the runner begins to steal second base. The fielder moves to cover second base. Players will probably find it easier to move from shortstop than from second base to get into position straddling the base to make the tag play. Practicing this drill from both positions will increase a player's overall skill as an infielder and make her a more valuable and versatile team member. Whatever technique is used for covering second base, make sure the player does not have her left foot and leg on the first-base side of second base between the base and the oncoming runner.

The runner must slide into second base. The preferred slide would be a hook slide to the outfield side of second, hooking the base with the left foot, in order to make the tag more difficult for the fielder. Before starting the slide, the runner should look to see if the throw gets by the fielder. If so, the runner should use the down-and-up slide and be prepared to advance to third base. After completing her steal attempt, the runner then joins the runners waiting in foul territory.

If this is a team practice, rotate position players into their respective positions, for example, pitchers into pitching, catchers into catching, and so forth. If all players are practicing all positions, rotate position players into the running position and runners into the fielding positions after all runners have had five

stealing attempts. All players should get experience as the runner stealing second base.

Although pitchers, catchers, and fielders have an important role in this drill, the practice task is stealing. Therefore, the success check and scoring are only for the runner. The on-deck person acts as observer and verifies the runner's scoring.

Success Check

- Time your leave of the base with the pitcher's release of the ball.
- Use the correct takeoff for your preferred technique.
- Determine the appropriate sliding method based on the position of the fielder and the throw.
- Execute the appropriate slide.

Stealing Drill 2. *Second to Third*

Set up this drill in the game situation described in the previous drill. The third baseman takes a fielding position one-third of the way toward home plate (about 20 feet [6.1 meters]). The shortstop takes her normal fielding position, as do the pitcher and catcher. A right-handed batter takes her stance in the middle or deep in the batter's box. Runners position themselves to run from second base or from first and second. The on-deck runner acts as observer and umpire. Each runner gets five attempts at stealing third base. The third baseman

and the shortstop alternate covering third for the throw from the catcher. The batter can alternate taking the pitch and swinging at the pitch without making contact. In either case, the batter may not move from the batting position to intentionally interfere with the catcher's throw.

Success Check

- Use the hook slide to the outfield side of third base.
- Be safe at third.

Stealing Drill 3.
Double Steal (Runners on First and Third)

This drill is set up the same as the previous two drills. Runners are on first and third, with a batter up to bat. The batter needs to remember that her responsibility is to do nothing that will interfere with the catcher's throw, so she should not swing or fake bunt. She is taking the pitch all the way. The runners will run based on the number of outs and the option that the teacher or coach calls. All

running options should be practiced. The defense should work on the defensive options, reacting to what the runners are doing on the bases. Each runner should have the opportunity to run from each base at least two times with less than two outs and two times with two outs before rotating into a fielding position.

HIT-AND-RUN

The hit-and-run is an offensive tactic that requires a more experienced batter in order to be successful. The batter must be a contact hitter and should not strike out often. This tactic is typically used with a runner on first, but it can be used with a runner on second or runners at first and second.

The baserunner leaves the base on the pitch, stealing the next base. The batter is obligated to protect the runner by making contact with the pitch, whether it is a strike or not. Therefore, the batter must have a positive count (more balls than strikes), increasing the potential for a hittable pitch. The only exception is if the pitch is so poor that the catcher will not be able to catch it (wild pitch). The batter attempts to hit the ball on the ground, with the best result being that the batter hits the ball behind the runner, to the right side. But even a ball hit to the left side can be effective, especially if the shortstop leaves her position early to cover the steal and the ball is hit to the vacated spot. If successful, the results of the hit-and-run can range from avoiding a double play to allowing the runner to go from first to third or from second to home. This tactic can be used effectively with runners who do not have above average speed.

The most effective way for the defense to counter the hit-and-run is to get ahead of the batter early, which will enable the pitcher to make pitches off the plate that might be difficult to hit. If the offensive team is known for hitting the first pitch, the defense could pitch a high pitch early with the intent of forcing a fly ball or pop-up. The defense could even consider using the pitchout on the first pitch. Defensive players, especially the shortstop, must hold their positions until the ball passes the batter so that a ground ball to the shortstop doesn't become a base hit because the shortstop is standing at second base. If the ball is hit, the defense should expect the runner to attempt to take an extra base, especially if the ball is hit behind the runner. The defense should look to get the ball in quickly to the lead base.

RUN-AND-HIT

The run-and-hit takes some of the pressure off the hitter, but it can be a little more risky for the runner. In the run-and-hit, the runner is basically stealing, but the batter has the green light to hit a good pitch or not swing if it is not her pitch. This tactic is designed to be used with baserunners who have above average speed and can successfully steal bases. The baserunner may get the run-and-hit signal without the batter knowing. The sign should be given when there is a positive count on the batter. This allows the batter to respond to the pitch and not worry about what the runner is doing. There is a risk that the batter will hit a fly ball or line drive, resulting in a double play, but if successful, the run-and-hit can result in extra bases or prevent the double play.

The defensive strategy for the run-and-hit is similar to the defense for a steal. With a runner on first, the shortstop must anticipate the potential steal. The shortstop must hold her position until the ball goes by the batter. She must also be able to get into position to cover second for the steal. If the ball is hit, the fielders must be aware that the runner will attempt to take an extra base.

A pitchout can be an effective deterrent to a team that uses the run-and-hit. If the offense thinks there is a chance that a pitchout will be used, they will be more careful about when they call this offensive tactic. A positive pitch count for the batter is the best time to run this play, so the pitcher must try to stay ahead of the batter.

Hit-and-Run or Run-and-Hit Drill 1. *Batting Machine*

A batting machine is used for consistency in pitches to allow for adequate practice opportunities. Place a runner at first with a full defense in the field. The batter starts with a count of two balls, zero strikes. The teacher or coach can call the hit-and-run or run-and-hit on one of the next two pitches. The objective is for the batter to hit the ball on the ground, preferably behind the runner. The runner leaves on the release of the pitch (when it shoots out of the machine) and should attempt to get all the way to third if the ball is hit. The defense should anticipate the attempt when making the play. Each batter should have at least four times at bat.

Hit-and-Run or Run-and-Hit Drill 2. *Live Pitching*

The setup of this practice activity is identical to drill 1, but instead of a machine, a live pitcher is used. This is more gamelike and forces the batter to react to the pitch, which might not be a great one to hit!

ANGLE DOWN

Angle down is an offensive tactic used with runners at second and third with less than two outs. The angle down offense seems to go against some of the basics of softball. With less than two outs and runners on second and third, if a ground ball is hit in the infield, the runner at third will typically wait for the throw to first (if the ball is hit slowly to the right side, she may break for home). In angle down, the runner on third breaks for home and the runner on second breaks for third if they anticipate the ball will be hit on the ground. The batter attempts to run all the way to second base if the initial play is made to home. With this aggressive play, even if the out is made at home, the offense will still have runners at second and third with one or two outs. This is the same situation that would have occurred if the runner had stayed at third. This tactic forces the defense to make a more difficult (and pressure-filled) play at home plate to get an out.

When the offense uses the angle down tactic, the defense is forced to attempt to get the runner who is running from third to home. Therefore, in this situation, the defense should play in (as they normally should with a runner on third) but should anticipate that the first throw will go directly home, without the need for a check of the runner at third. Good communication is needed on the field so that the fielder is aware that the runner on third is breaking for home on contact. Immediately after the play is made at home, the catcher needs to anticipate that the batter will attempt to run to second. It then becomes a first-and-third situation, and the defense needs to play it as such.

Angle Down Drill 1. *Pitching Machine*

A pitching machine is used in this drill to facilitate successful practice attempts. The pitching machine pitches consistently at the same speed and basically in the same location every time. This gives the batter a better chance to hit the ball on the ground and provide the fielders and runners with more opportunities to practice the play. Place a full defense in their positions on the field. The pitcher can feed the machine, and the catcher can either catch the machine pitch or stand behind a catch net and move into catching position after the ball has been contacted. Either way, the catcher should be in full gear. The runners take a lead on the release of pitch out of the machine and react to the hit ball. As soon as contact is made and they believe the ball will hit the ground, they should move to the next base. The batter runs out the hit, attempting to get to second base if the throw goes home.

Angle Down Drill 2. *Live Pitching*

This is the same practice activity as drill 1, except a pitcher is used instead of the machine and the catcher (in full gear) is in position behind home plate.

SUCCESS SUMMARY

Practicing offensive tactics and understanding how to counter those tactics from a defensive perspective are critical to being able to play the game of softball. Players need to understand what options the offensive team has in different game situations, based on the number of outs, the score, the inning, and so on. Review the checklists before every class, practice, or game so that you are ready to play and make good offensive and defensive decisions. Take advantage of practice opportunities so you are ready to play.

In the final two steps, a variety of modified games are presented that you can play to improve your skills. Go play and have fun!

Modified Games

The purpose of modified softball games is two-fold. First, you have the opportunity to see how well you can execute various skills under simulated game conditions. For example, an infielder in a real game gets only one chance to cleanly field the ball and make an accurate throw if the batter hits the ball to her. In addition, in a real game, you never know when the ball will come to you until it is hit. Modified games can be set up to give you the opportunity to see just how proficient you are at reading, reacting, and executing skills in specifically designed game situations. Second, modified games provide you with the opportunity to further develop your understanding of, and ability to execute, techniques of position play and game strategy.

The modified games in this step are presented in progressive order from simple to more complex and from more controlled to less controlled. Players without much game experience should start with the first game presented. More experienced players can look over the games provided and select games that will provide the opportunity to work on skills and strategies appropriate for their current level of play.

GROUNDERS-ONLY TEE BALL

Modified games focus on specific skills, sometimes to the exclusion of other skills. As the name implies, Grounders-Only Tee Ball provides practice opportunities in fielding ground balls that have been hit off a batting tee. Using the tee is not gamelike; it does, however, ensure that the ball is hit on every swing, which provides opportunities for a great number of fielding plays in a relatively short period of time. Despite the fact that this is not the same as hitting off a pitcher, this modified game provides the opportunity to work on hitting technique without having to wait for a pitcher to make good pitches. Also, players get a chance to practice baserunning. The major purpose of this game, though, is to work on fielding ground balls and throwing out runners.

During this game, you are asked to focus on both your skill execution and your ability to apply your knowledge of position play. To be a successful softball player, you must not only have good skill techniques but also know when and how to execute those skills in game situations. The good "four o'clock hitter" is a hitter who hits the ball out of the park during warm-up but doesn't get a base hit during a game.

On defense, knowing how to make the force-out is important, but being able to make the play with the runner coming at you in a game is the mark of a good softball player. Participation in this modified game will help you become a better game player by practicing specific skills. The skills you will use in this game are discussed below. Coaching tips are included for each skill; these tips are primarily intended to help coaches and teachers focus on key elements in order to cue the performance of less experienced players and give feedback to all players. However, you should look over the tips for all of these skills before starting the game. They are your *success checks* and serve as a quick review of the key technique and tactic points you will need for the game.

Basic Skills

The basic skills in Grounders-Only Tee Ball include hitting off a tee, fielding ground balls, making overhand throws of various distances, catching balls, and baserunning.

- When hitting off the tee, use the high-to-low swing to produce a ground ball. Keep your head down and focus on the ball. Adjust your position at the tee to place hit the ball to different infield locations. Defensive players should focus attention on these same hitting points so that they can work on the anticipation skills of reading and reacting to the hit ball.

- When fielding ground balls, move into position to field the ball in front of the body. Keep your head down and watch the ball go into the glove. Remember to field and throw the ball in one smooth, continuous motion.

- When making overhand throws of various distances during infield play, use proper technique for the overhand delivery and move your body in the direction of the throw. Avoid the sidearm throw except where appropriate, such as from the second baseman to first or a feed at second for a double play.

- When catching the ball, focus on the ball. Give with the ball using soft hands.

- For baserunning, focus on the necessity of running full speed over first base, turning to the left toward the field of play, and returning directly to the base. Review what constitutes making an attempt to go to second base after overrunning first base. Remember, just a step toward second is considered an attempt. Work on the spooning technique of rounding a base when there is the possibility of advancing more than one base. Remember the responsibilities of base coaches and their use of both verbal and visual signals to assist baserunners.

Infield Position Play

Area coverage and base-covering and back-up responsibilities are reinforced during the modified game. While working on area coverage, players should define position coverage areas and interaction areas. Focus on calling for fly balls, even if a certain hit ball is an automatic out. Go over base-covering and back-up responsibilities. Review the general principles that apply to ground balls hit to the right side and left side of the infield. Discuss the specifics of base coverage depending on the situations that could develop. Coaches can verbally cue more experienced players just before the batter hits the ball. However, the coach should stop play and set the situation for less experienced players if they appear confused.

Defensive and Offensive Tactics

All kinds of situations can be covered during modified games, including force plays, tag plays, baserunning, and place hitting.

For force plays, review all base-covering responsibilities. Emphasize the importance of the covering fielder moving to the ball side of the base to receive the throw (to cut down on the distance of the throw). Review footing the base and stretching for both on- and off-target throws. Less experienced teams should focus on getting the lead runner. More experienced teams can work on turning the double play.

For tag plays, work on proper footwork to move from the fielding position to a cover position at the base. Review how positioning at the base is based on the runner's path and the direction of the incoming thrown ball. Stress the importance of the fielder placing the ball in the glove at the edge of the base so that the runner coming into the base tags herself out, and then sweeping the glove and ball out of the way to prevent the runner from dislodging the ball from the glove.

For baserunning, review the concepts of being forced or not forced to advance to the next base. Remind runners to take a few steps off the base on a pop-up to the infield. In this game, a pop-up is an automatic out and the ball is dead; no further play can occur, and baserunners must return to the base. Baserunners should watch base coaches for signals.

When working on place hitting, discuss the concept of hitting behind the runner. Emphasize reading the defense and taking advantage of open spaces to hit into. For this game, players should place hit only in the infield area.

Game Rules

1. The infield area, both fair and foul territory, is the only area in which the ball is in play. The outfield is out of play.

2. When hitting the ball off the tee, the batter must hit a ground ball (a hit that makes initial contact with the ground within the infield).

   - Any ball that first lands in the outfield or is touched by a player in the outfield is an automatic out for the team at bat. The ball is dead and baserunners cannot advance.

   - Any fly ball or pop-up is an automatic out. An infield pop-up need not be caught to be an out. However, infielders should practice their fielding skills and attempt to catch the pop-up.

   - Any line drive is an automatic out. As with the pop-up, fielders should practice their fielding skills and attempt to catch the line drive.

   - Any ground ball that is misplayed by an infielder standing in the infield is a legally hit ball. If the misplayed ball goes into the outfield, the ball is out of play. However, the batter takes first base on an error credited to the infielder who misplayed the ball. All other baserunners

advance one base. If the misplayed ball stays in the infield area (including nearby foul territory), the ball stays in play and play continues.

   - Any ball that is not touched by a fielder but first lands in the infield area and goes into the outfield is a base hit. The ball is out of play, the batter takes first base with a single, and all other baserunners advance one base.

3. Each team is made up of six players: pitcher, catcher, first baseman, second baseman, third baseman, and shortstop.

4. Each team gets six outs per turn at bat. These six outs constitute a half inning. Teams change offensive and defensive roles after each half inning.

5. Use a batting tee. The pitcher plays at the defensive position of pitcher but does not pitch the ball to the batter.

6. The batting order follows the order of position number—1 through 6, or pitcher through shortstop.

7. A baserunner cannot leave a base until the ball is hit.

8. All other situations are governed by the official softball rules, such as those found in the *ASA Official Rules of Softball*.

Scoring

Every offensive and defensive play executed correctly adds 1 point to your team's score. For every error you commit, 1 point is subtracted from your team's score. The team with more points at the end of the game (an equal number of half innings of play) is the winner. Note: The purpose of the game is to work on game concepts and the execution of skills during gamelike conditions. Therefore, performance points, not runs scored, determine which team does better.

Look over the player score sheet (figure 10.1) to see the actions that typically occur in this game, actions for which you can both earn and lose points. Use the player score sheet to keep track of the points you contribute to your team's score. A team score sheet is also provided so that each player's points can be tallied into the total team score.

Figure 10.1
Grounders-only Tee-ball score sheet

Name _____ Position _____

Skill or concept	Plus performance points	Minus performance points

Hitting off the tee
   Ground balls
   Fly balls
	____
	____
		____
		____

Baserunning
   Overrun first base
   Round a base
	____
	____
		____
		____

Defensive skills
   Field grounder
   Overhand throw (not toss)
   Catch thrown ball
	____
	____
	____
		____
		____
		____

Area coverage
   Cover base
   Cover area
   Back up play
	____
	____
	____
		____
		____
		____

Game concepts
   Force play
   Tag play
   Baserunning
	____
	____
	____
		____
		____
		____

Totals	____	____

Team Score Sheet

Position	Player	Plus points	Minus points	Total
1				
2				
3				
4				
5				
6				
			Team score	

When you are out in the field playing defense, you need to remember the plays you make and whether they were correctly executed. Then when your team goes on offense, write down those defensive plays on your player score sheet. When your team is at bat, you can easily keep a record of your offensive tallies.

POSITION-PLAY HALF-FIELD GAMES

The next two modified games use the skills and tactics of position play, ground ball and fly ball fielding, fungo or soft-toss hitting, and baserunning. These games require you to analyze each situation, anticipate the action of the other team, react as the play develops, and apply teamwork skills. This is where the real fun begins—putting together skills and strategy.

These modified games are for the purpose of practicing anticipation and reaction in as many different gamelike situations as possible. Although less experienced players benefit from the repetitions received playing just one position, players should seek to increase their overall tactical knowledge and softball skills by playing different positions during these modified games.

Try to keep yourself in the game for every play. Remember, no one is perfect. Even the most experienced player will make an occasional physical error, such as having a ground ball go between her legs. However, these modified games will give you the opportunity to learn how to forget the error and concentrate on the next play. That is what you must do in a real game! Mental errors also occur, such as forgetting to back up a play at a base or to cover a base when it is your responsibility. Unlike the physical error, mental errors really should not happen. Mental errors occur because you either were not paying attention to the game situation as it developed or you did not know what your responsibilities were in that situation. By this stage of your development as a softball player, neither of these reasons for the mental error is acceptable. Work hard to overcome, not quickly brush off, mental errors. Figure out why you made the error so that you won't make it again. Then get ready for the next pitch!

Half-Field Game, Left Side

There are two half-field games, one that uses the left side of the playing field (from the second baseman's fielding position to the left-field foul line) and one that uses the right side (from the shortstop fielding position to the right-field foul line). Each game requires nine players, organized into three groups of three. In an inning, each of the three groups has a turn to score (as the baserunner group), and each turn is composed of three outs. An inning has three "half innings" for a total of nine outs. Several rules are common to both games:

- A caught fly ball is an out.
- A person can be put out at a base by a force play or a tag play.
- Only the team running the bases can score. Keep track of your group score when you are the baserunner group.
- If the covering player blocks the base when a runner is approaching, the runner is safe, no matter what happens.
- A hit to the wrong side of the field (to right field in the left-side game and to left field in the right-side game) is an automatic out.

For the half-field game, left side, fair territory is the area bounded by the left-field foul line and a line that extends from home plate to the outfield fence, passing just to the right of the second baseman's regular fielding position. One group of three players consists of a catcher, fungo hitter, and third baseman positioned for either slow pitch or fastpitch. A second group contains a center fielder, left fielder, and second baseman. The third group is the baserunners, who are lined up at first base, with one person on the base and the others in foul territory (figure 10.2).

The game begins with one baserunner on

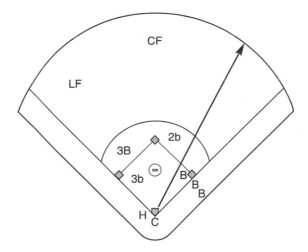

Figure 10.2 Half-field game, left side.

first base. The fungo hitter, though belonging to a different team, acts as the baserunners' teammate. She hits the ball (either fly or grounder) to any place on the field of play. Remember that this game uses only the left side of the field. The fungo hitter should think about where to place the ball to help the lead runner advance. Hint: Try to hit the ball into an area that would be difficult for an infielder or outfielder to field the ball. When possible, hit the ball away from the base to which the lead runner wants to advance.

The defense attempts to make a play on the baserunner. The runner runs to second on a grounder or tags up on a fly ball. The runner must decide whether to try to advance on a fly ball. In any case, if the baserunner is forced or tagged out, it is an out on the running team. If the baserunner makes it safely to second base or beyond, once the play is completed, the ball is returned to the catcher at home. A second runner moves onto first base. Play continues with the fungo hitter again hitting the ball and the fielders making plays on the lead or succeeding runners.

The object of the game is for the baserunners to score as many runs as possible by crossing home plate safely before there are three outs. The infielders, outfielders, and catcher work together to get three outs on the baserunners as quickly as possible.

After three outs, the baserunners rotate to the outfield and second-base positions. The outfielders and second baseman rotate to the hitter, catcher, and third-base positions. The hitter, catcher, and third baseman become the baserunners.

Every inning, rotate roles within your group so that by the end of the game you will have played every position. In doing so, you will play at least a three-inning game (27 outs).

Half-Field Game, Right Side

At the beginning of the section on the half-field game, left side, the rules common to both games were noted. In the half-field game, right side, fair territory is the area bounded by the right-field foul line and a line extending from home plate to the outfield fence, passing just to the left of the shortstop's regular fielding position (figure 10.3). The three groups for this game are as follows:

1. Fungo hitter, third baseman, and first baseman (either slow-pitch or fastpitch position)
2. Shortstop, center fielder, and right fielder
3. Baserunners located at home plate

Because the third baseman's starting position is not in fair territory for the right-side game, her major role is to cover third base and make a tag or force play on any runner coming to third. Any ball hit to her outside of fair territory is an out.

The game begins with one runner at first and the other two at home. The fungo hitter hits the ball anywhere on the modified playing field. When the ball is hit, the first runner at home plate runs to first base as the batter-runner. If the hit is a caught fly ball, the batter-runner is out, and she returns to home plate and goes to the end of the baserunner line.

The runner on first base, meanwhile, runs to second base on a grounder or tags up on a fly

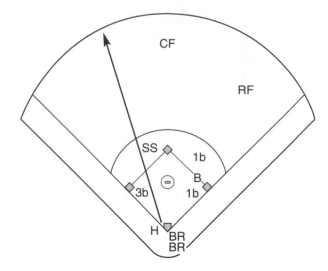

Figure 10.3 Half-field game, right side.

ball. The defensive players attempt to make a play on the lead runner. Once an out is made or play has stopped (baserunners are safe at their bases), the ball is rolled back to the fungo hitter. Play then continues with the fungo hitter hitting another ball.

The object of this game is for the baserunners to score by advancing safely to third base, not home. The object of the game for the defense is to get three outs on the baserunners as quickly as possible. Rotation is similar to the left-side game, and this game is also three innings long.

Another offensive strategy to be practiced is hitting behind the runner. With a runner on first base only and less than two outs, the hitter tries to hit a line drive or ground ball to right field. The baserunner rounds second base and tries to get to third base on the hit to right field.

SITUATION BALL

The modified game Situation Ball requires you to make judgments about how and when to use the various skill responses and game concepts you have developed to date. Although game play in this modified game is less controlled than in previous games in this step, play is still more controlled than in a regulation game; therefore, you will have some time to prepare yourself both physically and mentally for each situation.

Before starting this game, all players should look over the checklists for reading a defensive situation and for reading an offensive situation in step 9 (figures 9.1 and 9.2, page 182). These checklists list factors that you should quickly run through in your mind before every pitch when you are playing defense and when you are at bat. Looking at the lists should provide a quick refresher for all players. Carefully study the list.

Players with little game experience may need to be cued by more experienced teammates or coaches during game play.

Skills to Practice

In a regulation softball game, it may be difficult to get experience with a specific situation because that situation may never present itself in the game! For example, say you and the other outfielders on your team feel that you all need work on throwing out a runner tagging up and trying to score on a fly ball. However, if your opponents never have a runner on third base with less than two outs (or, if they do, the batter doesn't hit a fly ball), you won't get a chance to practice that type of throw. With Situation Ball, however, you can set up almost any situation to practice. For instance, in the case just cited, put a runner on third base, set the situation with no outs, and the offensive team must try to hit a sacrifice fly.

Basic skills to work on include pitching, hitting pitched balls, fielding ground balls, fielding fly balls, throwing overhand, catching the ball, and baserunning. Work on game concepts as well, including position-play area coverage; position-play covering and back-up responsibilities; force and tag plays; double plays; advancing runners with base hits, placed hits, and sacrifice flies; and tag-ups after caught fly balls (fair and foul). Situation Ball also gives you plenty of time to review your knowledge of the rules, including fair and foul balls, pitching and batting regulations, ways a batter may be put out, ways a baserunner may be put out, in-play and out-of-play situations, the infield-fly rule, and the number of innings for a regulation game.

Before playing Situation Ball, be sure you have all necessary equipment (gloves, catcher's gear, batting helmets) and that the equipment is in good condition. Inspect the playing area for any hazards or obstacles.

Game Rules

The following rules and method of playing the game have been established to both facilitate play and ensure that opportunities are presented to work on specific offensive and defensive situations under gamelike conditions. Before the start of the game, members of each team should get together and decide on a specified number of offensive and defensive situations that the teams want to work on. The number of situations will depend on the anticipated number of innings to be played. Next, determine the order for selection of situations to be practiced. For example, team A selects the situation for the odd-numbered innings, and team B selects for the even-numbered innings. Teams should check with each other to see that similar situations are not repeated. Examples of situations you can practice include the following:

- Runner on first base, no outs, 1 out, 2 outs
- Runner on second base, no outs, 1 out, 2 outs
- Runner on third base, no outs, 1 out, 2 outs
- Runners on first and second base, no outs, 1 out, 2 outs
- Runners on first and third base, no outs, 1 out, 2 outs
- Runners on second and third base, no outs, 1 out, 2 outs
- Bases loaded, no outs, 1 out, 2 outs

Until you're familiar with the key factors for reading offensive and defensive situations, you may want to put the checklists on an index card to keep in your pocket and review from time to time. During Situation Ball, new game situations will undoubtedly arise as plays unfold. Keep a list of those different game situations so you'll remember to practice them another day. Noting the situations that continue to give you trouble will also help you develop your anticipation and reaction skills. Mentally practice these situations to acquire an edge the next time you play Situation Ball or a regulation game.

Specific rules of the game are as follows:

1. Use the regulation field of play. Establish ground rules for out-of-play areas.

2. The game is played with 10 players for slow pitch or with 9 players for fastpitch, one player at each official position for the game being played.

3. The batting order follows position numbers 1 through 9 (or 10 for slow pitch). Starting with the pitcher (position 1) as the first batter, progress to the right fielder (position 9 in fastpitch or position 10 in slow pitch) as

the last batter. The player who makes the last out in an inning serves as baserunner for the situation setup in the next inning. More experienced players who are members of an established team may use their regular batting order.

4. Each half inning of a single inning starts with the same specified situation setup. For example, in the first inning, the team selecting situations for odd-numbered innings sets the situation. For the team that bats first in the inning, play continues from the original situation until three outs have been made. The team starting the inning on defense then comes to bat, sets up the same situation, and plays until they get three outs. At the beginning of the second inning, the team selecting situations for

even-numbered innings sets the new situation. Because each team has the opportunity to play through the same situations, it is important that complete innings be played.

5. Once the situation to start the half inning has been established, all play is governed by the official softball rules for either slow pitch or fastpitch.

6. The game is facilitated by using an umpire, coach, or more experienced player to call balls and strikes.

7. A coach or more experienced player should pitch in games for less experienced players; however, a player on the team in the field should play the pitching position defensively.

SCRUB

The preceding modified game provided opportunities to respond to predetermined game situations in controlled settings. It was designed to give you specific offensive and defensive situations to work on in gamelike conditions. Because the situation was set at the beginning of the inning, you had the advantage of knowing in advance the particular strategy or technique that you would be called upon to use. The rules were designed to increase the number of opportunities you had during the game to execute a particular technique.

The modified game of Scrub is less controlled and much more like a regulation game. In this game, situations result naturally. Thus, if no one gets on first base with fewer than two outs, you will not be able to work on the second-to-first double play. You now must recognize situations as they spontaneously occur and be able to effectively respond both mentally and physically.

This final game is modified only to a limited extent, primarily to increase participation. The rules of regulation softball are modified so you can play different defensive positions. The official rules govern the remainder of the play situations. Thus, you can develop your knowledge and understanding of the rules of the game. Also, you should review the defensive and offensive check-

lists from step 9 to enhance your softball game sense as you participate in this game.

You may play a game for a variety of reasons. Having fun, enjoying the company of others, and soaking up the rays are all legitimate reasons for playing softball. However, playing a game can also be looked on as a fun test. It is a chance to see what you can do with the skills you have learned. The game skills of hitting a ball, running the bases, fielding ground balls, making a force-out on a baserunner, and so forth, can provide challenges for you to self-test.

As you play modified games, list the skills you know and execute with ease and success. Also, list the skills that you have difficulty with. The problem areas should become your focal points as you play additional innings in these games and as you play future games. Your weak areas can become your strengths. To make this happen, however, you need to recognize the skills, tactics, and concepts that give you problems and then work hard to master them. A complete softball player executes the skills proficiently and knows what every game situation calls for.

Scrub is a good game to play when you do not have enough players for two full teams. It is also a good game for increasing your understanding of the total game because it requires you to play all defensive positions.

Game Rules

1. Use the regulation field of play. Establish ground rules that apply only to a given field for out-of-play areas.
2. The number of participants should be 13 to 15 players for fastpitch or 14 to 16 players for slow pitch. A full defensive team starts in the field, and the remaining players start as the team at bat. Original defensive starting positions do not matter because you will be changing positions throughout the game.
3. A player remains in the group at bat until she makes an out. A player hitting a ball that is caught in the air by a fielder (a fly ball, pop-up, or line drive) immediately exchanges places with that fielder before play continues. The fielder comes in to join the group at bat and hits at the end of the batting order. A player (either batter or baserunner) making an out on any other kind of play goes out into right field, the number 9 position in fastpitch, the number 10 position in slow pitch. All fielders then rotate to the next lower numbered position—10 to 9, 9 to 8, and so on. Remember, shortstop is 6, so the left fielder (7) rotates into the infield there, not to third base (5). The shortstop (6) rotates to third base (5), not around the infield to second base (4). The pitcher (1) moves in to the end of the batting order of the group at bat.
4. After three outs have been made, clear the bases of runners and start a new half inning. Remember, players remain on the team at bat until they make an out.

Scoring

There can actually be no team score in Scrub. Scoring, if desired, must be oriented toward the individual player. For example, keep track of the offensive statistics of each person: the number of times at bat; the number of base hits (singles, doubles, triples, and home runs); the number of walks; and the number of runs scored. At the

Figure 10.4
Offensive Player Scorecard

Name _____

Times at bat _____ × 2 points = _____ points
Walks _____ × 1 point = _____ points
Runs scored _____ × 3 points = _____ points

Base hits

Singles _____ × 2 points = _____ points
Doubles _____ × 3 points = _____ points
Triples _____ × 4 points = _____ points
Home runs _____ × 5 points = _____ points

Total offensive score = _____ points

Figure 10.5
Defensive Player Scorecard

Name _____

Fielding
Ground ball attempts _____
+ successes _____ × 2 = _____ points
Fly ball attempts _____
+ successes _____ × 1 = _____ points

Throwing plays   *Attempts* _____
On-target throws _____ × 1 = _____ points
Off-target throws _____ × -1 = -_____ points
To proper position _____ × 2 = _____ points
To improper position _____ × -2 = -_____ points

Covering and back-up plays
Correct covers _____ × 2 = _____ points
Correct back-ups _____ × 2 = _____ points
Incorrect covers _____ × -2 = -_____ points
Incorrect back-ups _____ × -2 = -_____ points

Pitching *(include pitches that are hit)*
Balls _____ × 1 = _____ points
Strikes _____ × 2 = _____ points

Total defensive score = _____ points

end of a predetermined amount of time, winners could be declared in each category, or you can use the player scoring system given at the end of this section. Use the offensive player scorecard (figure 10.4) to record your score for this game. If you wish to keep track of your individual defensive play, use the defensive player scorecard (figure 10.5).

You can use these scorecards in Scrub and in all softball games that you play. If you analyze the scorecards after you play, they can indicate your physical and mental levels of play. If you see areas in which scores are not satisfactory, challenge yourself to work harder on those areas next time you play.

SUCCESS SUMMARY

These modified games have given you the opportunity to execute all of the skills and strategies used in the game of softball under both controlled and real-game conditions. The various charts have outlined for you the game concepts and the responsibilities that various players have in given situations. The cognitive aspect is probably the most difficult part of the game of softball to master, and it can only be practiced in game or modified game settings. Your participation in these modified games is a means for you to increase your ability to read and react spontaneously to game situations.

By now you have mastered some skills and you know the areas of weakness that demand your continued practice. The only experience left for you now is to become a member of a team and play in an official competitive game; that is, of course, if you have not already done so! In the final step in this book—slow-pitch games—you will have the opportunity to continue practicing your individual skills and your knowledge of tactics. Pair up with another player and use the offensive and defensive scorecards to evaluate each other's play in either a modified or real game. Continue to play and enjoy the satisfaction that comes from getting a hit, making a throw to the proper base, and sliding into home with the winning run!

Players who primarily play fastpitch might also enjoy participating in the slow-pitch games in the next step. You will have lots of opportunities to work on your defensive skills because the ball is hit a lot. Although hitting off slow-pitch pitching won't help you hit the rise ball in your fastpitch games, it can be a lot of fun!

Slow-Pitch Games

This final step presents slow-pitch games that are particularly appropriate for class use. The game of slow pitch can be effectively used in instructional settings because it allows for more participation, students generally have more success, there is more action, and the highly specialized fastpitch pitching and catching skills are eliminated. Slow-pitch pitching is a bit easier to learn, and because slow pitch is a hitter's game, it provides more action for both the offense and defense, helping to retain interest. Slow-pitch softball is also a lifetime activity with many opportunities available for participation on recreational leagues of varying competitive levels.

Softball is not a game that can be played alone. Even practicing individual skills isn't very easy to do alone. You can play catch with yourself using a wall, hit a ball off a tee, or run around the bases all by yourself, but only for a short time. Others have to join you if, indeed, you are going to make much progress in your quest to become a skillful softball player. Softball is a team sport, and the ultimate enjoyment occurs when two teams take the field together and challenge one another's skill and knowledge in game situations.

If the slow-pitch games presented in this step are used in an instructional setting, the scoring can be modified to give points for using skills appropriately during the game as well as scoring runs. Points could be aligned with lesson objectives or team goals. For example, if the focus is on making accurate throws, the defense could get a point for an accurate throw even if the runner is safe. Points could also be given for making the appropriate play, such as attempting to get the lead runner or backing up a throw to a base. On offense, teams could get points for hitting line drives, placing the ball to right field with runners at first or second base, or hitting hard hit ground balls. Using a point system such as this helps to keep all players involved in the game and promotes using and applying game skill and knowledge appropriately.

Each of the games presented in this step—coed, one-pitch, and mat ball—are variations of the official game of slow pitch, have official rules of their own, and can be modified to suit individual needs. Have fun and enjoy the game!

Success Check

- Make good decisions regarding strikes and balls.
- Play the game without making any errors.
- Perform the skills correctly.
- Demonstrate an understanding of the game rules.

- Attempt the appropriate offensive strategies.
- Make the appropriate defensive decisions.
- Score more runs than the other team.

COED SLOW PITCH

Most physical education classes are coeducational, with females and males learning and participating together. Many corporate and recreational leagues offer coeducational playing opportunities. To facilitate play in coed settings, specific rules have been developed for coed slow-pitch softball. Only the basic rules are presented here. You will need to refer to an official rule book for a description of the complete set of rules.

Participation in coed softball takes place in a setting that is reflective of society. Males and females working together toward a common goal is an everyday occurrence in the workplace and in the family, but usually not so in sport, especially team sports. Softball is one of the few team sports (volleyball being another) that has an official game designed specifically for coed play. Coed softball provides class and recreational play opportunities in which women and men can learn to work together and develop respect for one another's abilities. In 1981, the ASA added a coed slow-pitch tournament to its offerings of national championships. Currently, the coed game is one of the fastest-growing versions of the game of softball. Whether you have aspirations of playing in a national championship or playing with friends in a local league, opportunities abound for young and not-so-young adults to participate in the game of coed slow-pitch softball.

The prerequisites for playing coed slow pitch include skill proficiency, decision-making ability in the strategies of game play, and the ability to participate in accordance with the rules of play. Most of the skills and knowledge that you have worked so hard to develop over the past 10 steps (remember, no stealing or bunting in slow pitch) are now put to use in an official game between

two teams. There are no special rules to ensure that you have ample opportunity to practice a particular skill or use a specific game concept. This game is for real! It can be a part of a tournament, or you can direct the focus of the game each day to be playing with friends, playing for fun, or even working on certain aspects of the game.

Uniforms and a freshly lined field are not a prerequisite for enjoyment of a class version of coed softball, but teams made up of five females and five males are a must. Most of the rules that you have learned for slow-pitch softball are applicable to the coed game. Some of the rules that specifically apply to the coed game follow:

1. Use a regulation field of play. Establish ground rules for out-of-play areas.
   - Baseline distances: 65 feet (19.8 meters) for adults and for youths (girls and boys) 13 to 18 years old; 60 feet (18.3 meters) for youths 11 and 12 years old; 60 feet (18.2 meters) for youths 10 years and younger.
   - Pitching distances: 50 feet (15.2 meters) for adults and for youths 13 to 18 years old; 46 feet (14 meters) for youths 11 and 12 years old; 40 feet (2.2 meters) for youths 10 years and younger.

2. Defensive positioning must include five females and five males:
   - Outfield: two females and two males in any of the four positions.
   - Infield: two females and two males in any of the four positions.
   - Pitcher and catcher: one female and one male in either position.

3. Adhere to the batting rules.
   - Batting order alternates between the genders.
   - When a male batter is walked (base on balls), he is awarded two bases. If there are two outs, the next batter (female) may choose to hit or to take an automatic walk before stepping into the batter's box. Note: This is the official rule. It could be modified (or even not used) in an unofficial class game, if desired. The official rule's purpose is to prevent the pitcher from intentionally walking the male batters in order to have to pitch only to female batters.

However, in a class setting, this rule may send the message that females are not as skilled as their male classmates, which is not an appropriate message for either gender.

4. Keep score. Official rules concerning scoring runs and deciding the winner apply. The team with the most runs wins the game.

If playing in a tournament or league, the ultimate goal is to win. However, in a class or practice setting, it is more important to demonstrate success check criteria that illustrate the purpose of playing the game.

ONE-PITCH

One-pitch is played exactly like a regulation game, except that the batter is allowed only one pitch per time at bat. If the pitch is a ball, the batter walks. If the pitch is a strike, the batter must swing or is called out. This pitching-rule modification speeds up the game, which makes it very appropriate for an instructional setting. For less experienced players, the teacher or coach should pitch so that the pitching is more consistent. Once the skill of slow-pitch pitching has been mastered by most of the class (refer to step 3), the students should be encouraged to pitch in the game.

One-pitch provides you with opportunities for practicing all softball skills and game concepts. You might want to review the scorecards you used in Scrub in step 10 (page 204). If you are weak in any particular skills or concepts, you should concentrate on them when relevant situations occur in the game. Anticipate the actions that might be called for by each situation; then your reaction is likely to be appropriate.

Playing different positions during the game will help you become more versatile. Do not be afraid to change positions. In fact, you can become very skillful and knowledgeable by practicing all the infield and outfield positions. And don't forget the pitcher and catcher positions. You know the old saying, "Try it, you'll like it!"

The following rules govern the method of play:

1. Use the regulation field of play. You must establish ground rules for out-of-play areas.
2. Use official teams in terms of the number of people on a team and the positions played. You may choose to play coed rules or not.
3. Official rules govern play, except that the pitcher delivers one pitch per batter with the following results:
   - If the pitch is a ball and the batter does not swing at it, the batter gets a walk (base on balls).
   - If the pitch is a strike and the batter does not swing, the batter is out on a strikeout.
   - If the batter fouls off the pitch, the batter is out.
   - If the batter hits the pitched ball fair, the hit ball is played out.

If playing in a tournament or league, the ultimate goal is to win. However, in a class or practice setting, it is more important to demonstrate success check criteria that illustrate the purpose of playing the game.

MAT BALL

Mat ball is an appropriate game for instructional settings because it eliminates the need for umpires and makes the decision about balls and strikes very clear. A mat extends home plate, making the strike zone easy to determine. Any pitch with the appropriate arc that lands on home plate or on the mat is a strike. Mat ball can be played using regular, coed, or one-pitch rules. Like each of those games, the object of mat ball is to score more runs than your opponent.

If playing in a tournament or league, the ultimate goal is to win. However, in a class or practice setting, it is more important to demonstrate success check criteria that illustrate the purpose of playing the game.

SUCCESS SUMMARY

Being successful in game play depends on you and your team performing the skills, knowing the game, making the appropriate plays, and scoring runs. However, at times you may do everything right and well in a game, but the other team still wins. You need to put things in perspective and realize that by focusing on the skills, tactics, and strategies, eventually your team will score more runs.

◰ About the Authors

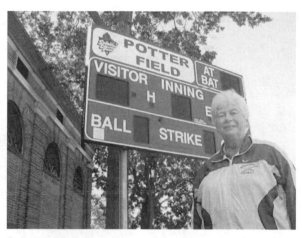

Diane L. Potter, EdD, is professor emerita at Springfield College in Springfield, Massachusetts. Dr. Potter has more than 40 years of experience in physical education teacher preparation, and she has coached the Springfield College softball team for 21 years. In addition, she played Class A fastpitch for 15 years in the Amateur Softball Association (ASA).

Dr. Potter has been an international clinician in softball, conducting clinics in Aruba, Italy, and the Netherlands. She took Springfield College teams to the Netherlands in 1971, 1975, and 1982, competing against the Dutch national team and various sport club teams in addition to conducting clinics for the Dutch youth programs. In 1982, she was awarded the Silver Medallion by the Koninklijke Nederlandse Baseball en Softball Bond (the Royal Dutch Baseball and Softball Association); she is the only woman so honored.

Dr. Potter is an outstanding leader in women's sport. She has served as a member of the AIAW Ethics and Eligibility Committee and was inducted into the National Association of Collegiate Directors of Athletics (NACDA) Hall of Fame in 1986. In 1989, she was inducted into the Springfield College Athletic Hall of Fame. The Springfield College softball field has been named in her honor.

Lynn V. Johnson, EdD, is an associate professor in the health and human performance department at Plymouth State University in Plymouth, New Hampshire. Over the past 30 years, she has taught K-12 physical education in Vermont and has been a physical education teacher educator at three institutions: Springfield College, the University of Vermont, and Plymouth State University. Johnson coached high school softball in Proctor, Vermont, served as the assistant softball coach at Springfield College for three years, and was the head coach at Springfield College from 1985 to 1989. In addition, she was the assistant softball coach at the University of Vermont from 1991 to 2006. Johnson played softball at Springfield College

from 1974 to 1977, playing in the College World Series in 1977. She continues to play slow-pitch softball on a tournament team that has competed together for more than 20 years.

Dr. Johnson is committed to the profession of physical education and sport. She is actively involved at the professional level, having served as the president of the Vermont Association of Health, Physical Education, Recreation and Dance and as vice president for the Eastern District Association of Health, Physical Education, Recreation and Dance (EDA). Johnson was awarded the Outstanding Professional Award from EDA in 2004 and the Higher Education Physical Education Teacher of the Year from VAHPERD in 2002.

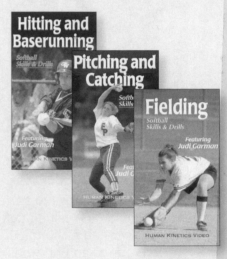

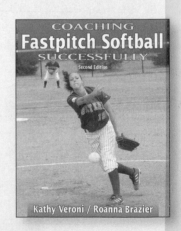